SoJourn

A journal devoted to the history, culture, and geography of South Jersey

SPECIAL EXPANDED ISSUE: THE REVOLUTIONARY WAR

Summer 2018

SoJourn is a collaborative effort. Local historians contribute the articles; Stockton students—in this issue, the editing interns of spring 2018—edit the articles, set the type, and design the layout; the directors of the South Jersey Culture & History Center at Stockton University oversee the publication.

Editors
Edward J. Arnold, Devyn R. Brown, Sara F. Brown, Mallory A. Caignon, Amanda V. Cook, Leah M. Fargo, Jackson Glassey, Nathaniel D. Hartsough, Caroline A. Linton, Madison E. Martorano, Mary K. McQuarrie, Alexa C. Novo, Edward T. Ochs, Kristin A. Robertson, Julio D. Sanchez, Margaret M. Simek, Gabriella Siwiec, Melissa Tucker, Samantha Wyld.

Supervising Editors
Tom Kinsella and Paul W. Schopp

ISSN: 2474-6665
ISBN-13: 978-1-947889-91-0

A publication of the South Jersey Culture & History Center
at Stockton University
www.stockton.edu/sjchc/

© 2018, the authors, South Jersey Culture & History Center, and Stockton University. All rights reserved.

Filler images, at the conclusion of articles, courtesy of the Paul W. Schopp Collection unless otherwise noted.

To contact SJCHC write:
SJCHC / School of Arts & Humanities
Stockton University
101 Vera King Farris Drive
Galloway, New Jersey
08205

Email:
Thomas.Kinsella@stockton.edu
Paul.Schopp@stockton.edu

Cover Image: Michel Capitaine du Chesnoy accompanied the marquis de Lafayette on his voyage to America during the Revolutionary War. A trained geographical engineer and cartographer, du Chesnoy served Lafayette in a variety of capacities as part of the marquis' entourage, including as an aide-de-camp. Part of Michel's role involved drafting beautiful full-color manuscript maps of Lafayette's exploits, as shown on this issue of *SoJourn*'s cover, depicting the Battle of Gloucester. A detail from this map with additional information can be found on page 66 of this issue. *Courtesy of Cornell University.*

Dedication

My friendship with Dave Munn (1941–2014) began in the mid-1970s, when he sat in the director's chair at the Cherry Hill Public Library. I had started researching local history and part of that investigation involved Dave's hometown, Gloucester City. Whenever I found new information or obtained a historic postcard of the city, I would trundle into Dave's office for show-and-tell. While there, I often watched a parade of local history apprentices, devotees, and icons enter and leave the same office. Some of these visitors would become close friends and confidants to me years later. Dave was a master at fostering younger people into the realm and mysteries of local history research. He soon engendered in me a passion for collecting books. He later said that if we combined our two libraries, we would have the finest research facility on local history south of Special Collections at Rutgers, New Brunswick. We became the best of friends and very few evenings passed without one of us calling the other. Sometimes the calls were short and other times, we would talk for well over an hour.

In addition to his fabulous book and ephemera collection, Dave was an indefatigable researcher who spent an inordinate amount of time at the Gloucester County Historical Society transcribing deeds and other documents related to the history of Gloucester City. Over time, he came to rely on me for my editorial and book design abilities as he embarked on a variety of writing projects, ranging from the contracted history of the Atlantic County Game Preserve, completed in 2007, to his magnum opus, *A Visit to Gloucester, 1677–1840*. The latter manuscript remains a work-in-progress, despite his death four years ago. This 199-page text features over 900 endnotes and should be ready for publication in two to three years. Among the works he produced while working for the State of New Jersey, but published after he left that position, was *Battles and Skirmishes in New Jersey of the American Revolution*, released in 1976 for the nation's bicentennial. For preparing this work and for his insatiable quest for knowledge about the American Revolution in South Jersey, we pay homage to David C. Munn by dedicating this special expanded issue of *SoJourn* to his memory. His imprint on local history will be long remembered, as will his imprint on me and on my career as a historian.

    Paul W. Schopp

        Assistant Director
        South Jersey Culture & History Center
        Stockton University

Dave Munn and I shared a common delight in library matters. Retired by the time we met, he had spent his career as a librarian and as a bibliophile, captivated by titles about the Delaware Valley and the State of New Jersey. I had spent quite a few years wandering the stacks of Philadelphia libraries under the careful tutelage of excellent librarians like Dave. During frequent visits to his Gloucester City home—where Dave's book collection overflowed every room—we traded modest stories about Philadelphia and New Jersey book luminaries and discussed titles we owned or at least had tried to own.

During these visits, I was cultivating Dave's trust. I hoped he would feel comfortable donating his collection to Stockton University, to feel convinced that Stockton would not neglect his gift, relegating it to some storage room to be cataloged later, "when resources become available." We both knew that nearly all libraries have such caches of unprocessed material, sometimes decades old.

I would visit Dave every six weeks or so, often bringing students with me so that they could experience the passion of an active book collector, and so that Dave could meet the sort of young people who would, hopefully, make use of his books. Stephanie Allen, class of '13 (she received her MA in '15), frequently accompanied me, and Dave became quite fond of her.

Dave Munn died in April 2014, a few weeks after officially donating his collection of South Jersey and New Jersey titles to Stockton. It is an honor to dedicate this volume of *SoJourn* to his memory. Our most lasting tribute remains, however, the on-going community effort that fosters and supports the study of South Jersey.

Tom Kinsella

Director
South Jersey Culture & History Center
Stockton University

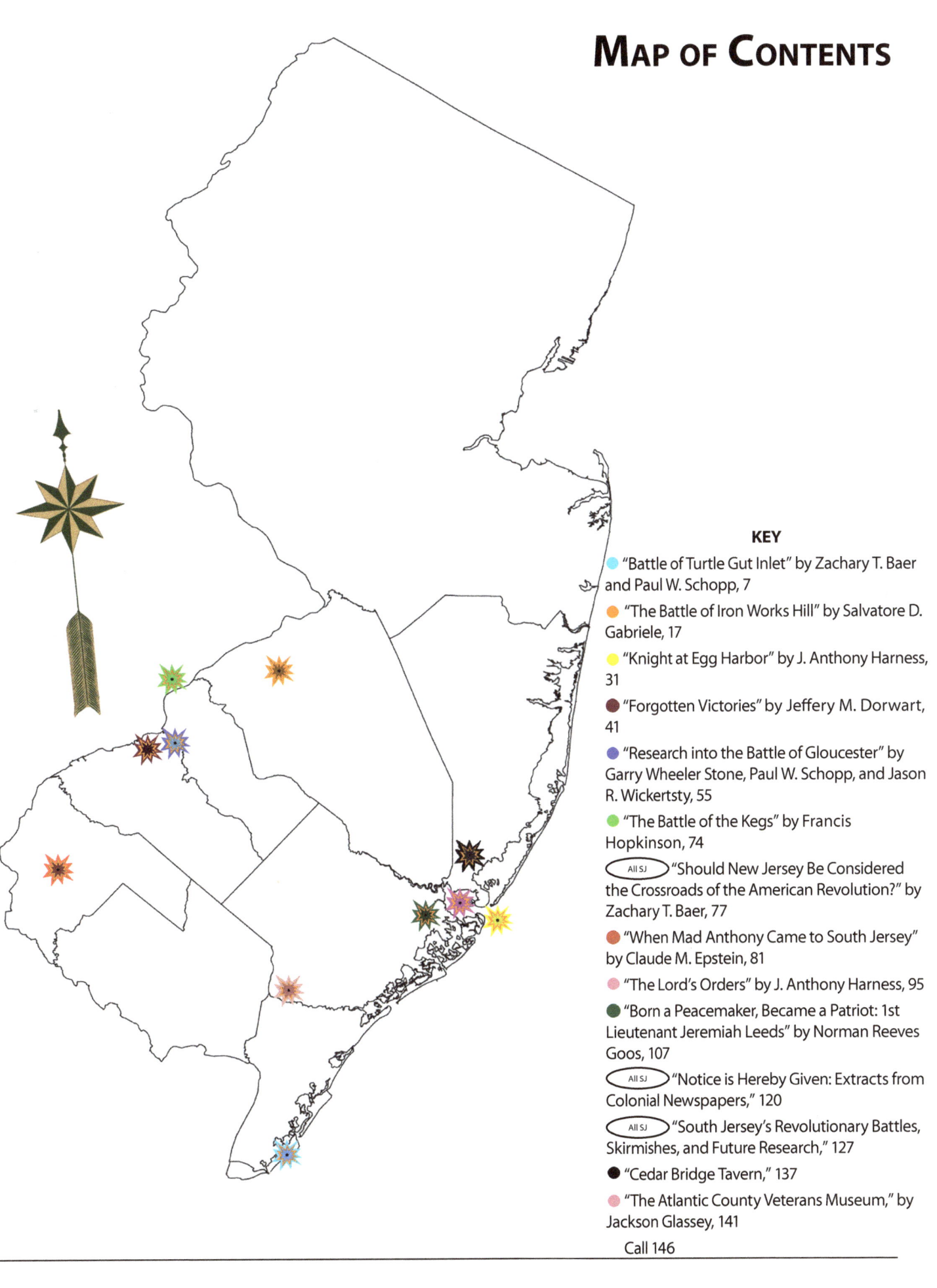

MAP OF CONTENTS

KEY

- "Battle of Turtle Gut Inlet" by Zachary T. Baer and Paul W. Schopp, 7
- "The Battle of Iron Works Hill" by Salvatore D. Gabriele, 17
- "Knight at Egg Harbor" by J. Anthony Harness, 31
- "Forgotten Victories" by Jeffery M. Dorwart, 41
- "Research into the Battle of Gloucester" by Garry Wheeler Stone, Paul W. Schopp, and Jason R. Wickertsty, 55
- "The Battle of the Kegs" by Francis Hopkinson, 74
- (All SJ) "Should New Jersey Be Considered the Crossroads of the American Revolution?" by Zachary T. Baer, 77
- "When Mad Anthony Came to South Jersey" by Claude M. Epstein, 81
- "The Lord's Orders" by J. Anthony Harness, 95
- "Born a Peacemaker, Became a Patriot: 1st Lieutenant Jeremiah Leeds" by Norman Reeves Goos, 107
- (All SJ) "Notice is Hereby Given: Extracts from Colonial Newspapers," 120
- (All SJ) "South Jersey's Revolutionary Battles, Skirmishes, and Future Research," 127
- "Cedar Bridge Tavern," 137
- "The Atlantic County Veterans Museum," by Jackson Glassey, 141

Call 146

About this Issue of *SoJourn*

With this issue of *SoJourn*, the South Jersey Culture & History Center enters the realm of thematic journal production. For the first time, you will notice that the covers lack the usual montage of postcard or photographic images. Instead, a beautiful full-color Revolutionary War map germane to the articles comprising this issue should catch your eye. The work of a number of new authors is found herein, along with a couple of regular contributors. While each article presents a facet of the American War for Independence in South Jersey, a quick check of the chronology of warfare at the end of the journal will demonstrate that many topics devoted to the theme remain to be explored.

The articles in this issue are sequenced chronologically to provide readers with a proper temporal understanding of the events documented. Careful readers will observe a recurring theme: important military actions occurred in South Jersey, but they usually fail to appear in the overarching narrative that most Revolutionary War historians provide. In many cases, these battles and skirmishes played critical roles in America winning the war, but larger military activities overshadow their importance. We are pleased to provide this special issue to reaffirm that what took place here in South Jersey was vital to the war effort.

We are grateful for the new authors who provided articles for this issue. Publication of *SoJourn* is dependent on people submitting articles for inclusion. Our student and staff editors will work with anyone to bring an article—or even an idea for an article—to completion for inclusion in a future issue. Whether it's the Revolutionary War, the bog iron industry, glassmaking, or one of myriad other topics, we welcome all submissions; and if we receive enough articles on a given subject, our readers will see yet another thematic issue in the future.

Paul W. Schopp

Battle of Turtle Gut Inlet

Zachary T. Baer and Paul W. Schopp

The Battle of Turtle Gut Inlet occurred on June 29, 1776, five days before the first public reading of the Declaration of Independence. Revolutionary War historians consider the fracas to be among the earliest and most noteworthy naval victories for the burgeoning colonial military. The battle also witnessed the first casualty resulting from the American Revolution in New Jersey.

Over the years since this brief encounter off the shores of Wildwood Crest, the Battle of Turtle Gut Inlet has gained meaningful attention.[1] Much ink has been spilled describing how Commodore John Barry and his unlikely band of sailors outwitted the British Navy to near embarrassment. In this fashion, the battle has become a quintessential "David versus Goliath" tale: a newly formed Continental Navy besting western civilization's most formidable opponent, the British Navy, with mere ingenuity. Entertainment, excitement, and patriotism aside, the historian is left with numerous questions of historical authenticity, accuracy, and methodology. For example, within what context does the battle occur? Why do so many published accounts not corroborate one another?

This article is focused on answering such historical questions; it will place the Battle of Turtle Gut Inlet within a proper historical context and piece together a coherent description of the battle from the primary sources available. In this fashion, the event is told in three parts: part one describes the events leading up to the battle from the perspective of the 31 year old Continental Captain, John Barry; part two describes the events leading up to the battle from the perspective of Barry's friend and captain of the Nancy, Hugh Montgomery; while part three concludes with the subsequent convergence of the two sides, Barry and Montgomery, taking on the pursuing British Navy.

Blockading Delaware Bay

The warm summer breeze swept across the beaches of coastal Cape May County and toyed with the ocean's whitecaps. Pods of dolphins dove and leapt just offshore, but no bathers or those seeking to gain a tan could be seen crowding the barrier islands and sand spits. It is the end of June 1776 and rebellious actions related to the

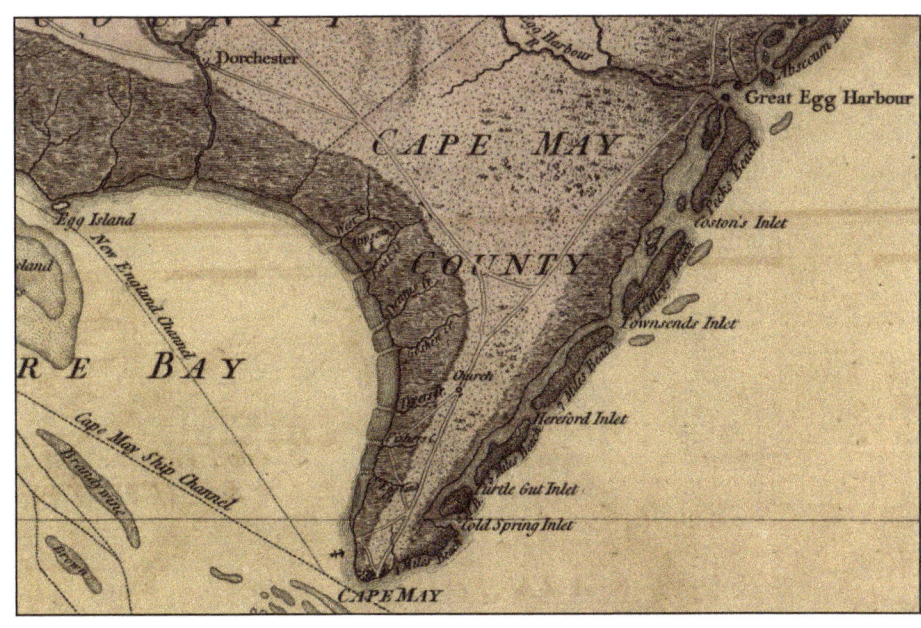

Detail from William Faden's map, *The Province of New Jersey, Divided into East and West, Commonly Called the Jerseys* (1777), showing Turtle Gut as the second inlet above Cape May. *Courtesy of the Library of Congress.*

Portrait of Commodore John Barry, US Navy, by V. Zveg, 1972, from the 1801 portrait by Gilbert Stuart. *Courtesy of Wikipedia.*

brooding American War for Independence were breaking out up and down the American eastern seaboard.

As numerous privateers and American merchantmen rode the waves at anchor proximate to the entrance of Delaware Bay in mid-1776, the captains on-board these vessels, with telescopes arrayed, cast a wary eye at the HMS Kingfisher and HMS Orpheus and their tenders. These two British man-o-wars actively patrolled the bay and nearby ocean day and night, blockading access to the Delaware River and the Port of Philadelphia. The blockade began when Parliament, the governing body of the entire British Empire, passed the Prohibitory Act in September 1775. Among its provisions, the act banned all commerce with the rebel colonies and authorized the seizure of all American ships. As a result, the British Admiralty issued orders to blockade all major ports in her colonies, including the largest port city: Philadelphia. The Royal Navy enforced a partial blockade until March 1776, when the full blockade became effective. British military vessels then actively engaged in full interdiction and continued to do so at Delaware Bay until June 1778, when the British land forces evacuated Philadelphia by marching overland to New York through New Jersey.

The blockade proved quite troublesome for American merchant ships and privateers, vessels manned by crews officially commissioned by the Continental Congress to engage in acts of war and deprivation. In their attempts to avoid the blockade, the American-flagged ships utilized shallow waters, various remote inlets, sounds, and rivers along the Jersey coastline, making intimate knowledge of local navigation essential for survival.[2]

John Barry

The newly established Continental Navy, created just a year earlier in 1775, also experienced the same challenges that merchantmen and privateers faced. Yet America's maritime military possessed amongst its fraternity skilled seamen like the Irish-born émigré, John Barry. At the start of the events that comprise the theme of this article, Barry and his ship, the Lexington, lay anchored at Fort Mifflin, approximately seven miles downriver from Center City Philadelphia. "Big John," as many called him due to his formidable six-foot-one-inch frame, had recently returned from the Capes of Virginia, where he successfully commandeered a British vessel and transported it to Fort Mifflin.[3] Now at Mifflin, Barry grew anxious to reenter the conflict and penned a letter expressing such emotion. "Sir," Barry wrote in May 1776 to Robert Morris, the well-known financier and weighty member of the Continental Congress, "I think if the Lexington Was Fited out to Come Down she might be of service."[4] Barry well understood the importance of a continued effort to pester the British blockade, which, by that time, had already inflicted "... a dreadful toll on rebel [American] shipping."[5]

In late May 1776, Barry's anxieties lifted as he received orders to leave Mifflin and reengage the enemy. The Lexington promptly weighed anchor and carefully sailed down the Delaware River.[6] Two friendly vessels joined Barry, the brig Reprisal, under the command of Lambert Wickes, and the schooner Wasp, under the command of Charles Alexander. While sailing downriver from Philadelphia, Barry avoided contact with the British. Despite early naval "victories" off the coast of New Jersey, like the grounding of the British transport Rebecca & Frances in early October 1775, the British remained in control of the waters.[7]

For the British, maintaining the blockade rendered myriad inconveniences to His Majesty's vessels. For example, the HMS Liverpool and HMS Kingfisher both appeared to be in rather dire physical condition. Lack of necessary supplies, including food and water, also plagued the vessels. Describing this situation, Captain Henry Bellew wrote in a letter aboard the HMS Liverpool,

> If Sir I should not meet with any Supplies of Provisions and Water Soon, or this Rage of Sickness among my people Continues under these Circumstances, I hope you will think me blameless in repairing to Halifax, tho' both my Main and Fore Masts are bad, nothing but the loss of One of them Can make me leave this Station.[8]

Struggles aside, the ships remained on station, as Bellew understood that leaving the bay meant ceding the waterways to the American privateers, merchantmen, and the Continental Navy. "I am well informed" Bellew wrote in a letter, "that these three lower Counties are ripe for Arms."[9] As Bellew would soon find out, the need for arms would bring the British Navy into conflict with a vessel carrying that very cargo.

Like Bellew, Barry understood the role the Delaware Bay played in ensuring civilian and military supplies reached Philadelphia and the adjoining territory. Barry was, in fact, well acquainted with the region. Decades before the colonies engaged in military conflict with Great Britain, Barry's merchant vessels, the Barbados and, later, the Black Prince, sailed in and out of Philadelphia on numerous occasions. Such experience taught Barry how to skillfully navigate the shoals and tides in the Delaware River, the bay, and off the coast

The brigantine NANCY, captained by Hugh Montgomery, flying an American flag at the Island of St. Thomas. Image drawn and engraved by John Sartain, originally published in Elizabeth Montgomery's *Reminiscences of Wilmington* (1851). The reader should notice the flag, which resembles Francis Hopkinson's flag for the U.S. Navy. This image, created nearly seventy years after the Battle of Turtle Gut Inlet took place, is representative of the NANCY, but the flag most likely either did not exist—or did not look like Hopkinson's flag. *Courtesy of Wikipedia.*

of Cape May.[10] Within a short time of his arrival in the bay area, Barry received a dispatch to maintain a vigil for the arrival of the two-masted brigantine NANCY, which was sailing north from the Caribbean with an important cargo of black powder, guns and victuals. Barry notified the two other Continental vessels in the area, REPRISAL and WASP, and the three anchored off the coast of Cape May County and waited.[11]

THE PRIVATEER NANCY

The NANCY received its letter of marque from Robert Morris of the Pennsylvania Committee of Safety in February 1775.[12] Under the command of Captain Hugh Montgomery, Morris contracted with the vessel to carry cargoes to "Porto Rico" and St. Thomas, Dutch West Indies, unload and sell the cargo, and then use the profits from the sale to purchase "Powder" and "Arms."[13] To ensure proper handling of the cargo, Morris, by this time a well-established businessman and financier, assigned Stephen Caronio to be the vessel's supercargo.[14] After

wasting nearly a month waiting in port for a break in the British blockade, Captain Montgomery finally decided to push the NANCY through the Delaware Bay blockade by flying false British colors.[15]

Montgomery safely delivered the NANCY to Puerto Rico and Caronio immediately engaged in selling the ship's cargo. After Caronio secured the desired cargo of ammunition and the stevedores stowed the lading in the hold, the brigantine cast off from port to continue its journey.[16] Montgomery caught a northerly wind and sailed the NANCY first to St. Croix and then north to St. Thomas. While in the West Indies, Caronio avoided suspicion by taking "in produce by day and munitions of war by night...."[17] At the conclusion of the trip's transactions, Caronio wrote a letter to Morris, dated April 30, that provided an account of the recent successful transactions.[18]

While in the islands, news arrived that the colonies would soon formally declare independence from Great Britain.[19] After learning the colors that Congress adopted for flags and ensigns, Montgomery allegedly commissioned a new flag to be sewn, upon which he drew down the Union Jack from the mast and replaced it with what has allegedly been called the first national flag flown at a foreign port.[20]

Within a few days, Montgomery left the Caribbean and plotted a course for Philadelphia. The cargo hold bristled with 386 barrels of gunpowder, 50 firelocks, barrels of rum, sugar, and guns. A crew of eleven sailors manned the Nancy.[21] Yet, this initial success soon faded as the Nancy neared Cape May, seeking to enter Delaware Bay. On the evening of June 28, 1776, documentary records indicate that two British vessels patrolling the blockaded waters in and around Cape May reported observing "18 Sail of Pirates and Merchant men at anchor off Cape May."[22]

Montgomery and his crew's trouble commenced sometime around 5 p.m. that night, when the HMS Kingfisher sighted the Nancy and hailed the HMS Orpheus, and the small fleet of tender vessels, to assist in the brigantine's interdiction.[23] Yet unknown to both Montgomery and the eleven-man crew of the Nancy, Commodore Barry's Lexington and two other Continental Navy vessels, the Reprisal and the Wasp, rode at anchor awaiting convergence.

Converging Sides

On the evening of June 28, Barry received signals from lookouts at Cape May that a chase between the Nancy and two British vessels was moving closer to his location. While it is unclear from the historical record

Painting by F. Muller, circa 1900, depicting the raising of the Continental Ensign on board the brig Lexington, commanded by John Barry, 1776. *Courtesy of Wikipedia.*

how Barry initially reacted, it is evident that Barry decided the Lexington and Wasp would sail out to shield the Nancy, while the Reprisal would remain behind. Captain Lambert Wickes of the Reprisal reported the winds being light and the water too shallow; he found it difficult to move his ship at that time. In an effort to provide as much aid as possible, Wickes ordered his ship's barge toward the developing conflict under the control of his brother, Lieutenant Richard Wickes. As all three Continental warships and two British vessels sailed towards the Nancy, the descent of nightfall on the well-shoaled sea forced each vessel to drop anchor, pushing any conflict to the following day.

Between 3 and 4 a.m. on June 29, the Orpheus and Kingfisher spotted and began chasing the Nancy.[24] Responding to the chase, Montgomery sailed his ship towards the shoreline and ordered his men to battle stations at the ship's guns. The Nancy soon navigated to shallow water just south of Five Mile Beach, offshore of a location known as Turtle Gut Inlet. The British ships quickly shortened the distance, forcing Montgomery to drop anchor and use the heavy fog to hide his attempts to salvage the ship's cargo by sending it ashore on the Nancy's boats.[25] Richard Wickes, commander of the Reprisal's barge, moved his vessel to the Nancy before the ship received any major damage from the British ships bounding toward her. Once there, Wickes climbed aboard and ordered Montgomery to cut his anchor rope and run the Nancy aground inside Turtle Gut Inlet in a desperate attempt to salvage as much cargo as possible. Montgomery acceded to Wickes command, and Wickes cut the anchor loose, and the Nancy soon grounded. Shortly thereafter, Barry arrived on a longboat with men from the Lexington and assisted in the effort to move cargo from the Nancy to the shore.[26]

Aided by the pea-soup fog and a group of local residents who apparently gathered on the shoreline to render aid, Barry and Montgomery's men unloaded "62 firelocks, 260 barrels of powder, and some dry goods."[27] The work continued until the fog lifted, sometime around 8 a.m., upon which time the British vessels commenced firing their cannons, while sailors from the Kingfisher rowed five longboats toward the now immobilized Nancy. Under so "Constant a Fire" and the realization of both the closing longboats and the vessel's impending doom, Barry devised a plan to blow up the vessel by opening "40 casks of powder in the cabin, and 50lbs. in the mainsail," then lighting a small fire in one of the mainsail's folds to serve as a time fuse. Barry hoped that by the time the fire reached the powder, he and his men would be well clear of the Nancy.[28] As the scene played out, his plan proved even more ingenious.

Seeing the Nancy abandoned, sailors on the Kingfisher's longboats boarded the vessel. As they boarded the ship, sailors from Montgomery and Barry's crew fired at the "pirate" sailors from the shoreline.[29] Within five minutes of the sailors gaining "Possession of the Brigg," the men on board gave "three cheers," and began to fire back.[30] As they fired toward the shoreline, the fuse set by Barry on the mainsail "took the desired effect" and exploded, sending "30 or 40 of them, as is supposed, into the air, some of them 30 or 40 yards high, who soon returned to the water, unable to tell who hurt them."[31] Besides this explosion, Montgomery and Barry's men "blue [blew] up one of their Boats and a great Number of their Men[;] on this Accident happening the other 4 Boats made off as fast as possible in a shattered Condition [and] weakly maned."[32]

With the explosion in the background, sailors on the shoreline continued to parlay shots back and forth with the British vessels. In that fateful scene, "a Cannon Shott" ended the life of Richard Wickes, becoming the only loss the Continental forces sustained.[33] Barry, with no purpose in continuing the fight, ordered his men to fall back. As the men retreated, Lambert Wickes took special care to bring along the body of his deceased brother, Richard.

Official losses for the British remain more obscured. Captain Alexander Graeme of the Kingfisher reported

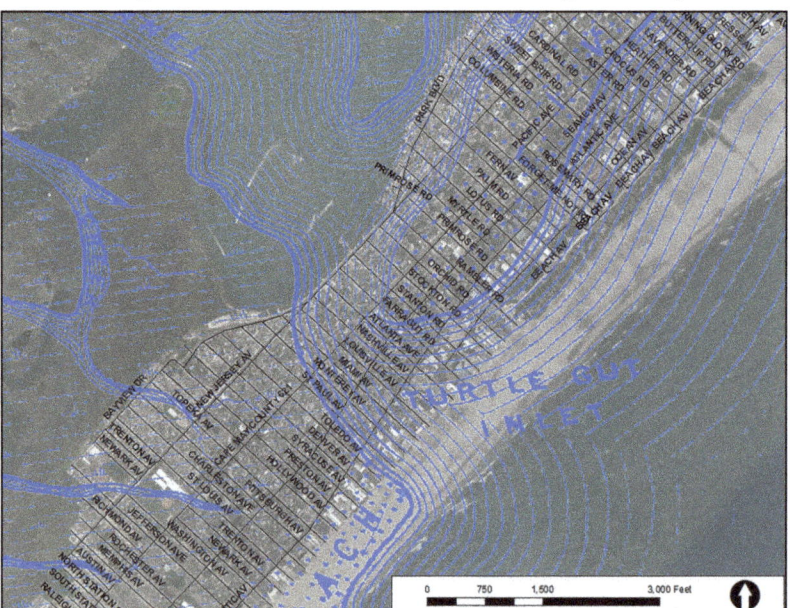

Turtle Gut Inlet Overlay Map. Through the wonders of GIS software, this map is a melding of detail from the nineteenth-century Beers map of Cape May County and a modern aerial photograph. The resulting composite not only depicts the original location of Turtle Gut Inlet, but also what streets now occupy its former path. *Courtesy of John W. Lawrence.*

Battle of Turtle Gut Inlet

Ships Involved in the Battle of Turtle Gut Inlet*					
Vessel	Commander	Type	Crew	Armament	Side
KINGFISHER	Captain Alexander Graeme	Swan Class Sloop	110	14 Guns	Great Britain
LEXINGTON	Commodore John Barry	Brigantine	70	16 Guns	Continental
NANCY	Captain Hugh Montgomery	Brigantine	12	6 Guns	Continental
ORPHEUS	Captain Charles Hudson	Lowestoffe Class 5th Rate Frigate	220	32 Guns	Great Britain
REPRISAL	Lambert Wickes	Brigantine	130	18 Guns	Continental
WASP	Charles Alexander	Schooner	48	8 Guns	Continental

*Names of the British tender vessels could not be determined, so the tenders are not included in this table.

the loss of "our Masters Mate & Six men" along with "the Long boat swivel muskets, pistols Long boat oars Sails &c," while Captain Charles Hudson of the ORPHEUS reported "one Man Wounded & Several of the Boats Oars lost."[34] No matter the official total, an account published in the *Virginia Gazette* states that those on the shore, "have taken up 11 bodies, two laced hats, a leg with a white spatterdash, both supposed to belong to officers." The letter also reports that "The water was covered with heads, legs, arms, entrails, &c. and one of the boats was towed off much shattered, with only six men. Thus did they huzza for a Scotch prize."[35] The explosion on-board the NANCY concluded the Battle of Turtle Gut Inlet.

In July, Hugh Montgomery and a handful of men from his privateering crew joined William Hallock, captain of the Continental Naval ship HORNET, in Cape May to observe the wreckage site. There, the men worked on salvaging as much from the NANCY as possible. According to reports from Hallock, the only available items included rigging and guns.[36] On July 11, the owners of the NANCY asked the Pennsylvania Committee of Safety for money to cover all losses suffered while engaging in privateering business for the committee. A transcript of the Pennsylvania Committee of Safety deliberations reads, in part:

> This Committee some time past Freighted & hired the Brig't Nancy, Capt. [Hugh] Montgomery, on a Voyage for procuring arms & ammunition, on Account of this Province, and having engaged to secure the Value of the said Vessel to the owners in case of loss: And Whereas, The said Brigt. Nancy, on her Return from St. Thomas with Powder and other goods, was Run on shore near Cape May and lost; In Consequence thereof, the owners of said Vessel exhibiting an Account against this Committee for the Value of said Brig't and other matters therein mention'd.[37]

The committee voted to pay the owners of the NANCY a sum of £1457/10s. to cover all losses.[38] Overall, however, the payment provided but little compensation when compared to the reward of escaping personal destruction and sweeping a victory away from the British Navy.

TURTLE GUT INLET TODAY

The Battle of Turtle Gut Inlet was the only recorded Revolutionary War action to occur in Cape May County in which men died. Despite New Jersey being often referred to as the "Cockpit of the Revolution,"[39] the Battle of Turtle Gut, like other South Jersey military actions during the American War for Independence, is virtually unknown to those that inhabit the state. During the ensuing two centuries, Turtle Gut Inlet was the site of frequent shipwrecks and groundings, so much so that it received its own lifesaving station after the federal government established the United States Life Saving Service in 1871. The inlet also served as a haven for duck hunters and fishermen until it finally disappeared under millions of tons of sand when the Cape May County Board of Chosen Freeholders, along with real estate developer Frank Shaw, began infilling the inlet in 1921, forever joining Five Mile Beach and Two Mile Beach and creating fast land for housing construction and extending highways. The county derived much of the sand from the area now known as Sunset Lake.

Today, it is hard to imagine how this locale looked prior to the infilling, but through the development of Geographical Information System technology, it is possible to overlay a modern aerial photograph with a historic map[40] to illustrate how the area once appeared. See overlap map on the previous page.

July 6.

" On Saturday last the brig Nancy, capt. Montgomery, of Wilmington, loaded on Congress account, with 400 barrels of powder, 50 or 60 small arms, dry goods, 101 hogsheads of rum, and 62 hogsheads of sugar, was drove on shore by the Kingfisher, at Cape May. The brig had six three-pounders mounted, with which, at one time, they beat off the boats, and one of their tenders; after which, being assisted by captains Barry and Weeks, they got out of her in a fog 62 firelocks, 260 barrels of powder, and some dry goods; but the fog clearing away, the ships came within shot, and sent five barges full of men, when the brig's people, finding they could not hold her, started about 140 casks of powder in the cabin, and 50lb. in the mainsail, in which they wrapped some fire, with an intent to communicate to the powder, and then quitted her. One or two of the men of war's boats soon boarded her, one was close under her stern, and others very near her. Those on board had given three cheers, and fired their arms at our people, when the fire took effect on the powder, and sent 30 or 40 of them, as is supposed, into the air, some of them 30 or 40 yards high, who soon returned to the water, unable to tell who hurt them. They have taken up 11 bodies, two laced hats, a leg with a white spatterdash, both supposed to belong to officers. The water was covered with heads, legs, arms, entrails, &c. and one of the boats was towed off much shattered, with only six men. Thus did they huzza for a Scotch prize. Some of our people had got one or two small cannon on shore, with which they fired at the boats boarding the brig; the men of war returned the fire, and killed the brother of capt. Weekes, who was 3^d lieutenant of the Reprisal, and wounded a boy in the thigh."

"Extract of a letter from Philadelphia, dated July 6," *Virginia Gazette*, July 26, 1776. Reset from a digital image of the original printing.

Plaque at Turtle Gut Inlet Memorial Park, 8000 New Jersey Ave, Wildwood Crest, New Jersey.

Monuments to the Battle

In 1976, Bicentennial fever raged across the United States. Nearly everywhere you looked, people walked around dressed in colonial garb and three-cornered hats. In the Borough of Wildwood Crest, historically minded residents joined together to form the new Wildwood Crest Historical Society in 1975. On May 31, 1976, the society opened its museum in a house on Cardinal Road. Almost a month later, the borough, in conjunction with the historical society, commemorated the Battle of Turtle Gut Inlet with creation of Turtle Gut Park, the first of several celebratory events for the Bicentennial. The society installed a bronze plaque on the flagpole.[41] Partners in Preservation, an organization formed in January 1997 ". . . to foster awareness of the community's historical sites throughout the Wildwoods by linking sites," installed a second historical marker at Turtle Gut Park on June 9, 2017.[42] This colorful plaque describes the battle with a map and other graphics.

Recent sign erected at the Turtle Gut Memorial Park in Wildwood Crest, New Jersey.

About the Authors

Zachary Baer is a history teacher at Shawnee High School. He is a member of the West Jersey History Roundtable and holds a deep, abiding interest in local history. Zachary resides in Gibbsboro, New Jersey, and looks forward to receiving feedback and comments from *SoJourn* readers. Comments can be sent directly to the author at zbaer@lrhsd.org.

Paul W. Schopp is the Assistant Director of the South Jersey Culture & History Center at Stockton University. He is a professional historian with over 44 years of experience working in the local history field. He is a well-known authority in the New Jersey history realm for his many reports, published articles, and books on state and Delaware Valley history. He is a member in long-standing of the West Jersey History Roundtable. The American War for Independence in New Jersey is a special interest for Paul.

Endnotes

1. There are numerous sources on the Battle of Turtle Gut Inlet, both print and digital, including Donald Grady Shomette, *Privateers of the Revolution: War on the New Jersey Coast 1775–1783* (Atglen, PA: Schiffer Publishing, 2016); Mark Donnelly and Daniel Diehl, *Pirates of New Jersey: Plunder and High Adventure on the Garden State Coastline* (Mechanicsburg, PA: Stackpole Books, 2010); Leonard Lundin, *Cockpit of the Revolution: The War for Independence in New Jersey* (Princeton, NJ: Princeton University Press, 1940); Elizabeth Montgomery, *Reminiscence of Wilmington in Familiar Village Tales, Ancient and New* (Wilmington, DE: Johnston & Bogia, 1872); David Petriliello, *Military History of New Jersey* (Charleston, SC: The History Press, 2014).

2. "There are no records of any Militia engagements in Cape May County, but along the Delaware Bay shore and the Atlantic Ocean shore there was privateering and several Cape May men were given by the Continental Congress commissions as Privateers and several captures of British merchant men were made." From Lewis T. Stevens, "Soldiers From Cape May in the Revolutionary War," *The Cape May County New Jersey Magazine of History & Genealogy* (June 1932): 44.

3. Anonymous, *Memorial to Commodore John Barry, Father of the Navy of the United States* (Philadelphia: Society of the Friendly Sons of St. Patrick, 1907), [4].

4. "Captain John Barry to Robert Morris, May 9, 1776," found in *Naval Documents of the American Revolution: Volume 5, American Theater: May 9, 1776–July 31, 1776*, ed. William James Morgan (Washington, D.C.: Government Printing Office, 1971), 15.

5. Donald Grady Shomette, *Privateers of the Revolution: War on the New Jersey Coast, 1775–1783* (Atglen, PA: Schiffer Publishing, 2016), 52.

6. "Commissioners of the Continental Navy in Account with the Brigantine Lexington," found in *Naval Documents of the American Revolution*, 5:193.

7. Peter Force, *American Archives: Fourth Series, Containing a Documentary History of the English Colonies in North America from the King's Message to Parliament, of March 7, 1774, to the Declaration of Independence of the United States*, vol. 3 (Washington, D.C.: M. St. Clair Clarke and Peter Force, 1840), 1313.

8. "Captain Henry Bellew, R. N., to Vice Admiral Molyneux Shuldham," found in *Naval Documents of the American Revolution*, 5:459.

9. Ibid. The term 'Lower Counties' refers to the three counties on the Delaware side of the river: New Castle, Kent, and Sussex.

10. Sarah A. Thomas, "John Barry, A Patriot of the Revolution," *The Cape May County New Jersey Magazine of History & Genealogy* 3, no. 2 (June 1932): 35. As one description of Barry suggests, he "could sail his vessel near to the Cape May shore, keeping shallow water between him and the blockading frigates"; Thomas, "Barry," 35.

11. Mark Donnelly and Daniel Diehl, *Pirates of New Jersey: Plunder and High Adventure on the Garden State Coastline* (Mechanicsburg, PA: Stackpole Books, 2010), 105.

12. *Naval Documents of the American Revolution*, 5:233–34.

13. "Journal of HMS Liverpool, Captain Henry Bellew,"

found in *Naval Documents of the American Revolution: Volume 5, American Theater: May 9, 1776–July 31, 1776*, ed. William James Morgan (Washington, D.C.: Government Printing Office, 1971), 234.
14 *Naval Documents of the American Revolution*, 5:234. A "supercargo" is a representative of the ship's owner (or in this case, the commissioner) who travels on board a merchant ship and oversees the cargo. Commissioners of privateering vessels commonly practiced this during the Revolutionary War.
15 Elizabeth Montgomery, *Reminiscence of Wilmington in Familiar Village Tales, Ancient and New* (Wilmington, DE: Johnston & Bogia, 1872), 154.
16 Ibid.
17 Ibid.
18 *Naval Documents of the American Revolution*, 5:234.
19 This does not equate to the Declaration of Independence, which the Continental Congress did not issue until July 4, 1776.
20 Montgomery, *Wilmington*, 155.
21 *Naval Documents of the American Revolution*, 5:952.
22 "18 Pirates and Merchant men at anchor off Cape May," *Naval Documents of the American Revolution*, 5:792.
23 Ibid.
24 H.M.S Sloop Kingfisher, *Naval Documents*, 5:818.
25 Montgomery, *Wilmington*, 154.
26 Montgomery, *Wilmington*, 155.
27 "Extract of a letter from Philadelphia, dated July 6," *Virginia Gazette* (Williamsburg), July 26, 1776.
28 Captain Lambert Wickes to Samuel Wickes, found in *Naval Documents of the American Revolution*, 5:882–83; "Extract," *Virginia Gazette*.
29 Leonard Lundin, *Cockpit of the Revolution: The War for Independence in New Jersey* (Princeton, NJ: Princeton University Press, 1940), 113.
30 Lambert Wickes to Samuel Wickes, *Naval Documents*, 5:882–83; "Extract," *Virginia Gazette*.
31 Lundin, *Cockpit*, 113; "Extract," *Virginia Gazette*.
32 Lambert Wickes to Samuel Wickes, *Naval Documents*, 5:882–83.
33 Ibid.
34 Journal Kingfisher, *Naval Documents of the American Revolution*, 5:817; Journal Orpheus, *Naval Documents of the American Revolution*, 5:818.
35 "Extract," *Virginia Gazette*.
36 *Naval Documents of the American Revolution*, 5:981.
37 *Naval Documents of the American Revolution*, 5:1048.
38 Ibid.
39 Leonard Lundin, *Cockpit of the Revolution: The War for Independence in New Jersey* (Princeton: Princeton University Press, 1940).
40 F. W. Beers, *Topographical Map of Cape May Co., New Jersey* (New York: Beers, Comstock & Cline, 1872). Environmental Systems Research Institute, ArcMap (Redlands, CA: 2017).
41 History of the Wildwood Crest Historical Society and Museum, https://cresthistory.org/index1.php.
42 Rachel Rogish, "Turtle Gut Inlet Recognized," *Cape May County Herald*, June 14, 2017, http://www.capemaycountyherald.com/community/culture/article_a8d83c76-5137-11e7-b215-b778073d2779.html.

A large Royal Naval brig-rigged sloop of about 20 guns is shown in broadside view running into an anchorage. There is a large amount of activity on board and the artist has shown some figures in the rigging. To the right and left of the ship are smaller American vessels captured by the sloop. They are flying the British Union over the American rebel merchant ensign of 1777, indicating they are prizes—presumably taken by the sloop. Painting by Francis Holman and dated 1778. *Courtesy of the National Maritime Museum, Greenwich, London.*

The Battle of Iron Works Hill:
The Forgotten Revolutionary War Battle of Mount Holly

Salvatore D. Gabriele

On that cold, Christmas night of 1776, George Washington led an army of 2,400 troops across the Delaware River toward Trenton, New Jersey.[1] Early the next morning, Washington and his men surprised the Hessian forces billeted at Trenton, who had dropped their guard while celebrating Christmas.[2] As they laid siege to Trenton, the American forces overwhelmed the Hessians, many of whom remained in a drunken stupor or suffered with a hangover from the previous day's festivities. The resultant victory provided the American military with a much needed boost in morale; Washington's total rout of the Hessians is often viewed as an early turning point in the Revolution. American forces grew stronger and more courageous as they continued in victory, eventually winning the war and the country's independence from Great Britain. Following his triumph at Trenton, George Washington gained renown as a leader, and, by the nineteenth century, had joined the pantheon of America's historic heroes. His legendary status as the nation's commander in chief and first president provided the impetus for German American artist, Emanuel Gottlieb Leutze, to execute his famous painting in 1851, *Washington Crossing the Delaware*.

Many history books omit the full story behind the victory in Trenton. Washington was triumphant due in large measure to a feint, known as the Battle of Iron Works Hill, which patriot militiamen and Virginia troops conducted in Mount Holly, Burlington County. Without this critical exercise in subterfuge, which the Americans employed to draw a large force of Hessians away from the Bordentown area, extrapolation suggests that the Battle of Trenton and, subsequently, the entire war might have had a different outcome. Although historians should refrain from delving into "what ifs," it is not difficult to imagine an alternate scenario where the Hessian reinforcements had remained in the Bordentown area, a mere few miles from Trenton, and easily marched to engage Washington's troops at Trenton and possibly repelled the American attackers on the morning after Christmas.

The Battle of Iron Works Hill, also known as the Battle of Mount Holly, usually fails to receive the discussion it warrants in historical accounts of the Revolutionary War. As a military engagement, the battle was a contrived American loss, but this skirmish virtually assured the greater American victory at the Battle of Trenton. What might be the reason this local battle has not received appropriate recognition in historical accounts for its vitally important role in the overall American military strategy? Some authors appear to romanticize key military actions like the Battle of Trenton and in their revere examine such battles so minutely that they miss the larger picture. This romanticist approach to retelling the story of these engagements, combined with the fact that the Battle of Iron Works Hill was technically an American loss, might provide a rationale for not acknowledging this battle's crucial importance to the events that transpired at Trenton.

The town of Mount Holly contains a rich revolutionary-era history, beginning with the Battle of Iron Works Hill and later, with the British evacuation of Philadelphia "through the Jerseys" to Sandy Hook and New York City. Examination of the skirmishes that occurred in and around the community provides critical insight into the American Revolution, and, more specifically, South Jersey's significance during the war. Deployment of militia forces, the British lack of confidence in American forces, and New Jersey locals' attitudes toward the war are a few of the key factors that play into this chapter of the American Revolution. The Battle of Iron Works Hill was a crucial event in New Jersey during the Revolutionary War.

Brief Background of Mount Holly and Iron Works Hill

The initial British settlement of Mount Holly occurred around three years after members of the Religious Society of Friends (Quakers) had arrived to develop the City of Burlington in the fall of 1677. John Cripps, the pioneering settler in Mount Holly—and the person who named the community—had 300 acres surveyed to him in April 1681 as part of his proprietary share of land rights in West New Jersey. The survey return of Cripps' land includes the phrase "... named by the owner thereof Mount Holley."[3] In November 1688, the Burlington Court created the Constabulary of Northampton, along with other political subdivisions, and Northampton's territory included Mount Holly. The New Jersey State Legislature formally incorporated the Township of Northampton 110 years later on February 21, 1798. In November 1931, local voters approved a referendum to rename the township Mount Holly, since lawmakers had taken most of Northampton Township's landmass to create new municipalities during the preceding centuries. State lawmakers memorialized the municipal name change within the volume of state session laws for 1932.[4]

Early Mount Holly commerce developed in the present town center, where settlers bought and traded goods. The Rancocas Creek's sinuosity through the village offered multiple opportunities for developing industries based on water power. The first operation to avail itself of this hydraulic horsepower was a sawmill, established in 1720, followed, three years later, by a gristmill.[5] In 1730, the creek provided power for an iron works in Mount Holly, at a site now known as Iron Works Park, located south of the creek and east of Pine Street.[6] The presence of the iron works caused a salient across Pine Street to be named "Iron Works Hill." The communicants of Saint Andrews Anglican Church acquired this prominence from the iron works owners and constructed their first edifice for worship. Around the mission church, the vestry laid out a burying ground for the interment of deceased members, which remains an active burial site today.[7]

The Military Situation in New Jersey Late in 1776

The cause for American independence began with a high level of enthusiasm, but the ardor among the citizenry quickly dissipated in the ensuing months leading up to the conclusion of 1776. British forces had crushed the American troops in every battle, and morale among the Continentals had reached a low ebb. British General William Howe, leading the campaign, forced Washington's armies out of New York, pushing the American troops across and out of New Jersey and into Pennsylvania.[8] Washington's demoralized soldiers suffered exhaustion, while various companies of the Crown's forces occupied much of New Jersey.

With the onset of colder weather in the fall of 1776, British forces, as well as their subordinate hired soldiers from Germany, a group of mercenaries known as Hessians, had bivouacked throughout Jersey and held command of various towns and cities. In Burlington County, the British command positioned outposts at Crosswicks, Burlington, Bordentown, Mount Holly, in addition to the cantonments at Trenton and Morristown, among other locations. The wide dispersal of the Crown's forces across New Jersey strongly suggests the utter contempt the King's commanders had for the Continental Army and the militia. In hindsight, this strategy proved disastrous for the British and Hessian troops.[9] Along with their military stranglehold on New Jersey, the British enjoyed increasing Loyalist support among the locals living across the state, partially based on Washington's repeated losses. Shortly after forcing the Continental Army out of Jersey, the British encountered approximately 1,500 of the state's natives seeking the Crown's protection.[10] With both military and political control of New Jersey, Britain appeared to be closing in on a final victory. American forces demonstrated discontent with their performance and defeats. With every loss, their morale and passion only further flagged. An American victory was needed and needed immediately.

Part of the British occupation of New Jersey included placing a deployment of Hessians at Trenton, under the command of Colonel Johann Rall. The German troops bivouacked in the town, including occupying the barracks constructed for housing British soldiers during the French and Indian War. Other Hessian mercenaries served to protect the main body of troops in Trenton, including those that Colonel Carl Emil von Donop commanded. On December 14, 1776, Colonel von Donop began occupying the southerly rear guard position at Bordentown, but this small community could not accommodate all of the foreign soldiers and their officers, so the Germans positioned satellite encampments at Black Horse (now Columbus), White Hill (present-day Fieldsboro), Jones Mill on Black's Creek, and at several farms around Bordentown.

The Battle of Iron Works Hill

Harassing the Hessians

During mid-December, General Washington initiated planning for a counterattack against the Crown and its military forces occupying New Jersey. In a letter to Massachusetts Governor Jonathan Trumbull, Washington noted that as soon as additional troops arrived, he entertained hope

> to attempt a Stroke upon the Forces of the Enemy, who lay a good deal scattered and to all appearance in a state of Security. A lucky blow in the Quarter, would be fatal to them, and would most certainly raise the Spirits of the People, which are quite sunk by our late misfortunes.[11]

With British troops situated only a day's march from the nascent country's national capital, General Washington appointed General Israel Putnam as military commander of Philadelphia in early December. Putnam, in command of "... a sizeable force,"[12] oversaw construction of defensive positions there.[13] Familiar with Washington's plans for harassing and then attacking the enemy, General Putnam ordered Virginia Colonel Samuel Griffin to take a patchwork of militia from Pennsylvania and Gloucester, Salem, and Cumberland counties in West New Jersey, along with two companies of his Virginia troops with two three-pound cannons, a total of about 500 men, into New Jersey. Griffin was already in Philadelphia, convalescing from the heel wound he had received during the Battle of Harlem Heights.[14] Putnam apparently took his own initiative in sending Griffin and his forces into New Jersey. While historians dither on whether Washington orchestrated all of Griffin's actions through orders, no documentation from Washington exists to verify such a posit. Writing in his three-volume history of the revolution, Benson J. Lossing notes,

> Unknown to General Washington, Putnam, who had been made acquainted with the design of attacking Trenton, sent Colonel Griffin, with a body of four hundred and fifty militia, across from Philadelphia into New Jersey, to make a diversion in favor of the Trenton expedition.[15]

Yet, Joseph Galloway, a moderate Continental Congressman who would prove a Loyalist in the end, provides the following passage, thereby muddying the research waters:

> ... He [Washington] therefore meditated an assault upon Trentown. But in order to draw Colonel de Donop from his post at Bordentown, and to prevent his supporting Colonel Raile at the time of the assault, he sent a corps of 350

Colonel Carl Emil Ulrich von Donop (1732–1777). *Courtesy of Wikipedia.*

Samuel Griffin (1746–1810). Portrait by Gilbert Stuart. *Courtesy of Wikipedia.*

militia, many of whom were boys picked up in Philadelphia, and the counties of Gloucester and Salem, to Mount Holly, with orders not to fight, but fly as soon as the effect of the manœuvre had taken place.[16]

The quandary of who issued the orders will not be resolved unless and until correspondence and orders from Washington to either Putnam or Griffin come to light.

Washington's adjutant general, Colonel Joseph Reed, left Colonel Cadwalader's headquarters in Bristol, Pennsylvania, crossed over the Delaware River to Burlington and traveled by night to Mount Holly. Once he had arrived, Reed met with Colonel Griffin and ascertained how Griffin and his forces could assist in the attack on Trenton. Reed found Griffin in poor health and later reported to Washington on his meeting with Griffin. When he asked about the troops under his command, Griffin responded that

> . . . his force was too weak to be depended on either in numbers or discipline, that all he expected was to make a division and draw the notice of the enemy before whom he proposed to retire if they should advance in any force.[17]

Colonel Griffin and his assembled troops certainly did not have the element of surprise on their side. Colonel von Donop learned of the Americans moving up from Philadelphia on December 16. On that date, the Hessian colonel dispatched a strong force of 200 grenadiers and mounted jägers to investigate. Three days later, von Donop and Colonel Block led a large party to Mount Holly, but the patriots had destroyed a bridge

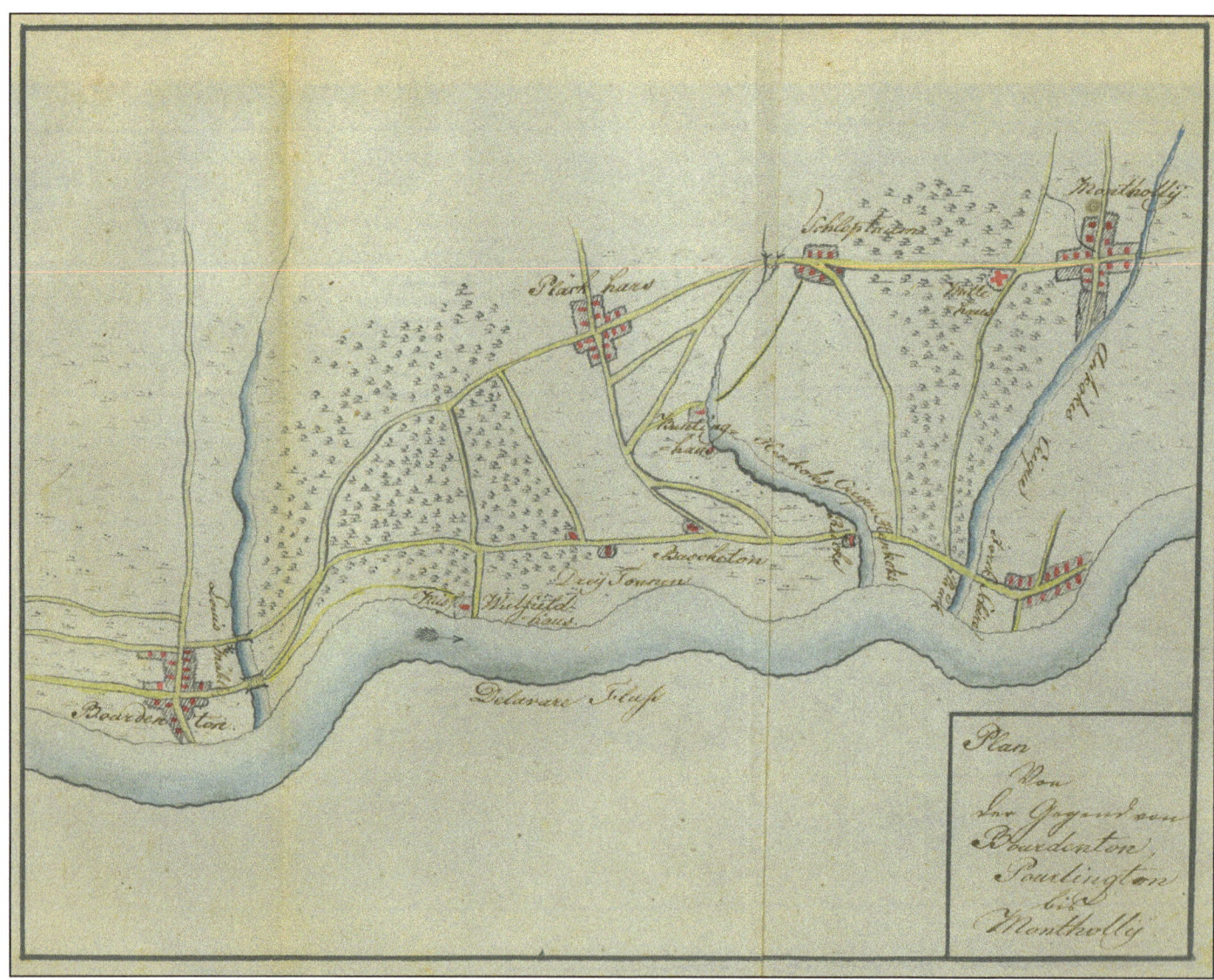

Captain Johann von Ewald's hand-drawn "Plan of the Area of Bordentown, Burlington to Mount Holly," which illustrates the territory in which Hessian Colonel von Donop, and his troops, and American Colonel Griffin operated during December 1776. *Used with permission, Joseph P. Tustin Papers, Andruss Library, Bloomsburg University.*

The Battle of Iron Works Hill

over the Rancocas Creek, so the Hessians returned to Bordentown. Colonel von Donop then dispatched a local Tory spy named Barzilla Haines to reconnoiter the troops in Mount Holly. Historian William S. Stryker notes Haines visited the town on December 21 and that he arrived at night "... and lodged in the rebel camp there. He was informed they had only two field pieces which he thinks were three pounders as he perceived them at the church."[18]

> ... they were not above eight hundred, near one half boys, and all of them Militia a very few from Pennsylvania excepted,—that he knew a great many of them who came from Gloucester, Egg Harbour, Penns Neck, and Cohansey. They were commanded by Colonel Griffin.[19]

Local military action that culminated in the Battle of Iron Works Hill began with minor skirmishing north of Mount Holly. On December 22, 1776, Griffin attacked and eventually overwhelmed a Hessian picket outpost at Petticoat Bridge, which spanned the Assiscunk Creek about a mile south of Blackhorse (present-day Columbus) and about a mile east of Slabtown (today's Jacksonville).[20] Burlington Quakeress Margaret Morris recorded the event in her diary:

> ... the intelligence brought in this Evening is seriously affecting aparty of our Men, about 200, Marchd out of Mount Holly, & meeting with aparty of hessians near aplace calld petti-Coat bridge, an engagement ensued,—the Hessians retreating, rather than advanceing, aheavy fireing of Musketry & some Cannon heard, we are informd that 21 of our Men were killd in the engagement, & that they returnd at Night to thier head Quarters at Mount Holly, The Hessians to thiers at the black horse.[21]

The Pennsylvania Evening Post published an account of this exchange:

> We hear from good authority, that on Sunday last, betwixt Slab Town and the Black Horse, in the Jersies, a party of our army, under the command of Col. Griffin, had a skirmish with the Hessians, and that the enemy were forced to retreat with precipitation, having some killed, and leaving behind them many knapsacks and other necessaries, amongst which was a hat shot through the crown.[22]

Regarding the battle, Colonel von Donop recorded that he

> ... went personally to Blackhorse [Columbus] but found that the enemy had not advanced any further than to the Meeting House this side of Mount Holly, except for some patrols. Hardly had I returned at 3 o'clock in the afternoon to Bordentown when the alarm-shots, for which I had arranged, were fired by the two battalions at Blackhorse....
>
> I then returned as fast as possible to Blackhorse and there I found every man under arms, since as soon as I had left there 400 to 500 rebels had attacked the outpost at Petticoat Bridge. They succeeded in nothing more than forcing the outpost troops, consisting of one under-officer and twelve Scottish Highlanders, to retire. Captain von Eschwege's company, stationed in a house nearby, came to their assistance as did the troops of the Scottish outpost and the grenadier post behind them, and this made it impossible for the rebels to advance one step further. Captain von Eschwege's company had two wounded and the Scottish command had two slightly wounded.[23]

Likewise, Captain Johann von Ewald, a Hessian officer with the Jäger Corps, recorded the events of December 22 from his side of the conflict:

> In the afternoon of the 22d I was reinforced with an officer and fifty grenadiers and took post at the Bunting house. This post was situated further on from Black Horse and Bustleton and consisted of a plantation lying upon a hill where the roads coming from Mount Holly and Burlington intersected. Toward the enemy I had woodland, through which these roads ran, and behind me was an extensive meadow.
>
> I had scarcely arrived at this post when the enemy appeared in the wood. I took the jägers to reconnoiter him and to learn with whom I had to deal. I skirmished with the enemy, who, since I attacked him quickly, withdrew toward Burlington with a loss of several dead and wounded. I pursued him for a short distance, and after I was certain of his retreat I returned to my post. One of my jägers was killed and another severely wounded.

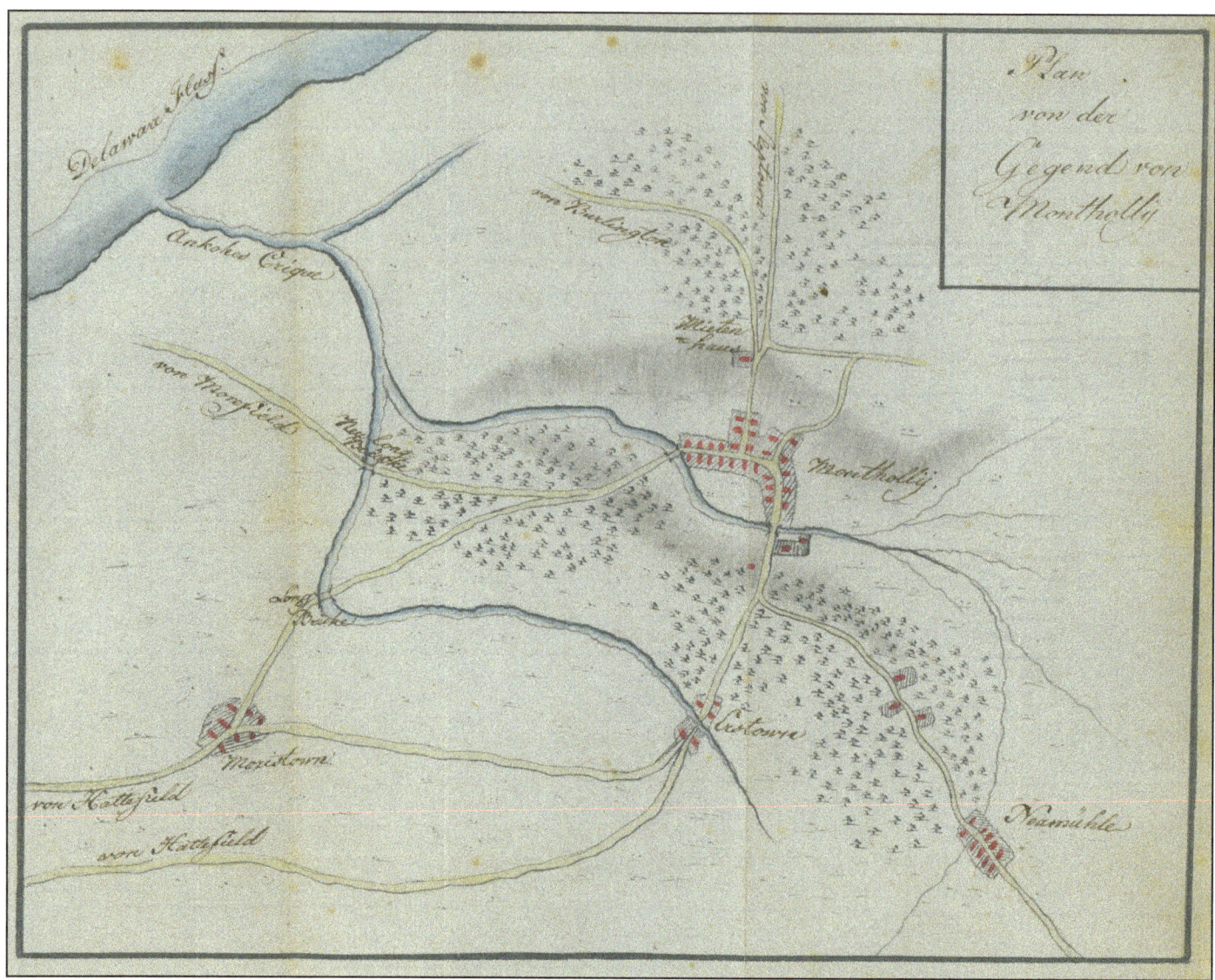

Johann von Ewald's hand-drawn "Plan of Mount Holly." Ewald depicted the area's two salient in shadow using a pencil. The higher Mount Holly overlooked the town from above and Iron Works Hill stood below the town. During the battle, the Hessians parked their cannons on Mount Holly for bombarding the Americans in Iron Works Hill. *Used with permission, Joseph P. Tustin Papers, Andruss Library, Bloomsburg University.*

No sooner had this skirmish ended than I heard heavy small-arms fire mixed with cannon fire in the vicinity of Black Horse or Slabtown. This firing caused me no little embarrassment because it was in my rear. I decided to investigate the firing and to fall upon the enemy's rear during his own attack. I hurried as fast as I could; however, the enemy had already been driven back by the grenadiers with heavy losses. Colonel Donop ordered me not to return to the Bunting house, but to choose a post in front of Black Horse.

During the night I received orders to draw back with the jägers behind the pickets of the grenadiers to give the men a few hours' rest, because the colonel intended to seek out and defeat the enemy the next day.[24]

Widely circulating rumors concerning General Putnam leading a force of 1,000 men to Mount Holly persisted. Diarist Margaret Morris noted: "22d—it is said Putnam with 1000 men are at Mount Holly—all the Women removed from the Town except one Widow of our Acquaintance."[25] Likewise, Scottish Colonel Thomas Stirling, who commanded the 42nd Highlanders assigned in a supporting role to von Donop, learned from "a gentleman of credit" that he reckoned "1000 of the rebels were certainly in Mount Holly" and "2,000 more were in the rear to support them."[26] Historian David Hackett Fischer states, however, that

> There was also some hope that Israel Putnam could lead another crossing from Philadelphia and join the South Jersey militia south of Mount Holly. About three hundred men had already

gone over the river, but Putnam's crossing was always very doubtful, and remained on the margin of the operation.[27]

The Battle of Iron Works Hill and Its Aftermath

In response to Stirling's report on the American forces in Mount Holly, von Donop sought the Scotsman's military advice on how to proceed. The Highlander replied,

> The rebels without doubt mean to beat up our Quarters and drive us from hence from their approaching so near to us. I am therefore of opinion, if it is necessary to keep this Country for the Winter, that we should not wait to be attacked.... You sir, with the troops at Bordentown, should come here and attack. I am confident we are a match for them.[28]

Colonel von Donop heeded Stirling's advice and issued orders for his Bordentown troops to go on the offensive against the ragtag American force. The morning after the skirmish at Petticoat Bridge, the Hessian colonel determined he would vanquish the Americans in finality. He writes,

> In order to get rid of these troublesome guests I marched early ... in the morning toward Mount Holly with the 42nd Regiment and the Block and Linsing battalions. I met several hundred rebels in front near the Meeting House. They took to flight after firing a few shots and retired with the others towards Moorestown. Their strength was about 1000 men and they were commanded by Colonel Griffin.
>
> It was the fault of one of my patrols, who had advanced too far against my will, that I could not go after the enemy as effectively as I wished. There were no casualties and the rebels were said to have lost only three men by my cannonade which consisted of only a few shots.[29]

Captain Johann von Ewald's account from the Hessian point of view provides additional details missing from von Donop's record of the events that occurred on December 23:

> On the morning of the 23d at five o'clock Colonel Donop set out toward Mount Holly with the 42d Regiment of Scots, the two

Captain Johann von Ewald (1744–1813), Hessian officer at the Battle of Iron Works Hill. He served in the Danish army from 1790–1813 and is here portrayed in uniform as Major General. *Courtesy of Wikipedia.*

> grenadier battalions, Linsing and Block, the twelve mounted jägers under Captain Lorey, and my jäger company. I formed the advanced guard, supported by Captain Lorey and a company of Scots.
>
> In the wood behind Slabtown we ran into an enemy party which took a new position at a Quaker church lying on a hill at the end of the wood, behind which the entire enemy corps was deployed. The colonel immediately ordered the Linsing Battalion to attack the hill on which the church stood. The Block Battalion was ordered to the left, and the jägers, with four companies of Scots under Colonel Stirling, moved to the right through the wood to cut of the enemy from Mount Holly or to gain mastery of the bridge across the Rancocas Creek, which intersects this town.
>
> The enemy, discovering this movement, withdrew in the greatest disorder through Mount Holly and across the bridge after the grenadiers had

taken possession of the church. Since the jägers and Scots pressed close behind them, a part sought to throw themselves into the houses near the bridge, but they were soon dislodged by the fieldpieces.[30]

Joseph Galloway states that von Donop marched ". . . with his whole corps of 2000 men (eighty left at Bordentown excepted)."[31] In so doing, he withdrew from his post at Bordentown, the southerly guard position for the German forces housed at Trenton. Von Donop's troops first met Griffin's militia at Petticoat Bridge, where the Hessians quickly retook the picket position. The account published in *The Pennsylvania Evening Post* on December 24, 1776, provides the following observations of what happened on December 23:

> . . . the next morning [23rd] the enemy advancing with considerable reinforcements, supposed to be about two thousand men with seven or eight fieldpieces, our little army was obliged to retreat (which they performed with great regularity) to prevent their being outflanked by superior numbers and in the evening they had another skirmish at Mount Holly in which an intelligent person informed had several killed and wounded. In both skirmishes our people had only two people killed and seven or eight wounded.[32]

Burlingtonian Margaret Morris notes:

> We hear the Hessians are still at Holly & our troops in possession of Church hill, alittle beyond—the account of 21 killd the first day of the engagement, & 10, the next, is not to be depended on, as the Hessians say our Men run so fast, they had not the Opp° [opportunity] of killing any of them.[33]

In his 1949 work *The Historic Rancocas*, local historian George DeCou mentions the cannonade exchange between the American and Hessian forces in Mount Holly:

> On arriving at Mount Holly on the afternoon of December 23rd, 1776, Colonel Griffin made a stand on Iron Works Hill; von Donop having mounted several pieces of artillery on the mount north of the village. An artillery duel was fought which the late Judge Slaughter described as the "Battle of Iron Works Hill" in an interesting article published in a county paper in 1926. Judging by the number of grapeshot and cannon balls that have been found in the vicinity of the hill it must have been a spirited engagement.[34]

Following the volley of cannonading between the Americans and the Hessian field pieces, Griffin's men quietly escaped into the woods, knowing they had achieved their objective: drawing von Donop and virtually all of his troops away from Bordentown. Captain Ewald recorded their retreat:

> . . . the greater part of the enemy gained the wood lying behind the town, through which the highway ran to Philadelphia, and by which the enemy saved himself. The jägers and Scots pursued the enemy for several miles through the wood, but he made no further stand. Almost two hundred men were captured, two cannon seized, and somewhat over one hundred men may well have been killed on both sides.[35]

Either prior to departing Mount Holly or on his way to Moorestown, Colonel Griffin dispatched a letter to General Washington, requesting permission to return to Philadelphia due to his falling ill. The skirmishing at Petticoat Bridge and in town must have overwhelmed what remained of his fragile health. Washington responded on December 23:

> Dr. Sir: I shall not object to your going to Philadelphia on Acct of your Health, but wish it would have permitted you to have gone to Bristol rather, in order to have conducted matters there in cooperation with what I hinted to you as having in view here.
>
> I fear their may be some little uneasiness about Command there, as some of the Continental Colonels have gone down with the Brigade that Marchd last. If you could only stay there two or three day to concert with Colonels Read [Reed] and Cadwalader a Plan, and direct in what manner it is to be conducted I should be glad of it. I am, etc.[36]

With Washington's granted, but reluctant, permission, Colonel Griffin returned to Philadelphia, taking his two companies of Virginia Troops with him after he had departed from Mount Holly. The Hessians, however, had no knowledge of the Americans' removal from West New Jersey and across the Delaware River to Philadelphia.

The Battle of Iron Works Hill

Hessian Colonel von Donop decided to remain in Mount Holly and celebrate Christmas, rather than return to Bordentown, particularly after meeting the young widow who stayed in town after the other women had vacated before the Hessians had arrived. Ewald described the Mount Holly then occupied by Hessian and Scottish soldiers, after vanquishing the American forces, and the deportment of the Hessian troops:

> The entire corps under Colonel Donop took up quarters in the town and I received mine at the exit to Philadelphia. Because of its position, this town is a very excellent trading place and inhabited by many wealthy people. Since the majority [of citizens] had fled and the dwellings had been abandoned almost the whole town was plundered; and because large stocks of wine were found there, the entire garrison was drunk by evening. Luckily for me, my quarters were in the section most poorly stocked, by which chance the jägers remained fairly sober. Meanwhile, the grenadiers were bringing in so much wine that the majority of the jägers became merry toward midnight, and I had great trouble to keep them together.[37]

Ewald reports that early the next day (the 24th), he

> ... was sent out with twenty jägers and fifty Scots to reconnoiter the road to Moorestown as far as the Long Bridge, to learn if it was occupied by the enemy or destroyed. The road there consisted of a succession of defiles through a thick wood. Toward ten o'clock I arrived unhindered at the bridge and found that it was ruined. Presently a few shots came from the other side where the Americans were hidden in several houses, through which a Scotsman was killed. I deployed the jägers along the creek to answer the enemy with brisk rifle fire and to reconnoiter the area more closely after which I withdrew and rendered my report [to Colonel von Donop].[38]

After Ewald and his troops returned to quarters,

> ... a trumpeter arrived in Mount Holly from General Washington, who presented a proposal to Colonel Donop concerning the exchange of some of his officers who had been captured at Mount Holly. The next two days would show that this was a ruse to find out whether the colonel was still in Mount Holly or was already marching back to Bordentown, which every reasonable man desired, since Trenton as well as Mount Holly were without any further support.[39]

Ewald and Hessian Captain Lorey, along with some troops, began ranging the countryside early in the morning on December 26, seeking horses and livestock as forage. While they were away from town, the first messenger arrived on horseback bearing the news to Colonel von Donop of Washington's successful attack on the Hessian troops at Trenton. While driving several hundred oxen, cows, pigs, and sheep, a messenger arrived from town informing the two captains of Washington's victory in Trenton and delivering orders that the animals should be left behind and all troops return to Mount Holly.[40] Regarding the situation, Ewald noted acerbically,

> ... for the colonel, who was extremely devoted to the fair sex, had found in his quarters the exceedingly beautiful young widow of a doctor. He wanted to set up his rest quarters in Mount Holly, which, to the misfortune of Colonel Rall, he was permitted to do. However, our control over this area came to an end today.[41]

The foragers had all arrived back in town by the afternoon and von Donop led his forces up through Crosswicks to arrive at Princeton. It was Captain Ewald's assignment to remain behind with 150 jägers and Scots and grenadiers and guard both entrances to Mount Holly. The colonel expected the American troops under Griffin's control to return quickly and attack from the rear. To prevent the citizenry remaining in town from engaging in mischief against the Hessians, Ewald filled a number of houses with brush and threatened to set them and the whole town ablaze at the slightest provocation or if the enemy attacked. The evening was uneventful and at midnight, Ewald received orders to withdraw and bivouac at Black Horse, leaving Mount Holly to recover from its occupation and depredations at the hands of the Hessian mercenaries.[42] Putting a final point on the whole affair, Ewald states, with remorse,

> This great misfortune, which surely caused the utter loss of the thirteen splendid provinces of the Crown of England, was due partly to the extension of the cordon, [and] partly to the fault of Colonel Donop, who was led by the nose to Mount Holly by Colonel Griffin and detained there by love.[43]

The Impact the Battle had on the Revolution

What occurred in Mount Holly had a great impact on the remainder of the Revolutionary War. It allowed Washington to gain a crucial victory at Trenton, thereby boosting the morale of both the troops and the patriotic citizens, and led to additional Continental victories. The tide had turned in the early days of the Revolution, and the Battle of Mount Holly played a crucial role in its final success, as noted in Ewald's quotation above.

Griffin's actions instigated Colonel von Donop's fateful decision to linger with his Hessian forces in Mount Holly through Christmas rather than trekking the eleven miles back to Bordentown. General James Grant, Colonel von Donop's British superior, certainly understood the importance of having reinforcements near Trenton, but Colonel von Donop failed to understand the full consequences of his remaining in Mount Holly. The colonel's choice to remain in town with his troops placed them eighteen miles away from Trenton and incapable of assisting in the event of an attack. It remains unquestionable that the Battle of Iron Works Hill diverted enemy troops away from Trenton, leaving the city without reinforcements on its southerly flank.

Late Christmas night in 1776, Washington and his commanders crossed the Delaware River at various points with a total of 2,400 men.[44] They reached Trenton early on the morning of December 26. Washington and General Nathanael Greene were at the head of the Continental command against Hessian Colonel Johann Rall and his 1,500 men.[45] Such an attack shocked the Hessians, as many were still drunk or hungover from Christmas Day celebrations, conditions that allowed Washington to easily overtake the enemy and capture Trenton.[46]

The Americans took the majority of Rall's unprepared forces prisoner at the time of the attack. On any other day, Colonel Rall's position in Trenton would have been complimented with an additional 2,000 men stationed at Bordentown for reinforcement in the case of an attack. However, not on this day, due to the troubles the militia caused down in Mount Holly and von Donop's ill-fated decision to remain there after routing the militia forces.

Washington's victory at Trenton, and then at Princeton, led to subsequent triumphs for the Continental Army and they eventually went on to win the Revolutionary War. Historians consider the Battle of Trenton as a key turning point in the war because it changed the morale of the American troops and set them on a path to victory. The Battle of Trenton receives attention and credit for being a significant factor in winning the war and, for obvious reasons, it is justified to give the battle such credit. However, the victory at Trenton and the triumphs that followed would not have been possible without the Battle of Iron Works Hill.

Today's Historic Mount Holly

The town of Mount Holly is proud of its history and promotes historical preservation and commemoration. Beginning in 2003, the town has held an annual commemoration of the clash between Colonel von Donop's troops and those of Colonel Griffin, complete with cannonading. The faux battle ceased being commemorated when reenactor and Burlington County resident Ian Johns retired from managing the yearly event after the 2015 reenactment. Others have made valiant attempts to revive the affair in 2016 and 2017, but failed for myriad reasons, ranging from insurance costs to complaints from local businesses. It is likely that future groundwork will be laid to again bring the sounds of cannons and gunshots to Mount Holly in December; only time will tell if success can be achieved.

Regardless of the present failure to continue the reenactment, Mount Holly is rich with American history. The town's heart is a historic district where the bulk of historical preservation recalls its Revolutionary War history. Various historical monuments, plaques,

Site maker located in Mount Holly, outside St. Andrews Cemetery, describing the events that occurred at the Battle of Iron Works Hill.

The Battle of Iron Works Hill

Stone monument within St. Andrews Cemetery in Mount Holly, paying tribute to those who fought at Iron Works Hill.

Reynolds. A United States flag flies on both graves.

There are some tributes to the Battle of Iron Works Hill found within St. Andrew's Graveyard. Off to one side within the cemetery, a stone monument and flagpole commemorates the battle. A metal plaque pays homage to those who fought at Mount Holly. The perimeter fence of the graveyard includes a site marker for the Iron Works Hill battle that offers a brief synopsis of the events that occurred there in 1776.

The Congregation of Saint Andrew's Church, located in town, commissioned the stone monument and dedicated it as a memorial to the late Reverend Canon Herbert R. Denton, who served as pastor and de facto ecclesiastical historian at this Episcopal Church.[48] In this capacity, he specifically focused on preserving the history of St. Andrew's Church in addition to his pastoral duties. Thus, the congregants, likely stricken with national bicentennial fever, dedicated this historical monument in his name following his death in 1976.[49] The monument contains two plaques. One describes the Battle of Iron Works Hill, while the other is the dedication to the Reverend Denton.

The Colonel Thomas Reynolds Chapter, National Society Daughters of the American Revolution, erected the Battle of Iron Works Hill site marker as part of the Daughters of the American Revolution Historical Markers Series.[50, 51] The series comprises thousands of historical site markers throughout the United States with the goal to promote historical preservation and education throughout the country.

and tributes, including some memorializing the Battle of Iron Works Hill, are scattered throughout the town. Other historical landmarks include the John Woolman Memorial Association property; the Shinn-Curtis Log House; the gristmill stone, retrieved from the millrace and erected in front of said log cabin; and Millrace Park. These landmarks have become part of the landscape and everyday culture of the town.

Part of this historic district is Iron Works Park, adjacent to Iron Works Hill. St. Andrew's Graveyard now sits on top of this hill along Pine Street, the same hill where the definitive battle occurred in 1776. Two soldiers who fought in the Revolutionary War lie in repose at the graveyard. John Lacey, a brigadier general with the Pennsylvania Militia,[47] and Colonel Thomas

Conclusion: Iron Works Hill History and Memory

The complete story of the Battle of Trenton includes underdog triumphs, success in battle, heroic bravery, and brilliant strategy. The retelling of this story usually fails to include the Battle of Iron Works Hill and the crucial role it played in Washington's victory. The Battle of Trenton became a legend of epic proportions in American history, overshadowing the essential nature of what happened at Mount Holly. A review of primary and secondary school curriculum across South Jersey failed to identify a single history class that teaches the Battle of Iron Works Hill, or any of the other events that occurred in and around Mount Holly and their role in winning the Battle of Trenton.

The Battle of Iron Works Hill is an intriguing tale of military strategy, involving deception, calculation, and an arrogant Hessian colonel. The underrated American militia forces served a critical role. It is clear that this battle was crucial during the American Revolution. Outside of Burlington County, however, it is barely remembered at all. Iron Works Hill was a key moment in the American Revolution, the memory of which has all but been erased from the historical knowledge of current society. We must preserve this significant history—the history of Iron Works Hill.

About the Author

Salvatore Gabriele grew up in Nutley, New Jersey, a small town located in North Jersey. Sal has always had a love for history, and he grew up fascinated with archaeology and prehistoric history. He developed an interest in local history as he researched New Jersey's significance during the Revolutionary War. Sal is currently a student at Stockton University, studying for a bachelor's degree in history. He aspires to teach high school history and, perhaps, even become a history professor someday.

Endnotes

1. Samuel Stelle Smith, *The Battle of Trenton* (Monmouth Beach, NJ: Philip Freneau Press, 1965), 16.
2. David Hackett Fischer, *Washington's Crossing* (New York, NY: Oxford University Press, 2004), 210.
3. West New Jersey Surveyor General's Office, Revel's Book of Surveys, 1681, 16.
4. John P. Snyder, *The Story of New Jersey's Civil Boundaries, 1606–1968* (Trenton: New Jersey Geological Survey, 1969), 97.
5. Henry C. Shinn, *The History of Mount Holly* (Mount Holly: Mount Holly Herald, 1957), 87.
6. Ibid.
7. Ibid., 36–37.
8. William A. Slaughter, "Battle of Iron Works Hill, at Mount Holly, New Jersey, December, 1776," *Proceedings of the New Jersey Historical Society* 4, no. 1 (1919): 20.
9. Slaughter, "Battle of Iron Works Hill," 20.
10. Slaughter, "Battle of Iron Works Hill," 20.
11. Smith, *The Battle of Trenton*, 10.
12. Fischer, *Washington's Crossing*, 146.
13. John C. Fitzpatrick, editor, *The Writings of George Washington, Volume 6, September 1776–January 1777*, (Washington, D.C.: United States Government Printing Office, 1932), 340.
14. Slaughter, "Battle of Iron Works Hill," 27.
15. Benson J. Lossing, *The American Revolution and the War of 1812*, vol. 2 (New York: New York Book Concern, 1875), 20.
16. Joseph Galloway, *Letters to a Nobleman, on the Conduct of the War in the Middle Colonies* (London: J. Wilkie, 1779), 53.
17. William M. Dwyer, *The Day is Ours!* (New York: The Viking Press, 1983), 211.
18. William S. Stryker, *The Battles of Trenton and Princeton* (Boston and New York: Houghton, Mifflin and Company, the Riverside Press, 1898), 337. The church mentioned in this quotation would be Saint Andrew's on Iron Works Hill.
19. Fischer, *Washington's Crossing*, 198.
20. Slaughter, "Battle of Iron Works Hill," 24.
21. John W. Jackson, *Margaret Morris: Her Journal with Biographical Sketch and Notes* (Philadelphia: George S. MacManus Company, 1949), 55–56.
22. William S. Stryker, editor, *Documents Related to the Revolutionary History of the State of New Jersey, Volume I, Extracts from American Newspapers, 1776–1777* (Trenton, NJ: The John L. Murphy Publishing Company, 1901), 243.
23. Dwyer, *The Day is Ours!*, 214.
24. Joseph P. Tustin ed, *Diary of the American War: A Hessian Journal, Captain Johann Ewald* (New Haven, CT: Yale University Press, 1979), 35, 38.
25. Jackson, *Margaret Morris*, 54.
26. Fischer, *Washington's Crossing*, 198.
27. Fischer, *Washington's Crossing*, 209.
28. Fischer, *Washington's Crossing*, 198–199.
29. Dwyer, *The Day is Ours!*, 214–215.
30. Tustin, *Diary of the American War*, 38.
31. Galloway, *Letters to a Nobleman*, 53.
32. William S. Stryker, editor, *Documents Related to the Revolutionary History of the State of New Jersey, Volume I, Extracts from American Newspapers, 1776–1777* (Trenton, NJ: The John L. Murphy Publishing Company, 1901), 243.
33. Jackson, *Margaret Morris*, 57.
34. George DeCou, *The Historic Rancocas* (Moorestown, NJ: The News Chronicle, 1949), 145.
35. Tustin, *Diary of the American War*, 38–39.
36. John C. Fitzpatrick, editor, *The Writings of George Washington, Volume 6, September 1776–January 1777*, (Washington, D.C.: United States Government Printing Office, 1932), 428.
37. Tustin, *Diary of the American War*, 39.
38. Ibid.
39. Ibid.
40. Tustin, *Diary of the American War*, 42–43.
41. Tustin, *Diary of the American War*, 42.
42. Tustin, *Diary of the American War*, 42–43.
43. Tustin, *Diary of the American War*, 44.
44. G. Bickham, "Contemporaneous Account of the Battle of Trenton," *The Pennsylvania Magazine of History and Biography* 10, no. 2 (1886): 203.
45. Smith, *The Battle of Trenton*, 64.
46. Bickham, "Contemporaneous Account," 204.

47 Mark Di Ionno, *A Guide to New Jersey's Revolutionary War Trail for Families and History Buffs* (New Brunswick, NJ: Rutgers University Press, 2000), 111.
48 "Mount Holly Historical Society," Home – Mount Holly, New Jersey, http://twp.mountholly.nj.us/.
49 "American Revolution Historical Markers," The Historical Marker Database, http://www.hmdb.org//results.asp?SeriesID=120.
50 "Colonel Thomas Reynolds Chapter," History of the Colonel Thomas Reynolds Chapter, NSDAR, http://www.rootsweb.ancestry.com/~njctrdar/history.html.
51 "American Revolution Historical Markers," 2017.

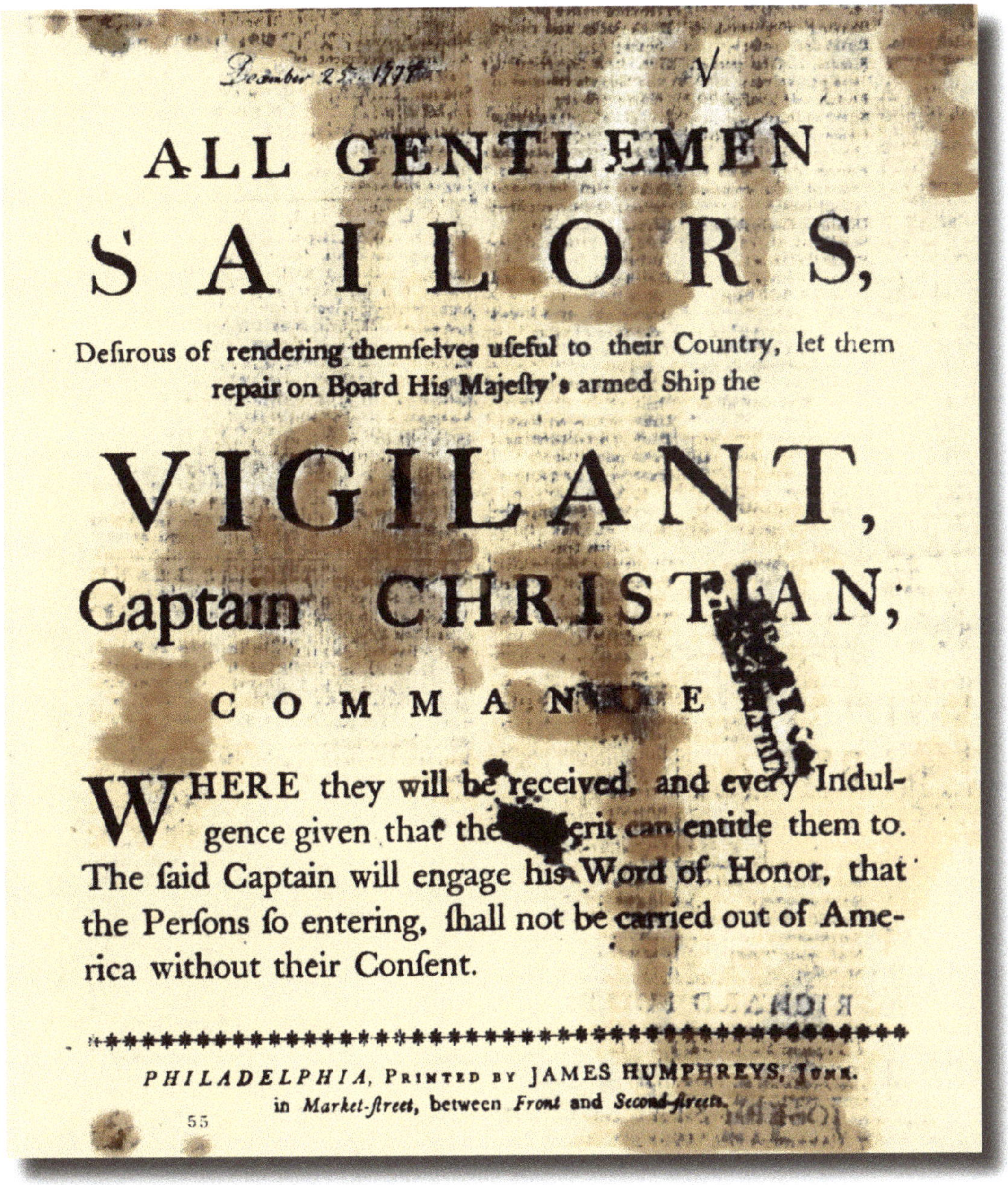

Broadside advertising for Loyalist seamen to join the Royal Navy on board His Majesty's Armed Ship the Vigilant. The handwritten date of December 25, 1777, suggests a promising time for British recruitment. The British Army had occupied Philadelphia since September 26, 1777. British victories at Fort Mifflin (in which the Vigilant played a pivotal role) and Fort Mercer certainly cheered the Loyalist outlook for success. Philadelphia: printed by James Humphreys Jr., 1777. *Courtesy of the Library of Congress.*

Tea House, Greenwich, N. J.

Greenwich Tea Burning. In what was the final tax protest before the American colonies formally revolted against the Crown, a group of about 40 young patriots learned that a loyalist named Daniel Bowen had received a consignment of tea from the British ship Greyhound. Bowen then secreted the shipment in the basement of his house at Greenwich, Cumberland County. The homeowner thought he could prevent rebels from taking action against the tea by storing it in his house before he shipped it on to Philadelphia. Like America's most famous tea party, the patriots donned Native American garb to mask their identity, but they did not dump the tea in the harbor as done in Boston. Rather, they broke into the Bowen house, removed the tea, and set the numerous chests containing the dried leaves ablaze on December 22, 1774.

On September 30, 1908, over 8,000 people jammed into the small town of Greenwich to witness the unveiling of a monument dedicated to the tea-burners. Conceived during the late nineteenth century, an appointed committee began planning the monument and collecting the funds for its creation. The local board of education contributed, as did school children. This would be Cumberland County's only memorial dedicated to revolutionary war activities in the county. The monument would include the names of many tea-burners from that night in 1774.

To assure the monument's completion, the Tea-Burners Chapter of the Daughters of the American Revolution stepped up and supplied the remaining funds necessary. On the day of its dedication, former governors and a host of dignitaries jammed the small platform, with each speaker delivering a historical discourse that made those present swell with pride over what our founding fathers had accomplished in bringing forth a new nation on this continent.

A passage from former Governor Edward C. Stokes summed up the pride that area residents felt:

> South Jersey is always modest. She has never properly unfolded her work in Colonial and Revolutionary days. Like the Roman Empress Cornelia, who counted her children her jewels, South Jersey has jewels in brave and worthy deeds. Her Red Bank, where Colonel Greene reserved his fire until his soldiers could see the enemy's eyes, her Hancock's Bridge and Tuckerton are glorious examples of her patriotism; and the waters of Great Egg Harbor Bay tell of the gallant work of the improvised navy of the Revolution, the "Mosquito Fleet" that sallied forth to attack and capture British ships and prevent prompt communication between British posts by sea.

Knight at Egg Harbor

J. Anthony Harness

In the middle of June 1777, Lieutenant John Knight, of the Royal Navy, proceeded north from the mouth of the Delaware in command of a small flotilla bound for New York City. He was to deliver two captured prizes and a number of American prisoners to the British Headquarters there, as well as convey a confidential report to Vice Admiral Lord Richard Howe, commander in chief, North American Station, from Captain Andrew Snape Hamond, Captain of HMS ROEBUCK and commanding officer of the Delaware Blockade.[1]

Captain Hamond's dispatch regarded his preparations for an amphibious invasion on the Delaware River above Newcastle, as he had been secretly warned earlier that spring by Lord Howe that his brother, General Sir William Howe, the commander in chief of British Army Forces in North America, had decided that the capture of Philadelphia would be his focus for the year's campaign. With that goal in mind, General Howe intended to transport his army by sea, landing it on the shores of the Delaware.[2]

Knight, however, had one more mission. Hamond had tasked him with conducting a quick raid on the American blockade runners and privateers based at Egg Harbor.[3]

Egg Harbor had already become quite a problem to the British by June 1777, along with the other principal smuggling and privateer bases of Boston, Salem, Portsmouth, New Bedford, New Haven, and New London. It has been estimated that at this time "… British ships in the Americas were being attacked at the rate of about one a week.…"[4] Mister Woodbridge, a London alderman, testified in early 1778 to the disruption of commerce by American privateers in the House of Lords. The "value of these (lost) cargoes was declared to be moderately estimated at over ten millions of dollars."[5]

Several privateer attacks prior to June 1777 are documented that concern the Egg Harbor area of operations. On June 6, 1776, Captain James Robertson's Pennsylvania privateer CHANCE, and the CONGRESS, a Pennsylvania sloop commanded by Captain George McElroy, brought into Egg Harbor the captured ships LADY JULIANA, JUNO, and REYNOLDS.[6] They had seized these vessels during May in the Florida Straits.[7] These prizes proved so important that John Hancock, then President of the Continental Congress, felt compelled to write of them to General George Washington.

> …This Morning two small Privateers arrived here after a very successful Cruise; having taken three West India Ships with 22,420 Dollars on Board—1052 Hhds & Trs. of Sugar 70 Pipes best Madeira Wine, and a Variety of other Articles. The Captain and Owners this Moment called to acquaint me, the Money is now in this City, and have generously made an offer of it to the Congress.[8]

The JUNO also carried a valuable quantity of gunpowder that was later convoyed up the Delaware to Philadelphia.[9]

Barely a month later, the same two privateers captured a British ship named the TAMAREA, bringing her into port at Egg Harbor on July 5, 1776.[10] Then again, the next month, according to the *Pennsylvania Evening Post* of August 1, 1776, Captain Craig, then in command of the CONGRESS, carried in the brig RICHMOND from Nevis said to be worth £20,000.[11]

At the end of August 1776, Congress's Marine Committee ordered the Continental Navy Schooner WASP to undertake a cruise to Bermuda. Before the year

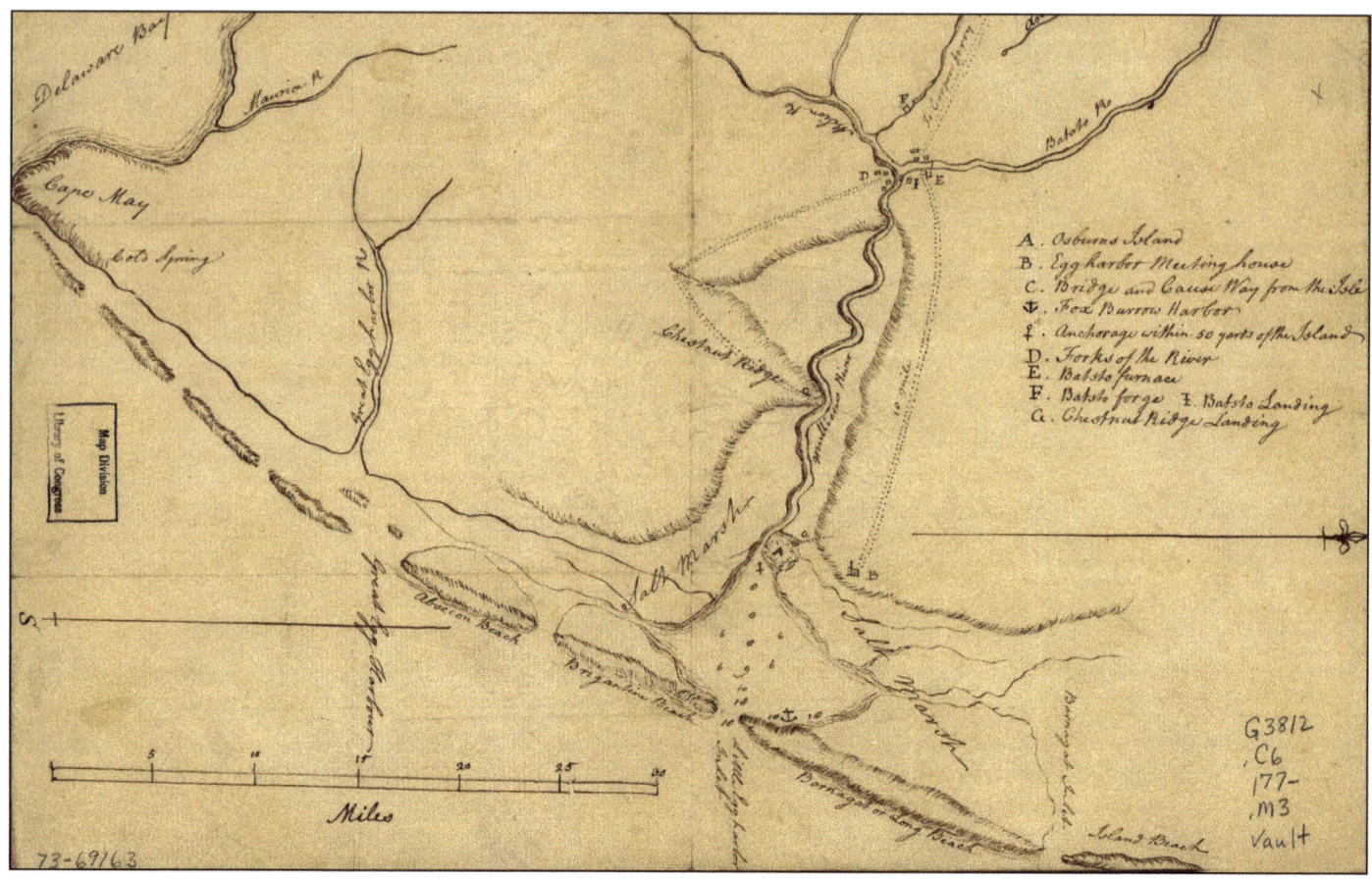

Little Egg Harbor Area. Detail of Map of the coast of New Jersey from Barnegat Inlet to Cape May. 1770s. *Courtesy of Library of Congress Geography and Map Division.*

was over, Lieutenant John Baldwin, her commander, had captured three enemy ships and sent them to Egg Harbor.[12]

The attacks by these American commerce raiders continued. And not always were the prizes seized far away; sometimes the capture occurred close along the Jersey shore. On March 1, 1777, only a few miles from Egg Harbor, Privateers captured a British brig off Absecon Beach.[13]

Likewise, Egg Harbor, for years a haven for tax smugglers,[14] excelled in her new role in evading the British embargo. Just the known war contraband deliveries there for the period between February and August 1776 are impressive—forty-eight tons of gunpowder, 60 tons of saltpeter, and 1900 stands of arms.[15]

However dire the above facts appear, the British attacked these problems vigorously. They retook 174 vessels from their American captors during the first two years of the war.[16] For the most part, their blockade of American ports during this period, though incomplete, proved effective.[17,]

Many successful British patrolling actions occurred between the Delaware Capes and Long Beach Island during these months. After the invasion of New York, the Royal Navy oriented its operations at maintaining the blockade of Philadelphia, protecting their vital lines of communication by sea along the Eastern Seaboard, and hunting down those who threatened these missions—be they Continental Navy, state's navies, smugglers, or privateers.

For example, just prior to Knight's mission to Egg Harbor, the Delaware squadron had a spate of coups in the South Jersey region. HMS Daphne, a frigate, took the brig Cornelia & Molly on March 28, 1777, loaded with gunpowder and sailcloth in Delaware Bay,[18] and chased the American ship Sally ashore at Cape May and burnt her and her cargo on April 1, 1777.[19] This was followed by the frigate HMS Mermaid destroying a schooner off Egg Harbor at the end of the month.[20]

But who was this British officer who would first take action against the American base at Egg Harbor?

John Knight was born in Dundee, Scotland, in 1747, the son of a Royal Navy officer. He followed his father to sea at the age of eleven and saw battle at Cherbourg in the Seven Year's War. In 1765, he transferred to the North American Station, where he took part in navigational surveys as a midshipman aboard the HMS Romney. In 1770, he was promoted to Lieutenant and given command of HMS Diligent and continued coastal surveys of New England and the Canadian Maritimes, assisting the noted Swiss-born cartographer, Joseph F. W. Des Barres with his major work, the *Atlantic Neptune*, for the British Admiralty.[21]

As captain of the Diligent, he pulled into port at Machias, Massachusetts (now Maine), for resupply during one of these survey missions, a month after the Battle of Lexington, unaware of the civil unrest in the area. His ship was seized by local rebels and he and the crew made prisoners.[22]

However bad that mistake, he was able to dispatch all of the valuable survey material amassed aboard the Diligent—what John Lyon, one of Knight's jailers, described in a apology to James Otis Jr., of the Massachusetts Provincial Assembly, as "all the plans of this continent."[23] Knight sent this material to British forces in a sea chest containing his personal belongings, right under the noses of the unsuspecting Machias authorities. He thus secured for the British a great wealth of naval knowledge that they could capitalize on through the course of the war.

He was exchanged a year later, and acquitted of any blame for the loss of his ship at courts-martial. Shortly afterwards, in February 1777, he was given command of HM Armed Sloop Haerlem and joined the Delaware Blockade.[24] The Haerlem was the former American privateer Harlequin that had been found scuttled in the Harlem River. The Royal Navy had purchased her for £700 from the New York authorities, raised her, armed her with twelve 4-pounders, and put a 65-man crew aboard.[25]

Two months later, at the end of May, Knight recaptured the schooner Apollo at Sinepuxent Inlet, Virginia. The Pennsylvania privateer frigate Oliver Cromwell, under the command of Harman Courter, originally captured the Apollo in the West Indies, after its Captain, Tobias Collins, had sailed out of Whitehaven, England, with a valuable cargo of cordage. Courter had placed William Forsyth as her prize master with orders to take her to Philadelphia.[26]

On May 29, 1777, three days after the recapture of the Apollo, the Haerlem and HM Brig Tender Stanley, Lieutenant Richard Whitworth of the Roebuck commanding, seized the American sloop Industry (Captain John Hutchins) as it sailed north from Bermuda with a cargo of salt.[27]

While Knight's return to active duty was marked with these successes, General Washington stood guard in New Jersey's Watchung Mountains. There, besieged with high desertion rates in his army, unmet recruitment quotas, and logistical and organizational difficulties, Washington still managed to repeatedly thwart General Howe's plans to lure him into a general engagement on the plains below New Brunswick.[28]

The artful American commander, however, knew that Howe had more options. Washington employed several intelligence networks in his efforts to ascertain British intentions for the new campaign season. Would Howe attack Philadelphia, and if so—by land or by sea—or would he move north, up the Hudson River to co-operate with General Burgoyne's drive down from Canada? Or, it was plausible that Howe might even descend on Virginia or South Carolina, or turn the other way and attack one of the New England colonies.[29]

It was in this tense period of the war, with the British believing they were on the eve of victory, that Knight sailed the Haerlem north out of Delaware Bay, skirting the Cape May coast. The Stanley and the Armed Sloop Hotham, Lieutenant Christopher Hele, commander, accompanied Knight on this voyage.

Knight's orders from Captain Hamond read as follows:

> You are hereby directed to take under your Convoy the Several Prizes now in the Delaware and proceed with them to New York, where you are to deliver the enclosed Letter to the Right Hon'ble the Lord Viscount Howe, and waite His Lordships Orders for your further proceeding.
>
> You are to receive on board the Sloop under your command the Prisoners named in the list sent with them and dispose of them at New York as the Commander in chief shall direct. And whereas I have received intelligence that several of the Enemies Vessels are lately arrived at Egg Harbour, You are therefore in your way to endeavour to look into that place, and if it shall appear to you to be practicable to cut them out or destroy them, You are to take the Hotham and Stanley Tenders under your command (who are directed to accompany you thither for that purpose) and use your best endeavours against the enemies Vessels; which Service being performed, You are then to give Orders to the Hotham Tender to join the Preston at New York, and Send the Roebucks Tender back to me with an Account of your proceedings; making the best of your way afterwards with the Sloop under your command to join the Admiral without further loss of time.

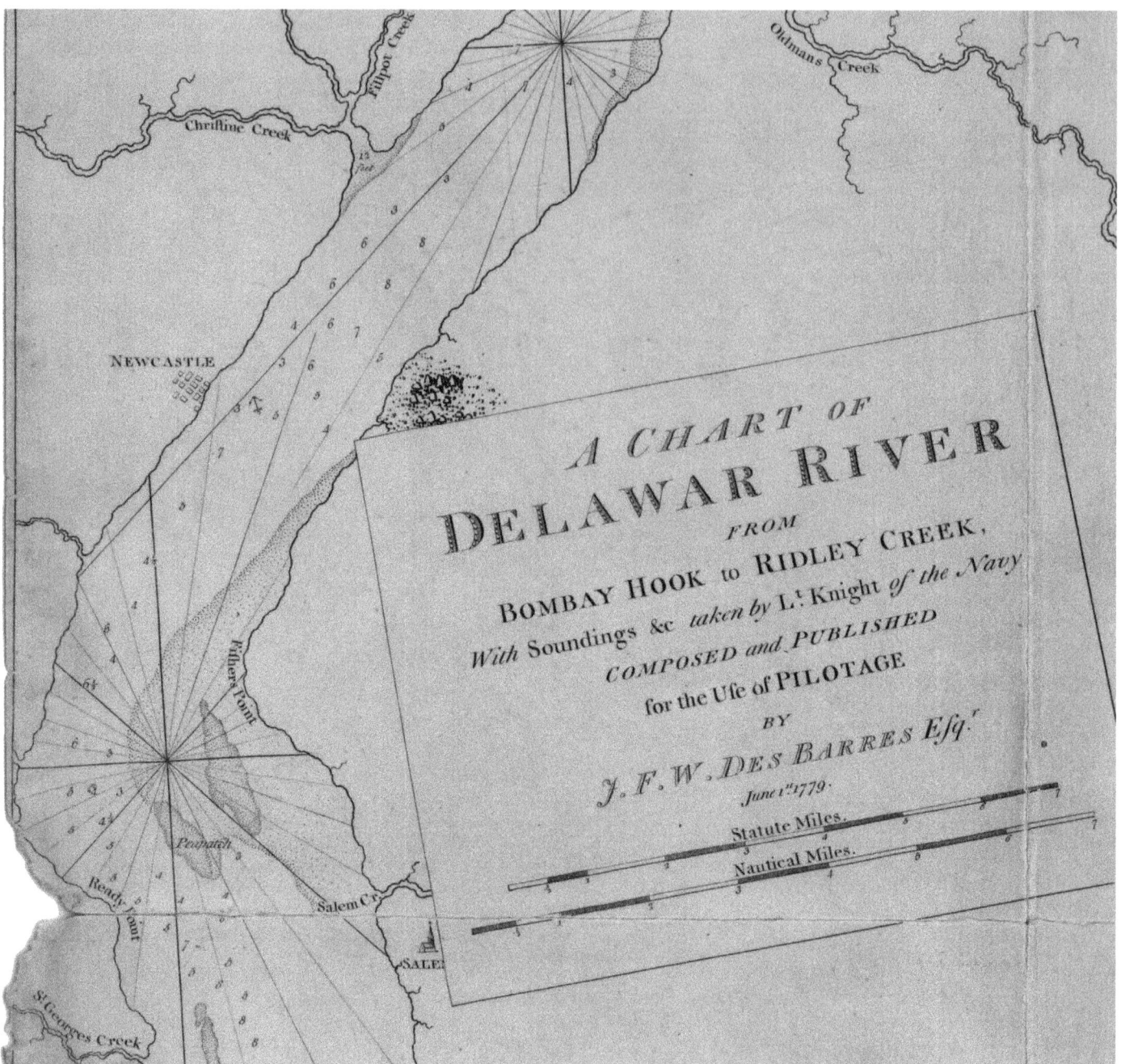

Detail of "A chart of Delawar River from Bombay Hook to Ridley Creek, with soundings &c taken by Lt. Knight of the Navy," 1779. *Courtesy the Library of Congress.*

Given on board His Majesty's Ship the ROEBUCK in the Delaware the 10th June 1777[30]

Lieutenant Knight followed those instructions. His small naval division arrived at the Little Egg Inlet on the evening of June 10, 1777. There, while the rest of his command stayed out of sight, he sent the STANLEY forward, pretending to be an American vessel in need of a pilot.[31] The unfortunate Joseph Sooy fell for the ruse and was captured along with the crew of his boat. Afterwards, Knight withdrew, and sailed eighteen miles south to attempt the trick again at Great Egg Harbor Inlet. With two pilots, he presumably was going to split his forces and attempt simultaneous raids on Egg Harbor and her sister smuggling/privateering community of Mays Landing.

Mister Golder, the pilot signaled for on the Great Egg Harbor Inlet, however, saw through the scheme and escaped, though he had to abandon his boat to the King's men.[32] This attempted kidnapping of Golder most likely took place on June 11, as it would not be until the following day that the next phase of the British plan evolved.

In the early part of the day of June 12, Knight struck with his force at Egg Harbor Inlet. Knight likely coerced

Knight at Egg Harbor

John Knight Esqr., Rear Admiral of the White Squadron, engraved by Smart, 1804. Courtesy of the National Maritime Museum, Greenwich, London. http://collections.rmg.co.uk/collections/objects/107590.html.

Joseph Sooy into guiding the British through the inlet to the harbor at Fox Burrows.[33] The Americans were ill-prepared to resist Knight's bold strike. The militia commanders at the Forks of the Little Egg Harbor River had been alerted, and rightly suspected that the kidnapping of pilots meant a British raid was in the offing, but they were still scrambling to reinforce the small outpost at the inlet with men, arms, ammunition and supplies when the attack commenced.[34]

Knight's sailors and Marines captured two vessels. One was the privateer brig NANCY under the command of Captain Montgomery. She was on a cruise out of St. Eustatius in the Dutch West Indies and had a small cargo of damaged salt on board.[35] The second vessel was the American merchant brigantine ANN under the command of Christopher Bradley. Her cargo was lumber and tar.[36]

John Cox, owner of Batsto Furnace, Lieutenant Colonel in the Philadelphia Associators,[37] and former intelligence officer[38] and scout for General Washington,[39] and Lieutenant Colonel Elijah Clark of the 3rd Battalion, Gloucester County Militia,[40] and former New Jersey Assemblyman,[41] chronicled certain of these events in a letter to Governor William Livingston, in his capacity as President of the New Jersey Council of Safety. The letter was sent to Livingston through the offices of Charles Pettit, New Jersey's Secretary of State, who was at Burlington, and had heard of the June 14 (Saturday) raid on Fox Burrows. Pettit had sent a preliminary account of it to Livingston the next day in a letter he wrote to the Governor on Sunday, June 15:

> ...I may, however, mention a report we had on Saturday last, (which seemed to come straight, and has not been contradicted,) that the enemy had invested Egg Harbor Inlet, and taken out two sloops and a larger vessel outward bound....[42]

But Pettit did not receive the Cox/Clark letter until June 18, a week after the attack. They most likely sent it to him because of the highly mobile nature of Livingston's wartime governorship. Pettit expressed concern about getting timely messages to the Governor. In April and May, Livingston was situated at Bordentown; in the middle of June, he was in Morristown; and by the beginning of August he was in New Town.[43]

Pettit forwarded the Cox/Clark letter to Livingston on June 19, enclosed in another missive of his own. He wrote:

> Last evening I received the enclosed letter from Col. Cox, and in order to convey it to you, I shall send this to the commanding officer at Bristol, with a request to forward it, either by the return of an express, or by some officer going to head quarters. I would beg leave to recommend it to your Excellency's consideration, whether it would not be proper to order a part of the militia to watch the motions of the enemy about the Egg Harbor Inlets....[44]

The Cox/Clark Letter:[45]

> Forks of Little Egg Harbor, June 12, 1777. The Hon. the President of the Council of Safety.
>
> Sir, — We this morning received information from Capt. Bradley, at the Foxborough, that on the 10th instant, about six o'clock in the evening, a brig appeared off Little Egg Harbor Inlet, and made a signal for a Pilot, on which Joseph Sowey with his brother and two boys went off to conduct her into port, and were unluckily taken and carried off.
>
> Immediately on taking them on board, the brig proceeded to the mouth of Great Egg Harbor Inlet, where she again threw out a signal for a pilot, on which Mr. Golder, a noted man in that way, went off with his boat, and on approaching near enough to discover what she was, finding her to be a vessel of force, and observing her to hoist out her boat to windward, which was managed with some degree of precipitation, he immediately put about, and pushed for the shore, the enemy's boat pursuing with only two men appearing, and on coming within about one hundred yards, a number of men instantly showed themselves, and fired on Golder and crew, who with some difficulty gained the shore, but were obliged to quit their boat, which fell into the hands of the enemy. As Sowey is one of our best pilots, and well acquainted with our Inlet, we doubt not he will be made use of by the enemy to bring in their tenders, and pilot them up the bay and river; which may be productive of the most fatal consequences, the inhabitants being in the most helpless condition and having a great number of cattle and other property that must immediately fall into the hands of the pirates, unless some spirited steps are immediately taken to prevent it; and being desirous of doing

everything in our power to disappoint them, we have presumed to take from Capt. Shaler eight or ten pieces of cannon, belonging to a sloop of his lately cast away on the coast, which we have this day ordered down to the Foxboroughs, under his direction, with orders immediately to throw up a battery to defend the Inlet, and to annoy the enemy as much as possible, should they attempt an entrance.

There is now at Foxboroughs a guard of about 20 men, and Col. Clark will immediately order down as many more, to assist in doing the necessary work. Powder and provisions for the people will be immediately wanted. Shot can be procured here. We doubt not the hon'le Council will think it expedient to lose no time in giving the necessary directions for effecting what they may think ought to be done on this alarming occasion.

We are, with great respect, your most ob't and h'e ser'ts,

John Cox Elijah Clark

Cox and Clark apparently wrote their dispatch before the two men had knowledge of Knight's success in cutting out the two ships. Unfortunately, as they were preparing to defend the anchorage at Fox Burrows, the attack must have been already underway, if not completed.

How long it took for the Cox/Clark letter to reach Livingston at Morristown (or indeed how long it took Pettit's first alarm of the British raid in his letter of June 15 to arrive) is not known. But the affair was well concluded as far as the Royal Navy was concerned by the time these messages did reach the Governor. Lieutenant Knight's flotilla reached New York City on June 15, bringing into port the captured vessels, APOLLO, INDUSTRY, NANCY and ANN. There they were tried by the Vice Admiralty court and condemned in the following weeks.[46]

After leaving command of the HAERLEM, Knight served aboard HMS EAGLE, Admiral Howe's flagship. There the commander in chief took great advantage of his knowledge of American waters.

He went home to England with Howe in 1778, but returned to the war in 1780. He served as First Lieutenant of HMS BARFLEUR, a 90-gun second-rate ship of the line, Rear Admiral Samuel Hood's flagship in the Caribbean theater. He was then briefly post-captain of HMS SHREWSBURY, a 74-gun third-rate ship of the line, in 1782, before returning to the BARFLEUR as her captain. His later years in the Royal Navy included very distinguished service during both the French Revolutionary Wars and the Napoleonic Wars.[47]

John Knight was knighted for his service to the Crown in 1815 upon his retirement, and promoted to his final rank, Admiral of the Red, in 1830, the year before he died at the age of 84.[48]

AFTERMATH OF KNIGHT'S RAID

Fully realizing the vulnerability of the Fox Burrows anchorage after Knight's raid, and the importance of the post there in safeguarding the approach to Chestnut Neck and Batsto, Colonels Cox and Clark, and Major Richard Wescott, also of the 3rd Battalion, Gloucester County Militia,[49] wrote to the New Jersey Council of Safety. Their appeal was heard by the Council at Newtown, Sussex County, on July 5, 1777.

> A Memorial from Elijah Clark, Richard Wescott, & John Cox was read, Setting forth that the Enemy's ships of War entered little Egg harbor, Inlet, and seized two brigs lying at the Fox-barrows, just within the Inlet & carried them off, with a considerable quantity of Stock &c, and praying that little Egg Harbor may be fortified &c, and that this Board would issue the necessary orders for that purpose.
>
> Agreed unanimously, That this Board is not competent to decide upon the subject-matter of the said Memorial; and therefore that it be referred to the Legislature.[50]

On September 20, 1777, the New Jersey House of Assembly took up the matter of Egg Harbor's defense. On their discovery that Clark and Wescott had fortified Fox Burrows at their own expense, they decided to repay the two Gloucester County Militia officers from the State's coffers.

> A Memorial from Elijah Clark and Richard Westcott, Esqrs. was read, setting forth, "That they had erected, at their own Expence, a small Fort at the Foxburrows, near the Port of Little-Eggharbour; and had purchased a Number of Cannon for the Defence of the said Port; relying on the Publick for Payment of the Expence on that Occasion: That they had disbursed a Sum of Money, an Account whereof is annexed to the said Memorial, and praying a Re-imbursement of

the Monies so advanced." Whereupon the House having taken the same into Consideration,

> Resolved,
> That the Treasurer pay the Balance due to the said Elijah Clark and Richard Wescott, being Four Hundred and Thirty Pounds One Shilling and Three-pence; and that their Receipt, or the Receipt of either of them, be a Discharge to the Treasurer for Payment thereof: That they be empowered and directed to sell such Stores as are not useful, and pay the Amount into the Treasury, and to take Charge of the said Cannon and necessary Stores for the Use of the State.[51]

But only a short six months later, the New Jersey General Assembly decided that the threat to Egg Harbor had evaporated. The legislators determined the Fox Burrows fortifications as superfluous and ordered them dismantled and the cannons sold.

> Whereas, by a Resolution of both Houses of the 20th of September last, Elijah Clark and Richard Westcot; Esquires, were empowered and directed to take Charge of a Number of Cannon belonging to this State near the Port of Little Egg-Harbour, for the Use of the State; and the said Cannon not being in Use,
>
> Resolved,
> That the said Elijah Clark and Richard Westcot be empowered to sell and dispose of the same, and pay the Amount of Sales into the Treasury; and that the Receipt of the Treasurer shall be a sufficient Discharge to the said Elijah Clark and Richard Westcot therefor.[52]

Then, of course, in October 1778, five months after the Assembly's unfortunate decision to sell-off Fox Burrows' armaments, Lieutenant General Sir Henry Clinton, the new British commander in chief, would send a more heavily structured force to return to Egg Harbor.

About the Author

J. Anthony Harness lives in Little Egg Harbor, New Jersey, with his wife, Victoria. He is a member of the Tuckerton Historical Society, the Atlantic County Historical Society, the American Revolution Round Table of South Jersey, and the Colonel Richard Somers Chapter of the Sons of the American Revolution. He is also a contributor of photographs and transcriptions to the online Historical Marker Database.

Endnotes

1. *Naval Documents of the American Revolution, American Theatre: Jun. 1, 1777–Jul. 31, 1777*, vol. 9. (Washington D.C.: United States Government Printing Office, 1983), 83.
2. Ibid.
3. The descriptor "Egg Harbor" or "Eggharbor," when used in eighteenth-century correspondence and newspaper descriptions, refers to today's "Little Egg Harbor," the inlet to the Mullica River and surrounding area. Maps from the period typically distinguish between Little Egg Harbor and Great Egg Harbor, the inlet to the Great Egg Harbor River, eighteen miles southwest of the Mullica. Throughout this article, Egg Harbor, mirroring common eighteenth-century usage, refers to Little Egg Harbor.
4. William Osborn Stoddard, *The Noank's Log* (Boston, MA: Lothrop Publishing Co. 1900), 1.
5. Ibid.
6. Granville W. Hough, "Granville Hough's Ship Listing C/D," *American War of Independence at Sea*, http://www.awiatsea.com/Other/Hough%20List%20C-D.html.
7. John Viele, *The Florida Keys: True Stories of the Perilous Straits* (Sarasota, FL: Pineapple Press, 1999), 70.
8. "To George Washington From John Hancock, 5–6 June 1776," *National Archives, Founders Online*, http://founders.archives.gov/documents/Washington/03-04-02-0354#GEWN-03-04-02-0354-fn-0003.
9. Hulbert Footner, *Sailor of Fortune: The Life and Adventures of Commodore Barney, USN* (Annapolis, MD: U.S. Naval Institute, 1940), 25.
10. David Munn, *Battles and Skirmishes of the American Revolution in New Jersey* (Trenton, NJ: Bureau of Geology and Topography, Dept. of Environmental Protection, 1976), 28. The David C. Munn collection of New Jersey materials is housed at Stockton University's Bjork Library in Special Collections.
11. "To George Washington From John Hancock, 5–6 June 1776" *National Archives, Founders Online*, http://founders.archives.gov/documents/Washington/03-04-02-0354#GEWN-03-04-02-0354-fn-0003.
12. Granville W. Hough, "Officers B," *American War of Independence at Sea*, http://www.awiatsea.com/Officers/Officers%20B.html.
13. Munn, *Battles and Skirmishes of the American Revolution in New Jersey*, 58.
14. Arthur D. Pierce, *Smuggler's Woods* (New Brunswick, NJ: Rutgers University Press, 1960), 32.
15. Don Williams, *Letters of Delegates to Congress: 1774–1789* quoted at H-net.org, http://h-net.msu.edu/cgi-bin/logbrowse.pl?trx=vx&list=h-oieahc&month=0302&week=a&msg=LplYLWm W5XBVFb6B9aYkYw&user=&pw.
16. William Osborn Stoddard, *The Noank's Log* (Boston, MA: Lothrop Publishing Co. 1900), 1.
17. Gary M. Walton, *The Economic Rise of Early America* (New

18 Granville W. Hough, "Granville Hough's Ship Listing C/D," *American War of Independence at Sea*, accessed on 1/01/2015, http://www.awiatsea.com/Other/Hough%20List%20C-D.html.

19 *Naval Documents of The American Revolution, American Theatre: Mar. 1, 1777–Apr. 30, 1777*, vol. 8 (Washington D.C.: United States Government Printing Office, 1980), 287.

20 Munn, *Battles and Skirmishes of the American Revolution in New Jersey*, 28.

21 "Lieutenant (later Admiral) John Knight," *Heritagecharts.com*, http://www.heritagecharts.com/product.php/217/0/john_knight.

22 Ibid.

23 Ibid.

24 Ibid.

25 Simon Harrison, "British Unrated Brig-Sloop 'Haerlem' (1777)," *Three Decks – Warships in the Age of Sail*, http://threedecks.org/index.php?display_type=show_ship&id=4581.

26 Granville W. Hough, "Oliver Cromwell," *American War of Independence at Sea*, http://www.awiatsea.com/Privateers/O/Oliver%20Cromwell%20Pennsylvania%20Ship%20%5BCourter%5D.html#T000007B.

27 Granville W. Hough, "Industry," *American War of Independence at Sea*, http://www.awiatsea.com/pl/Br/British%20Prizes%20June%201777/Industry%20Sloop%20%28John%20Hutchings%29.html.

28 "Revolutionary War Series: Volume 9," *The Papers of George Washington*, http://gwpapers.virginia.edu/editions/letterpress/revolutionary-war-series/volume-9-march-june-1777/.

29 "Revolutionary War Series: Volume 10," *The Papers of George Washington*, http://gwpapers.virginia.edu/editions/letterpress/revolutionary-war-series/volume-10-june-august-1777/.

30 *Naval Documents of the American Revolution, American Theatre: Jun. 1, 1777–Jul. 31, 1777*, vol. 9 (Washington D.C.: United States Government Printing Office, 1983), 83.

31 *Selections from the Correspondence of the Executive of New Jersey, from 1776 to 1786*, sourced at *Archive.org*, https://archive.org/stream/selectionsfromco00newje#page/n3/mode/2up ,61.

32 Ibid.

33 Joseph Sooy had been taken-in by another British ruse nineteen months earlier. On October 16, 1775, he had mistakenly helped British officers escape from a troop transport that had grounded on Brigantine Beach. For that foul-up, he had been brought for investigation to Burlington. His excuse was that the Britishers had taken off their regimentals and he did not realize that they were soldiers. "Joseph Sooy's Affidavit," *American Archives*, http://lincoln.lib.niu.edu/cgi-bin/amarch/getdoc.pl?/var/lib/philologic/databases/amarch/.7809.

34 *Selections from the Correspondence of the Executive of New Jersey, from 1776 to 1786*, sourced at *Archive.org*, https://archive.org/stream/selectionsfromco00newje#page/n3/mode/2up ,61.

35 Granville W. Hough, "Nancy," *American War of Independence at Sea*, http://www.awiatsea.com/pl/Br/British%20Prizes%20June%201777/Nancy%20Brigantine%20%28Montgomery%29.html.

36 Granville W. Hough, "Ann," *American War of Independence at Sea*, http://www.awiatsea.com/pl/Br/British%20Prizes%20June%201777/Ann%20Brig%20(Christopher%20Bradley).html.

37 "To George Washington from Colonel John Cadwalader, 27 December 1776," *National Archives, Founders Online*, http://founders.archives.gov/documents/Washington/03-07-02-0353.

38 "From George Washington to Joseph Reed or Colonel John Cox, 7 April 1777," *National Archives, Founders Online*, http://founders.archives.gov/?q=%22john%20cox%22&s=1111311111 &sa=&r=13&sr=.

39 "From George Washington to Joseph Reed, 14 January 1777," *National Archives, Founders Online*, http://founders.archives.gov/?q=%22john%20cox%22&s=1111311111&sa=&r=12&sr=.

40 George R. Powell, *History of Camden County, New Jersey*, (Philadelphia: L. J. Richards & Co. 1886), sourced at *The NJ Genweb project*, https://sites.google.com/site/camdencountynjgenweb/history/war-of-the-revolution-the.

41 Ibid.

42 *Selections from the Correspondence of the Executive of New Jersey, from 1776 to 1786*, sourced at *Archive.org*, https://archive.org/stream/selectionsfromco00newje#page/68/mode/2up, 67.

43 Deduced from William Livingston's letters, *National Archives, Founders Online*, http://founders. archives.gov/?q=William%20Livingston%20Author%3A%22Livingston%2C%20William%22&s=1111211111&sa=&r=1&sr=

44 *Selections from the Correspondence of the Executive of New Jersey, from 1776 to 1786*, https://archive.org/stream/

Armed Sloop at Sea, D. Tandy, 1799. Courtesy National Maritime Museum, Greenwich, London, http://collections.rmg.co.uk/collections/objects/124606.html.

selectionsfromco00newje#page/68/mode/2up, 69.
45. Ibid., 61.
46. *Naval Documents of The American Revolution, American Theatre: Jun. 1, 1777–Jul. 31, 1777*, vol. 9 (Washington D.C.: United States Government Printing Office, 1983), 83, 158.
47. "Sir John Knight," *Three Decks – Warships in the Age of Sail*, http://threedecks.org/index.php?display_type=show_crewman&id=1378.
48. "Admiral Sir John Knight, KCB RN," *Caro's Family History*, http://www.carosfamily.com/getperson.php?personID=I1945&tree=mytree.
49. "Revolutionary War Sites in Mays Landing, New Jersey," *Revolutionary War New Jersey*, http://www.revolutionarywarnewjersey.com/new_jersey_revolutionary_war_sites/towns/mays_landing_nj_revolutionary_war_sites.htm. For additional detail about Richard Wescoat's life and family, see Mary Jo Kietzman's "Made in Nesco: The Inter-Generational Project of Place-Making," *SoJourn* 2.2 (Winter 2017–18): 7–22.
50. *Minutes of the Council of Safety of the State of New Jersey*, sourced at *Archive.org*, https://archive.org/stream/minutesofcounci00newj#page/76/mode/2up/search/cox, 76.
51. *A Journal of the Proceedings of the Legislative Council of the State of New Jersey (1776-77)*, sourced at *Archive.org*, https://archive.org/stream/journalofproceed1776newj#page/110/mode/2up, 111.
52. *Votes and Proceedings of the General Assembly of the State of New-Jersey* (1777), sourced at Archive.org, https://archive.org/details/votesproceedings1777newj 107.

Enemy Fleet sighted off Little Egg Harbour. Draft of letter sent from George Washington to General Israel Putnam, July 28, 1777. The commander in chief reports the sighting of a portion of the British fleet off Little Egg Harbor in late July 1777. Washington believes that an invasion force, with Philadelphia as its target, will soon arrive in the Delaware Bay and he is making preparations for such an incursion.

A series of letters written at this time make clear the difficulties of interpreting intelligence during the war. Within this correspondence, Washington displays surprise that the British do not appear in Delaware Bay. In fact, General Howe had ordered that the fleet sail to the Chesapeake, landing at Head of Elk and marching north toward Philadelphia. From George Washington Papers, Series 4, General Correspondence. *Courtesy of the Library of Congress.*

> To Major General Israel Putnam
> 4 Miles East of Flemingtown [N.J.] July the 28. 1777
> Dr Sir
> We have certain advices that part of the Enemy's Fleet, Viz. Seventy Sail were beating off Little Egg Harbour on Saturday morning with a Southerly Wind. From this Event, there seems to be but little room to doubt but that their destination is into Delaware Bay and against the City of Philadelphia. I am now to request that the Two Brigades which I mentiond some time ago, to come this way in case Genl Howe turned his views towards Philadelphia, may be ordered to pass the River immedeately with All their Baggage & to hold themselves in readiness to march in a moment on your receiving further Orders from me. They will take the Rout through Morris Town (should they be ordered to proceed & from thence to Coryels Ferry where they will cross the Delaware[)]—You will direct the Brigadrs Genls or Commanding Officers to perform their March after they begin it, as expeditiously as they possibly can without injuring the Troops & to prevent every violation of property belonging to the Inhabitants by the Soldiery. I am Dr Sir Yr Most Obed. set.

Forgotten Victories

Jeffery M. Dorwart

On October 22, 1777, more than 3,000 elite Hessian mercenaries, fighting for Great Britain, attacked the American fortified earthworks on a high bluff at Red Bank, in Gloucester County, overlooking the Delaware River. Commissioned as Fort Mercer by the Continental Congress and General George Washington, this fort held out against repeated enemy assaults. The Hessian attackers suffered more than 100 dead, including their best commanding officers, and endured at least 300 front-line troops wounded. An hour after the land phase of the battle had begun, big warships of the British Navy arrived off Red Bank and began a fierce duel on the river with American gunboats and small warships. In the riverine phase of the battle, the British lost two of their finest warships on station in American waters.[1] Veterans agreed that they had not witnessed such a fierce land and sea fight before. "On the 22d, in the Afternoon," Colonel Joseph Reed of Philadelphia observed, "there was a heavy Cannonade, followed by the hottest fire of Musquetry I ever heard."[2]

Despite the fury of this Revolutionary War battle in southern New Jersey, few historians identify and discuss the prolonged attack that, along with the more famous New Jersey battles of Trenton, Princeton, and Monmouth, rendered New Jersey as the "Crossroads of the American Revolution." Even the name Fort Mercer obscures this Gloucester County battle, as the fort's namesake, General Hugh Mercer, is generally connected with the battle of Princeton, where he died, or Mercer County, which memorializes his name.

For many, Red Bank suggests a community by that name in Monmouth County, New Jersey. Founded in the nineteenth century, the popular Monmouth County fishing and resort town of Red Bank invariably steals the spotlight from the site of the battleground, located on the heights above the Delaware River. Moreover, little remains of the defensive works at Fort Mercer to identify it as a historic site, and, for more than a century, neither state nor local government appeared to hold any interest in preserving its heritage. Apparently, the local Gloucester County Quaker community sought to shun, from its collective memory, the violence and carnage that occurred on the farm of one of its peace-loving members, the Whitall family. When a veteran's association erected a monument to the defenders of Fort Mercer in 1829, the stone obelisk suffered constant vandalism at the hands of unknown miscreants, and, by 1900, the blue-veined marble shaft stood "ignored, neglected and forgotten."[3]

Nevertheless, the battle of Fort Mercer at Red Bank shares importance with the three more celebrated New Jersey Revolutionary War battle sites to the north. Discussion of this significant southern New Jersey military operation adds to our understanding of New Jersey's military history, and how Americans fought the Revolutionary War. The Gloucester County riverbank of red clay that rose forty feet above the Delaware River first drew notice as the possible site for a fort on June 30, 1775, when the Assembly of the Colony of Pennsylvania created the Philadelphia Committee of Safety (re-designated as the Council of Safety in 1776). Philadelphia leaders worried that as the site of the Continental Congress sessions since 1774, the city provided a prime target for the British military, which had engaged in open warfare in Massachusetts against Americans since April. So, they organized an association to protect the capital and elected longtime defense expert and fort designer Benjamin Franklin as president. The Philadelphia Committee of Safety immediately "Resolved, that the Committee go to Red Bank to-morrow, to take a view of the River and Islands."[4]

The emphasis on Red Bank indicates the unparalleled vista the high bank offered to the committee for viewing the Delaware and its archipelago. The committee's visit there likely stirred interest in placing a fortification atop this salient. Of course, far more strategic spots on the river existed to build fortifications. A partially completed stone fort already stood on Fort Island, just downriver from the Schuylkill River's confluence on the Pennsylvania side, nearly opposite Red Bank. A bit farther downriver on the Jersey shore, just below Mantua Creek, the land jutted into the river at Billingsport, close to the main channel, making it a good spot to guard any river obstructions that the committee might chose to sink in the narrowest part of the river. Indeed, Franklin's defense association selected Fort Island as the base for the so-called Pennsylvania Navy, a fleet of small gunboats and fire rafts assigned to guard the river. It also selected Billingsport as the location to construct a large fort and lay across the narrow river channel the first line of *chevaux-de-frise*, iron-tipped log assemblies sunk and anchored into stone-filled cribs on the river bottom. Projecting upward at an angle with the tips pointing downriver, the pikes stood ready to pierce the hull of enemy wooden warships. The Committee initially said nothing about gun emplacements at Red Bank; it lay too distant for guns mounted in any fort that might be constructed there to cover the main Delaware River channel or Fort Island.[5]

So, why did the Philadelphia Committee of Safety consider Red Bank as the site for a fort in the first place? Many city defense committee members held membership in the Gloucester Fox Hunting Club across the river and often hunted along the nearby Jersey shore and creeks. Prominent Gloucester County riverfront landowners like Benjamin Whitall of Red Bank, John Wood of neighboring Woodbury Creek, and David Paul of Billingsport (near present-day Paulsboro) offered to sell logs for constructing the *chevaux-de-frise* installations. Moreover, Red Bank's importance increased when the Philadelphia defense planners decided eventually to place a second series of *chevaux-de-frise* nearer Philadelphia as the last line of defense to a riverine attack. Fort Island would anchor and protect the Philadelphia side, and Red Bank would protect the Jersey side of the protective measures in the river.[6]

During late 1775 and early 1776, the Philadelphia defense committee, composed, in part, of shipbuilders, carpenters and merchants, funded the construction of a Pennsylvania Navy and a fort (later named Fort Mifflin) on Fort Island. It ignored the Jersey defenses until May 1776, when British troop movements in New Jersey raised concern for an invasion force reaching Philadelphia overland from the north. The committee resolved to fortify the Jersey shore "Particularly at a place called Billingsport," but complained that funding the navy, the *chevaux-de-frise*, and Fort Island barracks and blockhouses left nothing for additional river defenses. The Philadelphia defense committee appealed to Congress for help.[7] John Adams led the movement to fortify rivers "at the Continental Expence."[8] This included purchase, in July 1776, of the 96-acre Paul farm in Billingsport, on which to build a large fortification (the first Federal defense installation), provide "a skilful Engineer" to design the fort, and greatly expand the works on Fort and Mud Island for use as a naval base.[9] At the moment, Congress said nothing about any fortification at Red Bank.

Meanwhile, to the north, British forces drove the Americans across New Jersey and the Delaware River above Trenton. Hessian patrols probed as far south as Bordentown and Burlington. The Continental Congress feared an imminent attack through New Jersey on Philadelphia. In response during early December 1776, Washington dispatched his chief Continental Army engineer, General Israel Putnam, to fortify the city. Upon arriving, Putnam met with Colonel Thomas Proctor, a Pennsylvania artillery captain and the commander of the militia construction force working on Fort Island and Billingsport. Proctor warned the military engineer that something had to be done to prevent the British

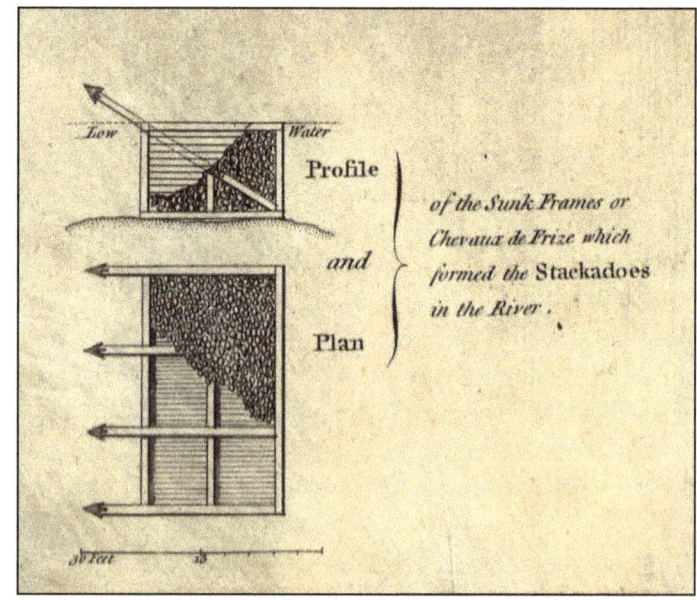

Chevaux-de-Frise in profile and overhead view. These long, heavy wooden pikes, iron-tipped and firmly weighted to the Delaware River bottom, presented formidable obstacles to the British navy. Detail from map of "The course of Delaware River from Philadelphia to Chester, exhibiting the several works erected by the rebels to defend its passage, with the attacks made upon them by His Majesty's land & sea forces." London: William Faden, c. 1777. *Courtesy of the Library of Congress.*

from "possessing themselves of Red Bank & Billings' Port." For the first time, Red Bank appears to be part of the evolving defensive scheme for the Delaware River approaches to Philadelphia. After slogging about in the mud on the low-lying Fort Island, often under water at high tide on the river, Putnam decided that the high and dry orchard and meadow of the Whitall farm at Red Bank held the key to the river defenses, not Fort Island. He "gave it as his opinion that works should be formed on Red-bank to prevent the enemy taking the advantage," Proctor informed the Council of Safety of Pennsylvania on December 23. "The Block houses at the Fort should be removed to Redbank to be fixed as redoubts, and form lines of communication to each and their flanks."[10]

Washington's surprise victories over the British-Hessian garrisons at Trenton in December 1776 and Princeton in January 1777 reduced the urgency for erecting a fort at Red Bank. No work began until the middle of April, when the Pennsylvania Council of Safety sent local builder Colonel John Bull and militia workers from Billingsport to Red Bank.[11] Meanwhile, Continental Congress, and the Supreme Executive Council of Pennsylvania, dispatched a special committee for viewing the works erected to guard the river. Led by Adjutant General Thomas Mifflin of Philadelphia and the Inspector of Ordnance and Manufactories, Philippe Charles Tronson du Coudray, a French military engineer and artillery officer recruited by Silas Deane in Paris, the fortification committee visited Fort Island, Billingsport, and Red Bank (soon referred to by some as Fort Mercer, since Congress had just passed a resolution on April 18, 1777, to order monuments erected to the memory of General Hugh Mercer).[12]

Du Coudray provided Congress with a detailed analysis of the three forts on June 11. Regarding Red Bank, Du Coudray thought the river was too wide in front of Red Bank for the artillery to be effective in preventing an enemy vessel from passing upriver between Fort Island and Red Bank and invading Philadelphia. Anxious to endear himself to Mifflin and other local leaders so that he could design the Delaware defenses instead of George Washington's favorite and his rival as military engineer, Louis Le Begue de Presle Duportail, du Coudray praised Colonel Bull's "natural good-sense unenlightened by theory" in making a huge earthworks at Red Bank superior to the works at either Fort Island or Billingsport, and advised preservation of the fort, that in conjunction with Fort Island opposite, served as a second line of defense.[13] Congress hired du Coudray to implement his fortification plans.[14]

George Washington read du Coudray's report, but favoring his own engineer Duportail's advice, claimed insufficient knowledge of the area to evaluate its merit. After all, Washington had never visited the Delaware River sites. Nevertheless, Howe's sailing from New York with 16,000 men and appearance off the Delaware Bay in late July forced Washington to act on a Delaware River defensive plan. He ordered his Continental army south from central New Jersey, and personally visited Philadelphia and Chester, Pa., where, on August 1st, the American commander in chief crossed the Delaware to visit Billingsport, Red Bank, and "Mud Island" (actually Fort Island).[15]

Ever cautious and meticulous in planning, Washington asked senior officers to convene a council of war and evaluate the three fort sites on the Delaware River. General Nathanael Greene and Colonel Joseph Reed of Philadelphia, Washington's aide, secretary and currently delegate to Congress, viewed Red Bank as useless. It stood so far from Fort Island and the second line of *chevaux-de-frise* that it was "very questionable whether it is worth retaining." They preferred Fort Island or Billingsport. General Anthony Wayne of Pennsylvania and Ordnance Commander Brigadier General Henry Knox disagreed, however, telling Washington that Red Bank remained a "post of Consequence" guarding one side of the river and providing a bastion of defense. Throw 500 men in the fort, Wayne insisted, and the fort could hold out and close the river to the enemy.[16]

Washington told Congress on August 9 that, despite flaws, a Red Bank fort should be developed. He accepted Congress's employment of du Coudray.[17] The French military engineer concentrated on building Billingsport and Fort Mifflin, while popular Philadelphia militia leader Bull and local militia workers from Pennsylvania and New Jersey, including African-American laborers, continued to raise earthworks at Red Bank. Meantime, Howe's army landed at Head of Elk at the top of Chesapeake Bay on August 25 and marched through Delaware and into Pennsylvania, where it engaged and defeated Washington's army at Brandywine on September 11. Howe crossed the Schuylkill and entered Philadelphia by September 26, 1777, beginning more than nine months of occupation of the Continental capital city. Still, the Americans held the Delaware River where the *chevaux-de-frise* prevented British supply ships from warping upriver to reinforce Howe in the city.[18]

In early October, British troops from the 42nd Regiment Scots and 10th Regiment fusiliers occupied the fort at Billingsport, while HMS Roebuck began clearing a passage through the lower line of river obstacles. With the fall of the first line of defense at Billingsport, desertion among local militia forces along the river and Pennsylvania Navy crews increased

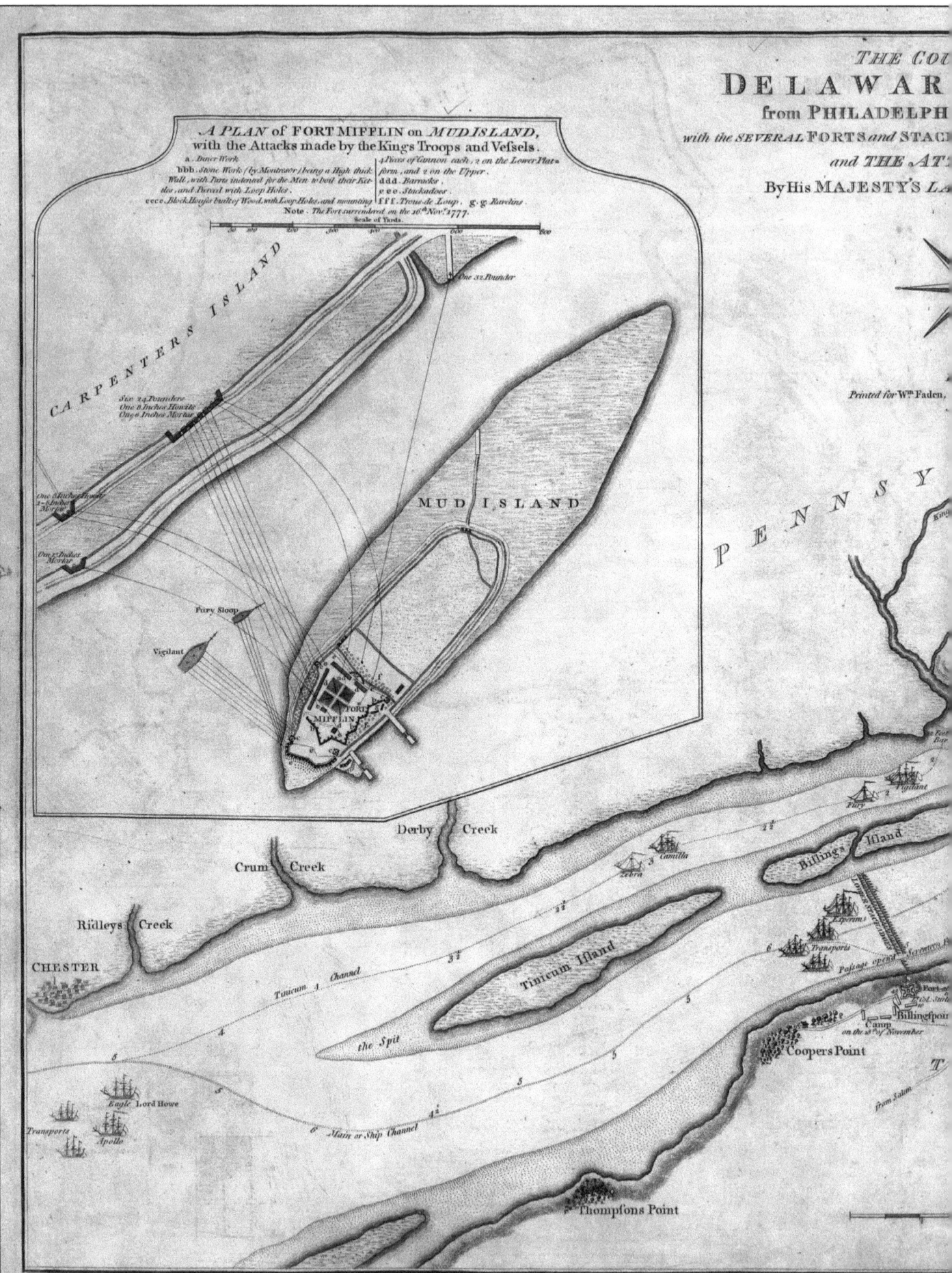

Forgotten Victories

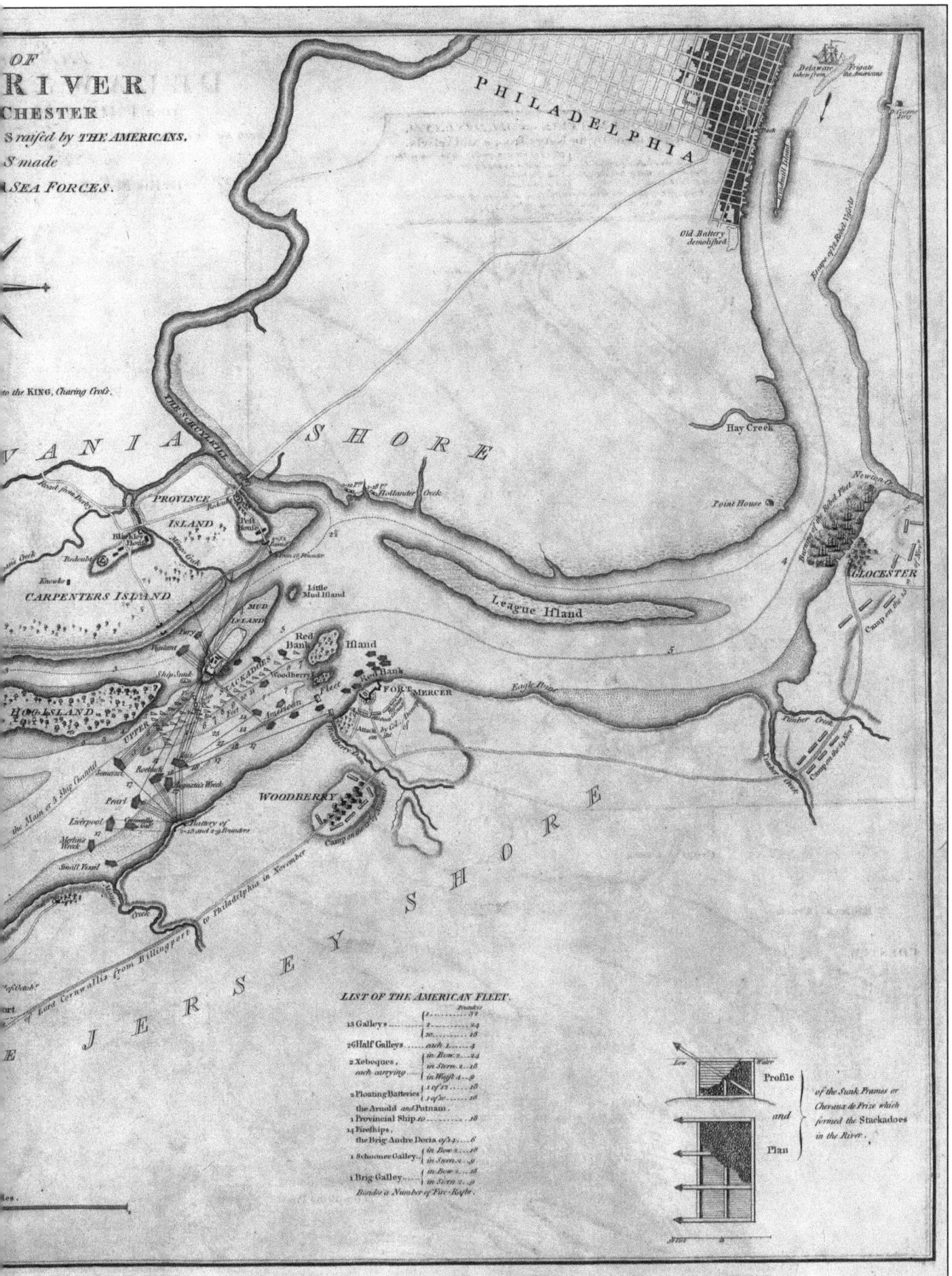

dramatically. Colonel Samuel Smith, commandant of Fort Island (Fort Mifflin), and Captain Joseph Blewer of the Pennsylvania Navy Board begged Washington to send Continental troops into the fort at Red Bank. The fort seemed vital to protect Commodore Hazelwood's retreating navy and preventing the British from removing the second line of *chevaux-de-frise* in the deep channel that passed between Red Bank and Fort Island.[19]

With Billingsport lost and Fort Mifflin under constant bombardment, desertion decimated the Pennsylvania Navy. Red Bank now took on new importance as a symbol of continued resistance along the Delaware River. Growing criticism in Congress of Washington's timid tactics around Philadelphia, combined with news of a "glorious victory" at Saratoga at the hands of General Horatio Gates, Congress' favorite to replace Washington as the commander of the Continental Army, made holding Red Bank vital to Washington. Leading critic Richard Henry Lee of Virginia offered to give Washington one more chance. "The General has sent a party to secure Red Bank, almost opposite to Philadelphia, in which case, Gen. Howe's situation must be a dangerous one," Lee told Patrick Henry.[20]

After Washington failed to penetrate British defenses of Philadelphia on October 4, 1777, at the battle of Germantown, the commander in chief focused on defense of the Red Bank fort (still not called Fort Mercer). On October 9, he dispatched Colonel Christopher Greene and the crack First Rhode Island Continental regiment with 244 men into the Red Bank earthworks. Also, Washington ordered Colonel Israel Angell's 2nd Rhode Island Regiment, with over 270 effectives, to march south from Coryell's Ferry, near Trenton, to join Colonel Greene. Later generations insisted that these Rhode Island regiments contained a number of African-American Continentals when they entered Red Bank in October 1777. However, Washington only gave Greene permission to raise black troops in December, two months after Red Bank, and Rhode Island never enlisted blacks in the Continental Line until the recruitment law of February 1778. Accounts made long after the battle of African-Americans defending Red Bank remain a part of tradition and folklore, not history.[21]

Colonel Christopher Greene, of Rhode Island, in command of Fort Mercer during the Battle of Red Bank. From a photograph of an oil painting owned by Mr. Edward A. Greene of Providence, Rhode Island.

Washington dispatched Captain Thomas Antoine, the Chevalier de Mauduit Du Plessis, General Knox's French artillery expert, to organize defensive positions at the Red Bank fort "where he united the Offices of Engineer and Commandant of Artillery," and "made several judicious alterations in the works at Red bank." Mauduit saw immediately that Bull's massive earthworks required a garrison of more than 1,000 musketeers and artillerymen. Washington had neither available in the area. Thus, the professionally trained French military engineer cut back the defensive perimeters, adding deep ditches filled with a barricade of logs with pointed stakes (*abatis*) and masked in heavy brush. He placed artillery and musket positions at angles to allow a devastating crossfire against assaulting troops trying to breach the abatis. Now, the fort at Red Bank might be defended by the 400-plus men of the two Rhode Island regiments and by the dozen cannon belonging to Captain James Cook's artillery company.[22]

General Howe recognized the significance of a fortified position, located high on the riverbank bluff of Gloucester County, overlooking the main river channel. Even if Fort Mifflin fell, Red Bank's guns promised to protect the remnants of the rebel navies seeking refuge under the high ground and make more dangerous the

Map on pages 44–45. "The course of Delaware River from Philadelphia to Chester with the several forts and stackadoes raised by the rebels, and the attacks made by His Majesty's land and sea forces." London: William Fadden, 1785. *Courtesy of the Library of Congress.*

lifting of the second line of *chevaux-de-frise*. The longer the forts held out, the longer the likelihood that winter ice would close the river to British supply ships desperate to reach Philadelphia. So, General Howe planned to attack Red Bank, dispatching across the river at Cooper's Ferry (now Camden) on October 21 a 4,000-man Hessian brigade under Count Carl Emil Ulrich von Donop. Howe's German adviser reported that the force included the

> grenadier battalions Linsing, Minnigerode and Lengerke, as well as the regiment Mirbach and the Hessian jaegers, all under the command of Colonel von Donop, [that] crossed over to Jersey at Coopers Ferry with orders to take the batteries and the fort at Red Bank.[23]

The expeditionary force marched to Haddonfield, where it camped for the night. The morning of October 22, von Donop's column reached the area of Mount Ephraim when either locals or an advance guard informed the Hessian colonel that the Americans had removed the bridge over Big Timber Creek. The Hessians turned southward and crossed William Harrison's milldam on their way to the next major crossing of Big Timber Creek at Clement's Bridge.[24] The Hessians then marched toward the riverfront fort past the major Gloucester County market town of Woodbury.[25] According to tradition, local Gloucester Fox Hunting Club guide Jonas Cattell ran from Haddonfield to the fort in front of the invaders to warn Greene's garrison of the impending attack.[26]

The force of German mercenaries arrived at Red Bank in the early afternoon, and deployed in two columns, one from the northeast and the other from the southeast, and von Donop, acting under an attitude of supreme superiority, demanded surrender of the fort, thereby losing the would be element of surprise. The Americans' defiant refusal to abandon the post caused von Donop to open fire on the earthworks with a battery of light 3-pounder cannon. The light-caliber guns made little impression on the rebel fort.[27] Howe ordered von Donop to wait, before attacking, for British warships to take up position in the river near Red Bank. However, tide and a "contrary wind" delayed the big British gunships from passing through the line of obstacles off Billingsport and making their way upriver to within cannon range of Red Bank.[28] Probably smarting from the humiliating defeat of his Hessians at Trenton by Washington the previous winter, von Donop

ordered Linsing and Minnigerode with 1,200 grenadiers and the Mirbach division of over 3,000 infantrymen to attack the fort before naval support appeared. The Hessian colonel held in reserve the Lengerke battalion and Hessian sharp-shooting jägers.[29]

The battle-hardened grenadiers fixed bayonets and, about 4 o'clock in the afternoon, marched to the beat of drums in two columns, one into the older portion of the fort to the north and the other directly into the new works from the southeast. The Mirbach division advanced into the old fort from the east. Receiving no resistance and thinking the Americans had retreated from the fortification, the Hessians rushed forward toward the nine-foot-high walls of Mauduit's smaller defensive work, getting caught on the abatis and brush in the ditch. Struggling to climb over the barricades,

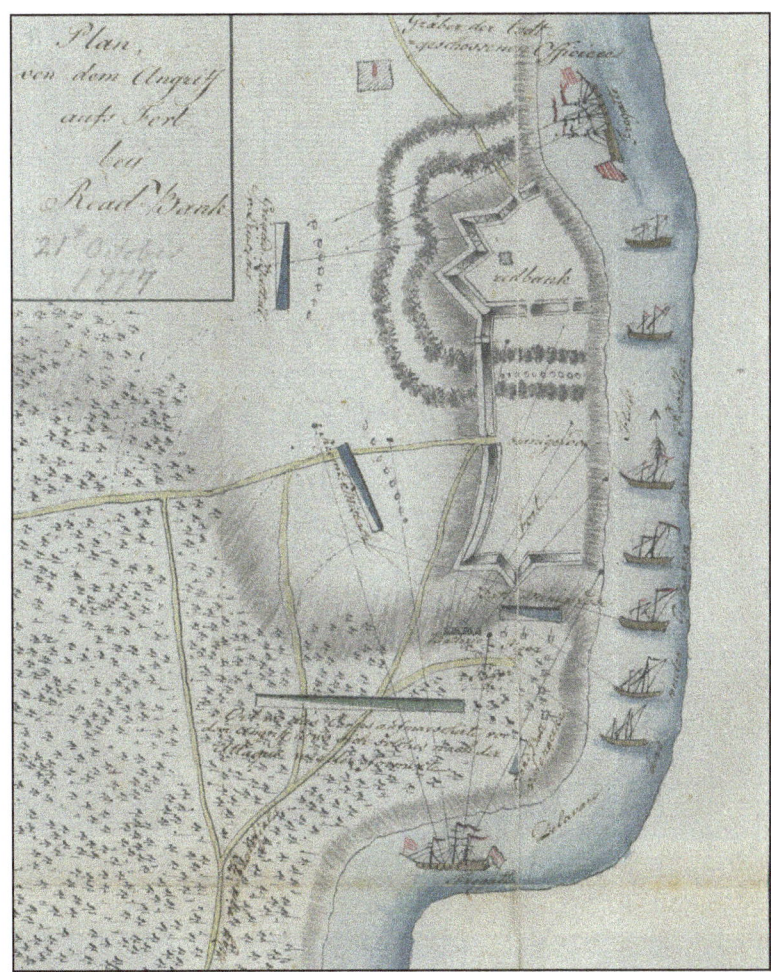

Johann von Ewald's hand-drawn "Plan of the Attack on the Fort at Red Bank, 21 October 1777." *Used with permission, Joseph P. Tustin Papers, Andruss Library, Bloomburg University.*

the Hessians took heavy crossfire from the muskets and cannon of the American defenders placed by Mauduit at the angles of the earthwork to cover every inch of the ditch with devastating musket ball and

Colonel Carl Emil Ulrich von Donop (1732–1777). Mortally wounded during the attack, von Donop was buried on the Red Bank battlefield. *Courtesy of Wikipedia.*

grapeshot.[30] Pennsylvania Navy galleys, unopposed by British ships, concentrated cannon fire on von Donop's land force.[31] After a firefight lasting nearly an hour, the Hessians withdrew with heavy casualties, including von Donop and his top commanders. Another 200 to 250 wounded lay about until the following morning when Greene ordered them brought to a makeshift hospital at the Whitall farmhouse nearby. In the end, more than 20 German officers and at least 120 infantry died. The garrison lost fourteen killed and twenty-three wounded.[32]

Meanwhile, the British naval force, led by Captain Francis Reynolds' 64-gun ship Augusta, arrived on station off Red Bank and engaged rebel naval forces until 7 o'clock when low tide and darkness stopped the battle. During the night, Augusta ran aground. The 20-gun ship Merlin tried to pull the bigger ship free from the sand bar, when suddenly the Augusta exploded and fire ignited on-board. Reynolds testified at the court-martial hearing later, that "Wads from her guns" accidentally ignited, destroying the warship. The Merlin grounded as well, and the British set the smaller ship on fire to prevent capture.[33]

The Americans believed that their naval forces set on fire the British warships. This, combined with Greene's repulse of von Donop at Red Bank, greatly boosted confidence in Washington's generalship. Seemingly, the battle fulfilled its promise to give the commander in chief a "glorious victory" comparable to that of Gates' triumph at Saratoga to the north. Erstwhile Congressional critics praised Washington. Lee predicted that the American commander would march south to Chester, Pennsylvania, below Philadelphia and cut off Howe's overland supply route. Washington's former military secretary and current Pennsylvania delegate to Congress, Joseph Reed, insisted that thus isolated in the city, Howe would quit Philadelphia in a week. "I assure you," he wrote Pennsylvania Supreme Executive Council President Thomas Wharton Jr., "there is a happy Prospect of a Speedy & glorious End to the Contest." On his part, Wharton hoped that Red Bank marked a turning point in the war. The American triumph ended traitorous desertions and brought "the day . . . near at hand when we can say with safety that . . . America is free and Independent."[34]

Massachusetts delegate to Congress John Adams placed the Battle of Red Bank in a larger setting. He told wife Abigail that news of the American victory would spread to Europe, secure diplomatic recognition for U.S. independence, and bring a much needed French diplomatic and military alliance. The usually cautious General Washington experienced a momentary and probably genuine exhilaration after Red Bank. The victory, he supposed, "will also be attended with the most happy consequences" of driving the British out of the Delaware Valley.[35]

In fact, the Red Bank fight momentarily disheartened the British command in Philadelphia. Admiral Howe ordered his ship captains not to talk about the loss of the two warships, while General Howe admitted to London that they had suffered a slight setback. But the Howe brothers had no intention of evacuating Philadelphia. If anything, the Battle of Red Bank merely increased the urgency of reducing the American defenses before ice closed the water supply route to the city. The British command would not repeat the mistakes of the Red Bank expedition. Naval and land forces would cooperate and employ heavy guns to reduce the rebel fortifications, and adequate manpower, mostly British regulars, would be employed to crush the American forces manning the fortifications.[36] To this end, Howe sent to New York for Major General Sir Thomas Spencer Wilson's 4,000-man army corps to reinforce Lieutenant General Charles Cornwallis in reducing the fort at Red Bank. Simultaneously, General Howe ordered additional heavy guns installed on the Pennsylvania riverfront directly opposite Fort Mifflin and for his brother to bring up the entire fleet to within cannon range of Fort Island.[37]

Washington suspected that Howe would send his best British regulars across the river to avenge von Donop's defeat, and that British warships would try to demolish Fort Mifflin and lift the final line of *chevaux-de-frise*. For the American commander in chief, the outcome of the battle for control of the river depended upon Colonel Samuel Smith holding Fort Mifflin and Colonel Christopher Greene preventing British seizure of Fort Mercer until Washington could assemble an army strong enough to engage Cornwallis and Wilson on the Jersey side of the river. Washington ordered all available forces south to Gloucester County in preparation for a great battle around Red Bank (that he referred to now as Fort Mercer for his fallen comrade, Hugh Mercer). These included Brigadier General Robert Ralston's Pennsylvania militia, Brigadier General David Forman's North Jersey militia, presently guarding the salt works in Monmouth County, Brigadier General Silas Newcomb's South Jersey militia, General James M. Varnum's Rhode Island regiment, General Jedidiah Huntingdon's Connecticut regiment, Colonel Daniel Morgan's Rifles, and Brigadier General Peter Muhlenberg's Pennsylvania Line. Washington placed the entire 8,000-man army in the South Jersey area under his best fighter, Major General Nathanael Greene.[38]

Unfortunately, Washington had been able to collect only a few thousand troops in South Jersey by early November, when the British launched an intense bombardment of Fort Mifflin. By November 15, British land and naval guns reduced the American fort to rubble. Smith evacuated the garrison across the river to Fort Mercer. Meanwhile, Cornwallis crossed from Chester to Billingsport on November 17 with 2,000 Scottish Highlanders, where he met Wilson's 4,000-man army corps, just arrived from New York. Washington's spies reported that the large British force planned to march

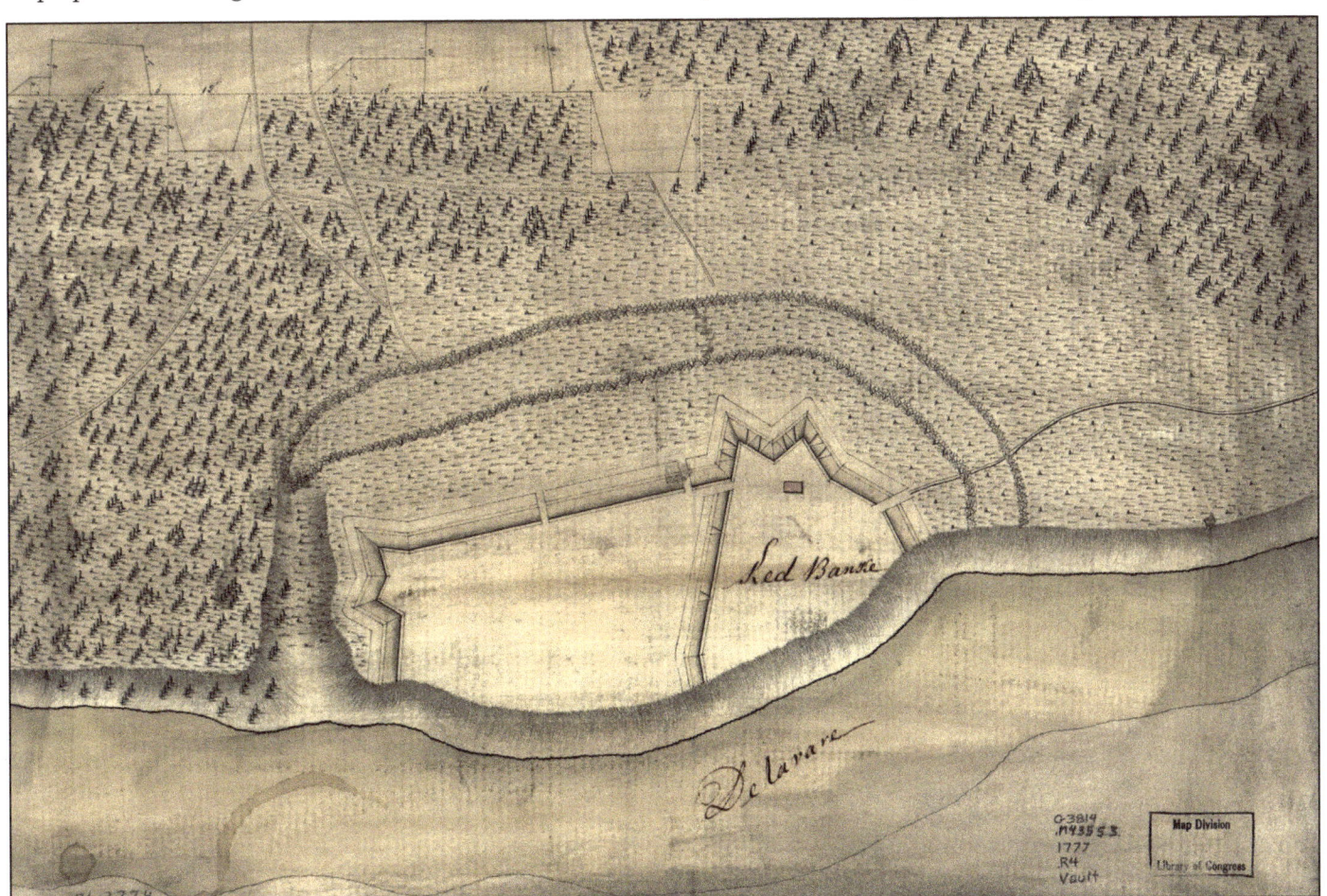

Red Banke. Map showing the size of the original fortification and how the Chevalier de Mauduit Du Plessis reduced the size of the fort to decrease the number of men required to defend it. c. 1777. *Courtesy of the Library of Congress.*

up the Jersey riverfront and besiege Fort Mercer. In response, General Washington ordered his three top staff officers to Red Bank to consult with local commanders as to the feasibility of holding the fort against this force. Generals Henry Knox, Arthur St. Clair and Johann Baron de Kalb arrived at Red Bank on November 17 and met with the commander of the river defenses, Commodore John Hazelwood, and area commander Varnum.[39]

Washington received conflicting and contradictory advice from his select military council. The committee felt that the fort could hold out if supported by the Jersey militia in the countryside. Yet, Hazelwood and Varnum reported that New Jersey militia commanders Forman and Newcomb feuded and that most militia had returned home for fall harvest. Meanwhile, Colonel Smith at Fort Mifflin complained that Hazelwood's naval force refused any longer to support the river forts. Varnum suggested that if the garrison dug bomb proofs, it could hold out against bigger British guns, but began to remove all the big American guns from Red Bank to avoid capture by the British. The collapse of Fort Mifflin made holding Fort Mercer tenuous. Still, Washington trusted that the fort would hold out until Huntingdon and General Greene arrived to engage the 6,000-man British column marching north from Billingsport. However, Washington ordered Varnum "not [to] hold [the] fort so as to endanger the safety of men."[40]

Lacking a decisive command decision, Varnum removed his brigade from Woodbury to Haddonfield as soon as Washington's committee returned to Whitemarsh headquarters. Greene reported that Varnum "retreated" farther the next day to Mt. Holly. Varnum's withdrawal of his men from the Red Bank area without consulting fellow officers stunned Hazelwood, who commanded American naval forces on the river. Lacking the protection of the land force, Hazelwood decided to burn his now vulnerable fleet.[41] Without Varnum's support, Colonel Greene at Red Bank loaded ammunition into wagons, removed the cannon and the fort's garrison and spread powder preparatory to blowing up the works.[42] He was not entirely successful. Lieutenant Colonel Francis Downman of the Royal Artillery found eighteen pieces of cannon and a "great quantity of powder," and "vast quantities of shot" in the abandoned fort.[43]

The British blew up the works at Red Bank, and, on November 25, leveled Fort Mercer completely. The British force withdrew from the Jersey shore to Chester on November 27, and went into winter quarters in Philadelphia. Washington had a momentary thought of attacking the British in Philadelphia with the large force that at last assembled in southern New Jersey. Certainly, General Greene urged an offensive to offset that depression caused by the loss of Fort Mercer and burning of the American fleet on the river. "I am anxious to do every thing in my power and more especially as the People seems to be dissatisfied at the evacuation of red bank fort," Greene advised the commander in chief.[44]

Other officers urged Washington to go into winter quarters, the usual eighteenth-century practice of warfare. Moreover, the British redoubts around the city seemed too formidable for an assault, and promised to inflict heavy casualties on the already depleted American force. General John Sullivan claimed that the lessons of Red Bank taught that a well-defended earthwork could withstand even the most intense assault, causing unacceptable losses to the attacking force.[45]

The political legacy of Fort Mercer proved far more lasting than the military lessons. "It is astonishing to think of the Precipitate retreat from Fort Mercer," William Bradford troubled; "they seemed determined not to see the Enemy."[46] Washington's critics returned to the attack. James Lovell of Massachusetts insisted that evacuation of Red Bank comprised another example of how Washington "fabiused" the war, alluding to comparison with the Roman General Fabius who used a strategy of delay to prolong war. Thomas Mifflin, Benjamin Rush, Jonathan Dickinson Sergeant and the Lees of Virginia called for Gates to replace Washington. Washington's influential friends in Congress, however, wanted to protect the general, so they accepted a resolution on November 28 "That an enquiry be made into the causes of the evacuation of Fort Mercer on the river Delaware, and into the conduct of the principal officers commanding that garrison." Thus, Washington escaped direct blame for losing the fort. This was not a time for recrimination or blame, friends of Washington insisted, and they voted to create a Board of War, where Gates, Mifflin and other critics could recommend organizational reforms to prevent similar defeats. The Board studied how to better supply the army and raise and train manpower in order to give Washington the means to defeat Howe come spring campaign time.[47]

Congress seemed anxious to forget the humiliation of evacuating, without a fight, the very same site of Colonel Greene's heroic stand against von Donop's grenadiers by eliminating memory of Fort Mercer. After the British evacuated Philadelphia in June 1778, Congress returned to the city and voted funds to rebuild Fort Mifflin and even Billingsport, but refused to restore Fort Mercer. It seemed that attempts to obliterate the fort succeeded. A recent history published in 2002 of the realities and mythologies of the Revolutionary War misspelled the fort as "Fort Mercier." Memory of the Battle of Red Bank faded, too. While other New Jersey Revolutionary War battles at Trenton, Princeton, and Monmouth continued to grow in importance, study of the Gloucester County activity faded into obscurity and distortion. A recent local history web page announced that the battle had no military significance in the Revolutionary War.[48]

Nevertheless, the Battle of Red Bank of October 22 and 23, 1777, held a significant place in the Revolutionary War. It buoyed American resolve in the mid-Atlantic theatre nearly broken by the British occupation of Philadelphia the previous month. It slowed the growing rate of desertion among American forces. It restored Congressional confidence in Washington's more cautious defensive strategy that had drawn recent criticism from political friends of General Horatio Gates, credited with a more successful offensive strategy in the Northern campaign along the Hudson River. Indeed, news of Gates' victory at Saratoga arrived in the Continental Congress capital-in-exile at York, Pennsylvania, concurrently with Washington's report to Congress about the Red Bank victory.

On the British side, Red Bank humiliated the Howe brothers: General Sir William Howe, commander of the British occupation army in Philadelphia, and Viscount Admiral Richard Howe, commander of the British naval forces on the Delaware. Though the Americans abandoned Fort Mercer on the Jersey shore in mid-November after the British army and navy crushed Fort Mifflin across the river, General Howe's reputation never recovered from von Donop's failure to take Fort Mercer and Admiral Howe's loss of two big warships during the Battle of Red Bank. After an uneasy winter of occupation in Philadelphia, the British government replaced General Howe with General George Clinton. Clinton decided that he had to abandon the city. In June 1778, the occupation army began the long march to New York through New Jersey. Washington intercepted the British column at Monmouth Court House. Here, Washington's army at last fought the British to a standstill, and Clinton withdrew from the battlefield and returned to New York under the cover of darkness. In the end, the final outcome of the war and Washington's military reputation had been influenced greatly by all four battles in New Jersey: Trenton, Princeton, Monmouth, and Red Bank.

About the Author

Jeffery M. Dorwart is a professor emeritus of military, naval, and New Jersey History at Rutgers University. He received his BA from the University of Connecticut and MA and PhD from the University of Massachusetts, Amherst. He has authored numerous books, including *The Office of Naval Intelligence: The Birth of America's First Intelligence Agency, 1865–1918*; *Camden County, New Jersey, 1616–1976: A Narrative History*; *Cape May County: The Making of an American Resort Community*; *Camden County, New Jersey: The Making of a Metropolitan Community, 1626–2000*; *The Philadelphia Navy Yard*; *Fort Mifflin of Philadelphia: An Illustrated History*; and *Invasion and Insurrection: Security, Defense, and War in the Delaware Valley*. He resides in Elmer, Salem County, New Jersey.

Endnotes

1. Samuel Stelle Smith, *Fight for the Delaware, 1777* (Monmouth Beach, NJ: Philip Freneau Press, 1970), 18–24.
2. Reed to Thomas Wharton Jr., October 24, 1777, *Pennsylvania Archives,* 1st ser., edited by Samuel Hazard, 12 vols. (Philadelphia: Joseph Severns, 1852–56), 5:701.
3. Alfred M. Heston, "Red Bank, A Paper Read Before the Monmouth County Historical Association, July 26, 1900, wherein is Given a True Account of the Gallant Defense of Fort Mercer" (printed by request, n.p., [1900?]), 23-24; *Crossroads of the American Revolution in New Jersey* (Philadelphia: National Park Service, 2002).
4. *Minutes of the Council [Committee] of Safety,* June 30, 1775, *Minutes of the Supreme Executive Council of Pennsylvania* [*Colonial Records of Pennsylvania*, vols. 11–16] (Harrisburg: Theo. Fenn & Co., 1852–53), 10:283.
5. Minutes of July 19 and 21, 1775, *Pennsylvania Colonial Records*, 10:283, 289.
6. Ibid. Also, see John W. Jackson, *The Pennsylvania Navy, 1775–1781: The Defense of the Delaware* (New Brunswick, NJ: Rutgers University Press, 1974); Samuel Stelle Smith, *Fight for the Delaware, 1777* (Monmouth Beach, NJ: Philip Freneau Press, 1970); and Mark Edward Lender, *The River War: The Fight for the Delaware, 1777* (Trenton: New Jersey Historical Commission, 1979).
7. Memorial to Congress, May 16, 1776; Council Minutes, May 21, and June 14, 1776, *Pennsylvania Colonial Records,* 10:572, 575, 601
8. John Adams to Isaac Smith Sr., June 1, 1777, John Adams to David Sewall, June 12, 1776, Paul H. Smith, ed., *Letters of Delegates to Congress, 1774–1789,* 23 vols. (Washington, D.C.: Library of Congress, 1976–), 4:112.
9. Ibid.; Smith, *Fight for the Delaware,* 9.
10. Proctor to Council of Safety, December, 17 and 23, 1776; *Pennsylvania Archives*, 5:118, 130.
11. Col. John Bull to Wharton, April 11, 1777, *Pennsylvania Archives*, 5:304–05.
12. John Hancock to Patrick Henry and Massachusetts Council, April 18, 1777, *Delegates Letters*, 6:611.
13. Supreme Executive Council minutes, April 14, 1777; Report on 'Fort at Red Bank,' enclosed in Resolution to Congress,

June 11, 1777, *Pennsylvania Archives,* 5:310, 359–63.

14 Supreme Executive Council to Washington, July 18, 1777, *Pennsylvania Archives,* 5:430–31.

15 Expense Account, August 1777, Financial Papers, series 5, *George Washington Papers in the Library of Congress* (hereafter, GWPLC).

16 See Worthington C. Ford, editor, *Defences of Philadelphia 1777* (New York: DaCapo Press, 1971), 5–39; Nathanael Greene, *The Papers of General Nathanael Greene,* edited by Richard K. Showman, Robert E. McCarthy and Margaret Cobb (Chapel Hill: The University of North Carolina Press for Rhode Island Historical Society, 1980), 2:135-137n3; 99n8.

17 Ford, *Defences of Philadelphia 1777,* 5–39.

18 Evidence of African Americans at fort as laborers, in Joseph Ellis and Robert Harris to William Bradford, October 14, 1777, series 4, General Correspondence, *GWPLC.*

19 Smith to Washington, October 2 and 3, 1777; Washington to Commodore John Hazelwood, October 7, 1777, both in Michael J. Crawford, ed., *Naval Documents of the American Revolution,* 10 vols. (Washington, D.C.: Naval Historical Center, 1996, 10:16–17, 28, 60 (hereafter *NDAR*); also, see Smith, *Fight for the Delaware,* 8–11.

20 Lee to Patrick Henry, October 16, 1777, in *Delegates Letters,* 8:127.

21 The folklore of heroic African-American Continental troops fighting at Red Bank arose from recollections of "Old Negro Mitch," who claimed to have been at the fort during the battle, and told local historians Isaac Mickle and Dr. Charles Clark that blacks fought in the battle, see Heston, *Red Bank,* 18. For the best evidence that no black troops fought at Red Bank, see Anthony Walker, *So Few the Brave: Rhode Island. Island Continentals, 1775–1783* (Newport, RI: Seafield Press, 1981), 42, and Jackson, *Pennsylvania Navy,* 440.

22 Washington to President of Congress, January 13, 1778, *GWPLC.*

23 Diary entry, October 14, 1777, *At General Howe's Side, 1776–1778: The Diary of General William Howe's Aide de Camp. Captain Friedrich van Muenchhausen,* trans. by Ernst Kipping and annotated by Samuel Stelle Smith (Monmouth Beach, NJ: Philip Freneau Press, 1974), 41.

24 William W. Leap, *Ashbrook's Burial Ground...* ([Runnemede, NJ]: William W. Leap, 1995), 15–16.

25 Diary entry, October 14, 1777, *At General Howe's Side, 1776–1778: The Diary of General William Howe's Aide de Camp. Captain Friedrich van Muenchhausen,* trans. by Ernst Kipping and annotated by Samuel Stelle Smith (Monmouth Beach, NJ: Philip Freneau Press, 1974), 40-41.

26 Jonas Cattell, "The Battle of Red Bank," from the *Woodbury Constitution,* March 10, 1846.

27 Smith, *Fight for the Delaware,* 18–21.

28 Diary entry, October 22, 1777, *At General Howe's Side,* 41.

29 Smith, *Fight for the Delaware,* 18–21.

30 Smith, *Fight for the Delaware,* 21–24.

31 Journal entries, HMS Pearl and HMS Camilla, October 22, 1777, *NDAR,* 10:239–40.

32 Smith, *Fight for the Delaware,* 21–24.

33 Viscount Howe to Philip Stephens, Secretary Lords Commissioners of the Admiralty, October, 25, 1777, Minutes of Court-Martial of Captain Francis Reynolds, November 26, 1777, *NDAR,* 10:603; Smith, *Fight for the Delaware,* 24–26; Jackson, *Pennsylvania Navy,* 194–99.

34 Reed to Wharton, October 24, 1777, Wharton to Hazelwood, October 24, 1777, Wharton to Blewer, November 6, 1777, *Pennsylvania Archives* 5:696, 746, 702.

35 John Adams to Abigail Adams, October 26, 1777, Washington to Congress, October 1777, *Delegates Letters,* 8:187.

36 Smith, *Fight for the Delaware,* 26–29.

37 Vice Admiral Viscount Howe to Capt. William Cornwallis, November 1, 1777, *NDAR,* 10:371.

38 See, *Defences of Philadelphia,* 54–157.

39 Washington to St. Clair, de Kalb, and Knox, November 17, 1777, St. Clair, de Kalb and Knox to Hazelwood, November 18, 1777, *NDAR,* 10:521, 533.

40 Washington to Varnum, November 19, 1777, *NDAR,* 10: 542–43.

41 Hazelwood to Wharton, December 1, 1777, *NDAR,* 10:645–647.

42 N. Greene to Washington, November 21, 1777, *Defences of Philadelphia,* p. 158.

43 Diary entries, November 19 and 21, 1777, Downman Diary, *NDAR,* 10:543, 559

44 Comstock to Greene, November 25, 1777, Greene to Washington, November 21 and 25, 1777, all in *Defences of Philadelphia,* 158, 200–201, 199.

45 Sullivan to Washington, November 25, 1777, ibid., 182.

46 Bradford to Wharton, November 22, 1777, *Journal of the Continental Congress,* November 28, 1777, both in *NDAR,* 10:568–69, 625–26.

47 Lovell to Horatio Gates, November 27, 1777, Dyer to Trumbull, November 28, 1777, William Williams to Trumbull, November 28, 1777, *Delegates Letters,* 8:329, 334, 341.

48 Robert Harvey, *"A Few Bloody Noses:" The Realities and Mythologies of the American Revolution* (Woodstock & New York: Overlook Press, 2002), 242, 466; "What is the historical significance of Red Bank Battlefield?" New Jersey History's Mysteries website, https://web.archive.org/web/20130501215908/http://www.njhm.com/redbank.htm (3/17/2018).

> This article is a greatly modified version of an article with the same title that appeared in *New Jersey Heritage* magazine, Vol. 4, no. 1, Winter 2005.

Representation of the action off Mud Fort in the River Delaware from the British point of view. Lieutenant W. Elliot, Royal Navy, claimed to have drawn the image "on the spot," and later engraved the image. Elliot describes the "Enemy's" fleet consisting of frigates, fireships, and Galleys which attacked His Majesty's Ships Augusta, Roebuck, Pearl, Liverpool, and Merlin on October 22, 1777. The Augusta took fire by accident and the Merlin was burnt to prevent her falling into the hands of the Americans. Published by W. Elliot, 11 Park Street, February 17, 1787. *Courtesy of The Miriam and Ira D. Wallach Division of Art, Prints and Photographs: Print Collection, The New York Public Library, http://digitalcollections.nypl.org/items/510d47d9-7af7-a3d9-e040-e00a18064a99.*

Map of the Principal Seat of War, 1777. "A map of that part of Pensylvania now the principle [sic] seat of war in America, wherein may be seen the situation of Philadelphia, Red Bank, Mud Island, & Germantown." London, 1777. Surveyed by Nicholas Scull, Surveyor of the Province of Pennsylvania; engraved by L. Jackson. *Courtesy of Library of Congress.*

Research into the Battle of Gloucester:
Progress and Prospects

Garry Wheeler Stone, Paul W. Schopp, and Jason R. Wickersty

November 1777 was not a good month for the young United States of America. During this time, the British Army and Navy broke the Continental Army's Delaware River blockade, thus ending the rebels' hopes of starving the enemy out of Philadelphia. Fort Mifflin fell on the night of November 15–16 and a large detachment, under Earl Cornwallis, forced the evacuation of Fort Mercer on November 20. This Anglo-Hessian detachment returned to Philadelphia on November 25–27 with minimal losses and several hundred head of cattle. The Continental Army tried to relieve Fort Mercer, but reacted too late with too little and the Continental and Pennsylvania riverine navies performed poorly. The rebels could look with pride at only two events: the heroic defense of Fort Mifflin during a five-week siege and a skirmish on November 25. During the skirmish, the marquis de Lafayette led a detachment of Continental riflemen and militia (300 to 400 men) in pushing a Hessian outpost two miles down the Haddonfield-Gloucester Town Road. The skirmish was of no military significance, but its results enabled Commander in Chief George Washington to convince the Continental Congress to give the marquis command responsibilities in the Continental Army. The marquis was anxious to serve the cause of liberty, but without real responsibility, he had been hinting that he would return to France. Lafayette's success on November 25 helped to cement the Franco-American alliance.

Introduction: September 1777, the Status of the War

March 1776, the new Continental Army forced the British to evacuate Boston. In July and August, the British reappeared in New York Harbor with a flotilla of over 400 ships and 33,000 troops under the command of Sir William Howe, the commander in chief of British forces in North America. In three months, Sir William and his older brother, Vice Admiral Richard, Lord Howe, out-maneuvered and outfought the Continental Army, driving it from Long Island and Manhattan Island and forcing a portion of it across the Hudson River into New Jersey. With Lord Cornwallis and a large detachment of the British Army in pursuit, George Washington's dwindling force had crossed the Delaware River by December 8 into Pennsylvania. New Jersey militiamen went into hiding, and the British occupied all of northeastern and central New Jersey. Then, Washington re-crossed the Delaware, won battles at Trenton and Princeton, and the British occupation collapsed. Left with only enclaves along the Raritan River and the shore of New York harbor, the British were soon struggling to cope with a re-energized New Jersey militia and the Continental Army. Every foraging expedition, every attempt to bring Washington to battle, resulted in more British and German casualties. From Christmas 1776 until April 1777, the British Army suffered more casualties in New Jersey than it had from forcing the rebels out of New York, August–November 1776.[1]

During the late spring and early summer of 1777, Sir William Howe wavered between plans to win the war by defeating the Continental Army in New Jersey, invading Pennsylvania by marching south from New Brunswick, or sailing from New York to capture Philadelphia, the rebel capital. Meanwhile, apparently demoralized by his losses at Trenton and Princeton, he did nothing until June 13, when he marched west to threaten the Continental Army's encampment in the hills above Bound Brook, New Jersey. Washington, however, refused the invitation to fight and—after five days—Howe withdrew his army to Amboy and returned to New York. When

Washington left the hills, however, and marched towards the British, Sir William Howe eagerly spun around and attempted to bring the Continentals to battle. While some fighting occurred, the Continentals again avoided a decisive battle. The Royal Army embarked for Staten Island on June 30, the month of June now gone.

Sir William made only one firm decision during May and June: to ignore his orders from London. The strategic goal of 1777 was to sever the thoroughly rebellious New England states from the reputedly more loyal Mid-Atlantic States through taking control of the Lake Champlain-Hudson River corridor. As planned, General John Burgoyne would advance down Lake Champlain and Howe would sail up the Hudson to Albany. Howe would invade Pennsylvania only if he could accomplish the invasion prior to coordinating with Burgoyne. Despite Burgoyne's rapid advance for laying siege to Ticonderoga, Howe dallied in New York and failed to sail up the Hudson as ordered to support the siege. Howe chose instead to assemble an invasion force for Philadelphia.

Preparations included providing a "battery ship" to cover amphibious landings. Admiral Howe purchased a large transport, removed its upper deck to reduce its weight and draft, and armed it with fourteen 24-pounder guns. The vessel featured newly cut gun ports to increase the firepower of either side, and the installation of special ballast tanks so that water could be pumped to either the port or starboard, thereby compensating for shifting three-ton guns. Admiral Howe renamed the battery ship VIGILANT.[2] On July 23, Sir William Howe and an army of 18,000 men sailed out of New York harbor.[3]

Sir William Howe's immense fleet of 260 ships arrived in Delaware Bay on July 29, but, to the consternation of his subordinates, he decided not to land there, but to proceed to the Chesapeake. August 25, they landed at Head of Elk at the top of Chesapeake Bay.[4]

Three times Washington tried unsuccessfully to block the British advance on Philadelphia. On September 11, Howe outflanked the Continentals and drove them from the field at Brandywine Creek. Five days later, Washington positioned his army on the hills protecting the best ford over the Schuylkill River, but, just as the British attacked, a violent thunderstorm arose, halting the fighting and forcing Washington to retreat and replace his men's rain-soaked ammunition. Next, the Continentals formed on the river's north bank to stop the enemy from fording it. The British, however, feinted a march to the west towards the important Continental supply depot at Reading. When Washington shifted his men west, the enemy marched east and forded the Schuylkill. The road to Philadelphia was now open.[5]

Philadelphia: Prize or Prison?

On September 26, 1777, unopposed British and Hessian grenadiers paraded into Philadelphia, fifes and drums playing, and the grenadiers' caps and the artillery horses decorated with greenery. While the British now held the largest city in their former colonies, they had no efficient way of supplying it. The rebels had blocked the shipping channel to Philadelphia with massive underwater timber barricades, barricades protected by the ordnance at Fort Mifflin on Mud Island and Fort Mercer at Red Bank, New Jersey. October 5, the British began making preparations to lay siege against Fort Mifflin but progress was slow. Impatient to break the rebel blockade, Sir William Howe decided to storm the forts. These attempts, however, led to a bloody repulse at Fort Mercer and the loss of two ships at Fort Mifflin. Meanwhile, the city experienced severe shortages and economic inflation.

General Sir William Howe, 5th Viscount Howe, Commander and Chief of His Majesty's forces in America. A color mezzotint by Richard Purcell, published by John Morris, 1777. From the Anne S. K. Brown Military Collection at Brown University. *Courtesy of Wikipedia.*

Research into the Battle of Gloucester

On November 1, Engineer Captain John Montresor noted: "We are just now an army without provisions or Rum, artillery for besieging [sic], scarce any ammunition, no clothing, nor any money."[6]

The British reconciled themselves to a long siege and continued constructing batteries on Province and Carpenters Islands and smuggling ammunition into Philadelphia. Parallel, the garrisons of Forts Mifflin and Mercer labored to improve their defenses. The weather, however, forced a time out for both sides. From midday on October 26 through late into October 30, torrential rain fell, flooding both Fort Mifflin and the siege works on Province and Carpenters Islands. The drenching washed away sections of earthwork. Then, the weather cleared and work resumed. On November 10, the British began their bombardment of Fort Mifflin. Captain Montresor wrote in his journal:

> We opened our Batteries against Mud Island Fort, the whole consisting of two 32 pounders, six 24 pounders Iron, one 18 pounder, two 8 inch Howitzers, two 8 inch mortars, and one 13 inch mortar.[7]

Fort Mifflin's construction featured stone walls on the east side of Mud Island facing the shipping channel to protect against a frontal riverine assault, but the defenses facing Province and Carpenters Island consisted of timber blockhouses and palisades. On November 10, the British gunners "much injured" the blockhouses—dismounting several of their guns, shattering a range of barracks and mowing down sections of palisades. By the 13th, the blockhouses were little more than heaps of timber and sections of palisades had to be rebuilt every night. More and more of the fort's artillery was dismounted. The fort's defenders' best ally was gale-force wind from the north, which pushed the river's water downstream, lowering high tide. Since the 11th, the British had attempted to move their two battery vessels—the VIGILANT ship and the FURY sloop—up the shallow channel on the western side of the fort. On the 15th, the wind moderated and the VIGILANT began warping itself up the shallow channel between Hog Island and Province Island.[8]

About noon, the VIGILANT and FURY sloop reached their positions alongside the fort. The VIGILANT lay so close to the fort that marines, standing on the mast tops, lobbed hand grenades into the fort, killing the defending gunners with the grenades or musketry. The first broadside from the VIGILANT's 24-pounders leveled the ruins of a blockhouse. From the shore, Royal Artillery Captain Francis Downman observed

a glorious sight. On one side of the fort was to be seen a number of galleys, floating batteries and ships keeping a constant fire on our ships; on the other side, all our batteries, the VIGILANT and sloop pouring in a tremendous fire on the fort, and from the men-of-war a no less vigorous fire was directed into the fort and at their galleys.

The cannonade continued all afternoon. "The fort seemed to be totally in pieces." That night, the garrison set the ruined barracks on fire and boarded boats rowed with muffled oars for Fort Mercer at Red Bank. When Captain Downman inspected the ruins in the morning, he found a dreadful sight. "It is in such a battered situation that it is past describing. In almost every place you see blood and brains dashed about."[9]

At the rebel camp at Whitemarsh, Washington hoped that Fort Mercer could hold out until ice "obliges their Ships to quit the River.... I am anxiously waiting the arrival of the [Continental] Troops from the Northward."[10]

THE RACE FOR REINFORCEMENTS

After the defeat at Brandywine on September 11, Congress and Washington desperately needed to muster more troops to contend with the British Army. The day after the Battle, Congress ordered Major General Putnam at Peekskill, New York, to send 1,500 men to Washington, but only on September 30 did Varnum's Brigade cross the Hudson. Meanwhile, Washington wrote Major General Heath in Boston on September 14 and Putnam at Peekskill for more troops. Heath had only a handful—Jackson's, Lee's and Henly's incomplete additional regiments. Washington ordered Putnam to send an additional 1,000 men and, if McDougal's Brigade had not marched, to hurry it along.[11]

In northern New York, Major General Gates had more men than Washington, but Gates was locked in combat with Major General John Burgoyne's forces. Washington was unaware of Gates's circumstances, and, on September 24, Washington wrote Gates that if Burgoyne had retreated to Ticonderoga, please return Morgan's Rifle Corps. On October 5, Gates wrote back that Burgoyne must soon attack or retreat—Morgan's is the corps that the enemy fear most. Not long after receiving Gate's letter, Washington received a letter from Putnam relating (prematurely) that Burgoyne had surrendered. Washington eagerly waited for confirmation from Gates. None arrived. Finally, on October 26, Washington received a letter from Putnam enclosing the articles of capitulation.[12]

With Gate's star in ascendancy, Washington had to proceed carefully. On October 29, he convened a Council of War at his headquarters north of Philadelphia. After reviewing the strategic situation, the council agreed that reinforcements should be sent to Red Bank and Fort Mifflin, and that twenty regiments should be drawn from the northern armies. The next day, Washington wrote Gates—congratulating him on his victory, chiding him for not properly reporting to Washington, and notifying him that he was sending his aide-de-camp, Lieutenant Colonel Alexander Hamilton, to inform Gates of the situation in Pennsylvania. Hamilton received orders to explain the "happy Consequences" of a large reinforcement. If reinforcements enabled the Continentals to maintain a blockade of the Delaware River, it would be possible to starve Howe out of Philadelphia. If Hamilton encountered Nixon's or Glover's Brigades, he was to hurry them on and Glover's regiments should march directly to Red Bank.[13]

Gates, Putnam, New York Governor George Clinton, and the New York Council expressed reluctance about sending Continental troops out of the state. November 2, Gates sent Washington a note that Morgan's corps had marched for Pennsylvania on October 17, but he enclosed a letter from Governor George Clinton. In the correspondence, Governor Clinton agreed that the New York British garrison was sending several regiments to Howe, but, for his own purposes, the Governor alleged that these troops would cross into Northern New Jersey and march the 90 miles to join Howe. Clinton opined that the Continental brigades needed to remain in lower New York, ready to intervene when the enemy troops crossed the Hudson into Jersey, but, in actuality, the troops embarked on transports for Philadelphia.[14]

Hamilton wrote reports to Washington on November 2 and 6, reporting that Putnam would send Poor's and Learned's Brigades, but Gates would release only Paterson's small brigade, insisting on holding two brigades at Albany to protect the military stores. The next day, however, Gates relented and dispatched Glover's Brigade as well, but time was fleeting. On November 7, Glover's Brigade was still 240 miles from Forts Mercer and Mifflin and, two days earlier, the enemy reinforcements had sailed from New York harbor.[15]

The Continental troops from New York arrived at a very slow pace. Not only were Gates, Putnam, and Governor Clinton reluctant to release them, but it took time to find provisions and wagons and the days were getting shorter. Varnum's Brigade had arrived in mid-October. The next to arrive were Morgan's riflemen. Worn out from almost a month of continuous combat, they had marched in easy stages, arriving at the Continental encampment at Whitemarsh by November 14. The small regiments from Boston would not arrive at Whitemarsh until the 19th. On the 18th, Learned's and Paterson's Brigades remained in the vicinity of Morristown, and Glover's Brigade had just approached the New Jersey border. Washington could no longer wait for reinforcements. With the British conquest of Fort Mifflin, Washington knew that the enemy would move against Fort Mercer. On October 27, Putnam warned Washington that the British troops were preparing to embark from New York. By November 8, the General learned that these troops had sailed, and, on the 12th, he learned that these transports had anchored off Chester, Pennsylvania. Washington had to act, despite the lack of more Continental troops arriving from the north.[16]

Washington Reacts

As Washington prepared to act, he did so with political caution by keeping the Continental Congress informed and consulting with others. During the afternoon of November 17, Washington completed drafting a long letter to Henry Laurens, President of the Congress. The letter provided both a report and a proposal. In it, Washington carefully explained why the Continental Army—not having received reinforcements from the north—lacked the ability to attack the British siege works on Province Island. However, the American forces still controlled Red Bank [Fort Mercer], and, if the army could maintain control long enough, ice might force the British fleet from the river. Thus Washington dispatched Generals St. Clair, Knox, and Baron de Kalb to view the ground, consult with the officers of the garrison and riverine navy, "and to endeavour to form a Judgment of the most probably means of securing it." Parallel to composing his letter to Congress, Washington drafted orders for the inspection committee, including six questions to be answered as a beginning point for the generals' report. By 11 p.m. on the 17th, St. Clair, Knox, and Baron de Kalb stood at the Delaware River, ready to cross."[17]

The next day, the issue of reinforcing Fort Mercer ceased being academic. During the afternoon, Washington received multiple reports that Lord Cornwallis, accompanied by a large column of grenadiers and light infantry, had marched out of Philadelphia the previous night and prepared to embark for New Jersey. At 10 p.m. that evening, Washington wrote to General Varnum at Woodbury that 1,500 to 3,000 enemy had left the city to "pay you a Visit" and that he was awaiting the report from St. Clair, Knox, and Baron de Kalb. During the night or early the next morning, a message arrived from the generals and Washington took action.[18]

Research into the Battle of Gloucester

During November 19, Washington dispatched two detachments of troops to Red Bank. In the morning, after receiving the message from the inspection committee, Washington ordered Brigadier General Jedediah Huntington to march his Brigade—about 1,000 officers and men—to Red Bank. That evening, upon receiving oral reports from St. Clair, Knox, and Baron de Kalb, Washington ordered Major General Nathanael Greene to New Jersey with his division—the brigades of Muhlenberg and Weedon, about another 2,100 men. During the day, Washington received information that Learned's Brigade was too close to Coryell's Ferry to divert to Red Bank, but he sent messages to Poor's and Paterson's Brigades that if they were not approaching Coryell's [and they were], they should march to Trenton and await orders. At 11 p.m., Washington sent a note to Glover's Brigade, reiterating his earlier order that they should march directly to Red Bank. The following day, November 20, from headquarters at Whitemarsh, Lafayette wrote Henry Laurens "I am just now going from this place with a detachment under Mjor. Gral. Greene. I hope my wound w'ont be much hurted,"[19] By evening, Greene—ahead of his troops—had reached the Delaware River at Bristol, Pennsylvania. There, from the comfort of a "fine country House," Greene wrote his wife:

> My dear
> I am now on my march for Red Bank fort. Lord Cornwallis crost over into the Jerseys day before yesterday to invest that place with a large body of troops. I am in hopes to have the pleasure to meet his Lordship.[20]

The next morning, Greene crossed the Delaware to Burlington. His division reached the Delaware at 10 a.m., but Greene expressed disgust at finding so few scows laying at the Bristol-Burlington Ferry; it would take all day for the baggage wagons and artillery to cross the river. At noon, he wrote Varnum that he was marching to join him, adding that Huntington (who had crossed on the 20th at Dunk's Ferry) probably would join Varnum that day. Morgan's rifle corps and Glover's Brigade were en route. Having heard reports of Fort Mercer's evacuation, Greene asked for information on the situation and the location where he could link-up with Varnum. At 5 p.m., Greene penned a letter to Washington. Greene had spoken to Varnum and Commodore Hazelwood, commander of the river fleet. Greene relayed the appalling news that the Continental forces had burned Fort Mercer along with all of the river fleet that could not pass upriver beyond Philadelphia. Varnum's Brigade retreated to Mount Holly. The United States' enormous investment in ships, floating batteries, artillery, and Fort Mercer was now lost. Greene would investigate the possibility of attacking the enemy, but he was not optimistic.[21]

Charles Cornwallis, First Marquis of Cornwallis. Portrait c. 1795 by John Singleton Copley. *Courtesy of Wikipedia.*

Early on the 22nd, Greene moved his headquarters to Mount Holly and, during the day, he consolidated all of his regular troops there. Mount Holly stood at a strategic road junction far enough inland to be safe from surprise attack. The town also hosted 200–300 militia under Lieutenant Colonel Joseph Haight, 2nd Burlington. Greene ordered Haight to march south to Moorestown and to keep outposts and videttes (mounted sentries) "advanced so as to annoy, and gain the best intelligence of the Enemy." A cadre of 170 men from Morgan's rifle corps under Colonel Richard Butler, 8 Pa., and a Major Morris also arrived at Mount Holly. These tough frontiersmen had marched the 36 miles from Whitemarsh to Mount Holly in one day. Greene sent them south to the militia's forward base at Haddonfield.[22]

November 23 and 24, Greene waited at Mount Holly for Glover's Brigade to appear. At 3:30 p.m.,

Greene expressed his frustration in a letter to Washington. At Mount Holly, Greene had a little more than 3,000 officers and men, while, from Haddonfield, militia Colonel Joseph Ellis reported that the British had 5,000 men. Greene was acutely aware of the political implications surrounding the Continental Army's successes and failures. If he attacked and suffered a significant defeat, it would be a political disaster. If he did nothing, it would expose the army to further criticism from an ignorant and impatient population. Just as he was closing his letter, Greene learned that Glover's Brigade had arrived at Black Horse (modern-day Columbus, New Jersey), only eight miles away. Greene already had issued brigade orders that the following morning at 7 a.m., troops would march towards the British. But just as it seemed that Greene's command would get a needed night's rest and then a battle, an express rider arrived from Washington with a dispatch—Greene was to remain at Mount Holly until he had spoken with Washington's aide, Lieutenant Colonel Richard Kidder Meade, who arrived shortly thereafter. The matter at hand: with Cornwallis and a large contingent of troops in New Jersey, should the Continental Army attack Philadelphia? Several reports—perhaps disinformation—had circulated that few enemy troops remained in Philadelphia after Cornwallis's excursion across the Delaware. At 9 p.m., Greene penned a letter to Washington for Meade to carry back. Greene thought that an assault on Philadelphia would be too hazardous, but if the Council of War decided to attempt it, Greene would support the effort. Greene would then cancel tomorrow's march and Glover's men would benefit from a day's rest.[23]

Much earlier that afternoon, the marquis de Lafayette began the eighteen-mile ride from Mount Holly to Haddonfield. The restless 20-year-old wanted to see action and grew weary of waiting. As a volunteer, he held no administrative responsibilities. No record exists of his conversation with Greene prior to Lafayette's departure, but it was likely similar to Greene's order for militia Colonel Haight, "annoy, and gain the best intelligence of the Enemy." Lafayette would not disappoint. With Lafayette rode his two aides and three French officers. Majors Edmund Brice and Jean-Joseph de Gimat served as Lafayette's aides-de-camps. Brice was the scion of a wealthy Annapolis, Maryland, family and had studied art in France, where he met and befriended Lafayette. Major Gimat was a 1st lieutenant in the French infantry who had joined Lafayette in 1776. Both men accompanied Lafayette to Philadelphia in June. The three French officers with Lafayette included Captain Thomas-Antoine de Mauduit du Plessis; Colonel Armand, the marquis de la Rouerie; and Jean-Baptiste-Joseph, chevalier de Laumoy. An engineer and artillerist, Du Plessis had fought bravely at Brandywine, Germantown, and Forts Mercer and Mifflin. Colonel Armand, a member of Pulaski's Legion of 3rd Continental Light Dragoons, was a man as brave and rash as Lafayette. Jean-Baptiste-Joseph, chevalier de Laumoy, was a colonel in the engineers. While du Plessis was traveling with Varnum, the other two officers had come from Pennsylvania, hoping for action. Lafayette may have had a "black Servant" attending him, which Major Brice purchased for the marquis in August. Lafayette and his entourage reached Haddonfield in the evening.[24]

Major General Nathanael Greene. Mezzotint by V. Green from portrait by Charles Wilson Peale. *Courtesy of Wikipedia.*

On November 25, Greene waited for word from Washington, received reconnaissance reports from Haddonfield, and prepared a detailed order of battle for attacking Cornwallis. The Continental troops would be arrayed in two main lines. Greene's and McDougall's Divisions would form the front line with a regiment from each brigade marching behind it as an immediate reserve. Greene posted the irregulars on the flanks of the front line: "The Militia and light troops are to endeavour to gain the flanks of the Enemy, but more especially to prevent them from gaining ours." Glover's Brigade would post as a second line, "ready to support any part that should be hard prest." Upon the order to march, the troops would form in regimental columns, carefully spaced to be able to form the line-of-battle. At the head of each regimental column, a company was to march as an advance guard. The prose order of battle was illustrated with an expertly drawn plan. Encouraging reports dispatched from Haddonfield fueled expectations. Captain Henry Lee and his light dragoons had arrived on the 24th, and the light dragoons, militia, and riflemen sent a steady stream of prisoners to Haddonfield. General George Weedon reported that prisoner interrogation revealed that the Cornwallis force consisted of 4,250 men with 100 light horse and 16 field pieces—"the marquis will inclose you a particular Acct." The enemy was now at Gloucester Town and embarking foraged cattle to Philadelphia. Greene ordered Generals Varnum and Huntington to advance and "fall on the enemies rear and prevent their getting off their stock." At midnight, Greene wrote Washington that he awaited word from the commander in chief before advancing with the remainder of the troops. The next morning, November 26, not having heard from Washington, Greene marched.[25]

General Howe orders reinforcements from New York

The Continental Army's October 4 attack on Germantown came as a shock to Sir William Howe. It reinforced his belief that he required more troops. October 8, he sent an express to New York for Sir Henry Clinton to reinforce the Philadelphia army with 4,500 men from the New York garrison. Howe directed Clinton to send the 7th, 26th, and 63rd Regiments of British Foot, the German regiments of Ansbach and Bayreuth, two recently arrived companies of Hessian riflemen (jägers) recruits, an artillery detachment, the 17th Light Dragoons, and all of the convalescents and recruits for the Philadelphia regiments. The express arrived in New York City on the 16th and then forwarded up the Hudson River, where Sir Henry was overseeing an attempt to get supplies to Albany for Burgoyne's expedition. Sir Henry received the order on the 18th. Apparently after determining that General Vaughan would not be able to reach Albany on October 22, Clinton ordered the British posts on the middle Hudson abandoned and the troops returned to the City. The troops arrived back at New York on the 25th, the Ansbach and Bayreuth regiments remaining on their transports for the trip to Philadelphia. A violent storm on October 28 and 29 slowed embarkation, but, by November 4, the troops with their horses, baggage, artillery, and supplies had been loaded. The flotilla of 36 ships sailed the next day. It arrived in Delaware Bay on November 8, moving up to Chester on the 11th, where it joined the upstream portion of a huge armada of transports and warships that clogged the bay and lower river. A German officer estimated this upper, or "second division" consisted of 200 ships. There, off Chester, the troops from New York remained on board their transports while the siege of Fort Mifflin entered its final days.[26]

After taking possession of Mud Island on November 16, Sir William Howe quickly and quietly (he issued no written orders that might reach Washington) began planning to lay siege to Fort Mercer. Word was sent to Major General Sir Thomas Wilson, commander of the New York reinforcements on the transports at Chester. A vanguard of troops was landed on the 17th. On the 18th, at the "Firing of 2 guns and Hoisting a Flag Blue and white at the mizen Top-Mast head of the Eagle," the remaining troops were to disembark and form up in defensive alignments. Later, some of the soldiers' wives joined their men on shore.[27] That evening, the New York troops comingled with men from the Philadelphia garrison. At midnight on November 17, Lord Cornwallis led five battalions and a detachment of 50 jägers south towards Chester, arriving at seven the morning of the 18th. Mid-afternoon, some troops embarked in flat boats while others, along with horses and baggage, boarded sloops and schooners.[28]

As Cornwallis's troops navigated up the Delaware River from Chester, ahead of them they could see the British Jack flying over the ruins of Fort Mifflin. On the east bank, the Stars & Stripes flew over Fort Mercer. Closer ahead, situated above Billingsport between Little and Great Mantua creeks, two small rebel batteries occupied the top of the bank. The ground around them was raw earth—plowed and harrowed by hundreds of cannonballs from the naval bombardment that occurred between November 5 and 15. Now the batteries' guns lay silent as all of the British warships had moved out of range—but, as the sailors rowed the flatboats carrying Cornwallis's troops towards shore, they carefully chose to land the troops south of Billingsport and out of the range of the rebel guns.[29]

On the 19th, the British officers and men prepared to march on Fort Mercer. More artillery was unloaded, wagons secured from the nearby countryside (purchased or stolen?), and Engineer Robertson reconnoitered—investigating the bridge at Sandtown over Great Mantua Creek and potential fords further inland. At a ford, a brief

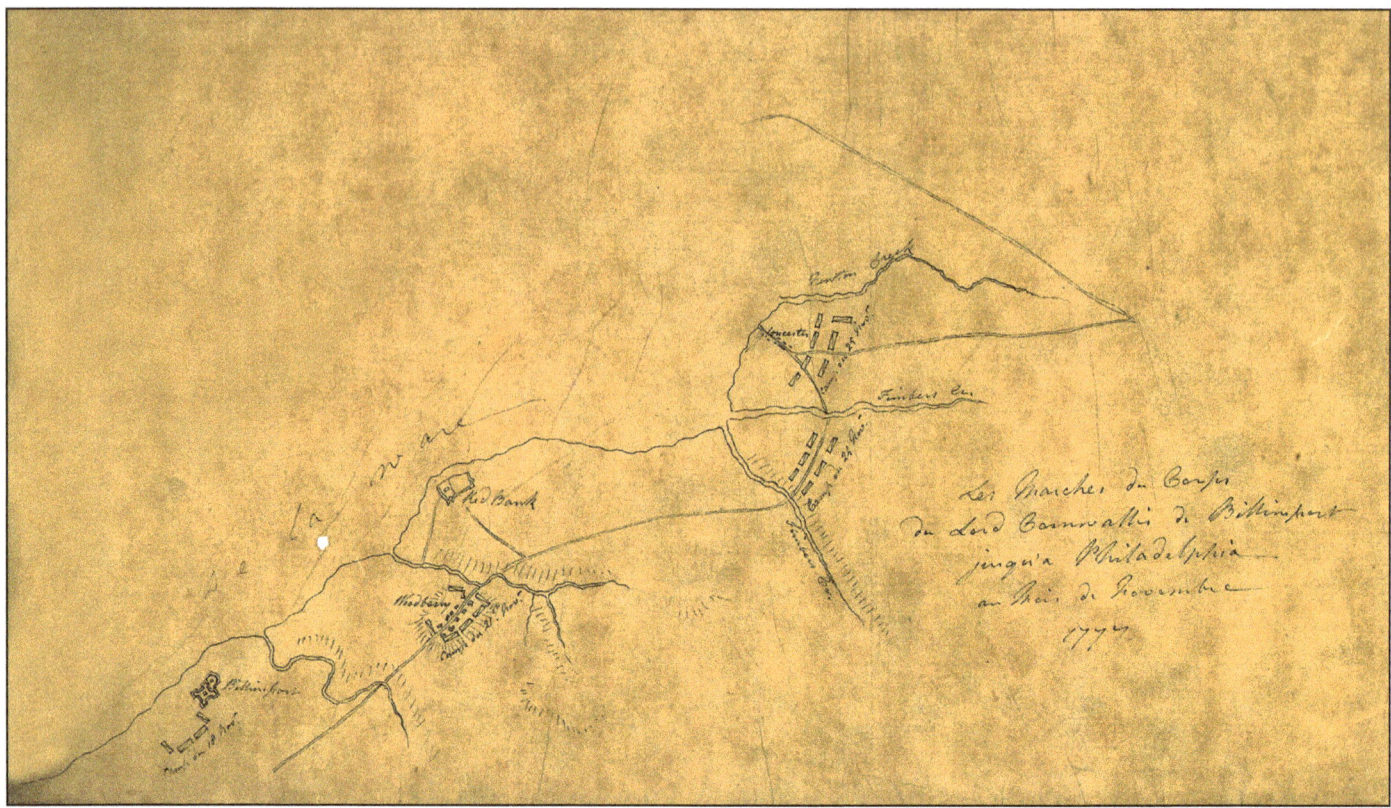

Friedrich Adolph Julius von Wangenheim, "The Marchs of the Corps of the Lord Cornwallis from Billingsport until Philadelphia in the Month of November 1777." Wangenheim was a 1st Lieutenant in the Hessian Jäger Corps and a botanist who studied and later published about North American trees. *Courtesy of the Library of Congress.*

skirmish occurred with some militiamen. Rumors swirled that the American forces had evacuated from Fort Mercer. That night, two companies of light infantry landed below the rebel batteries to confirm the evacuation rumor. When a rebel sentry fired upon them, they scrambled back into their boats.[30]

The next morning, two other light infantry companies landed below the southern battery. This time, the rebels had departed. When the light infantry returned, the battalion marched to Sandtown and repaired the bridge. That evening, the troops saw an explosion at Red Bank. Then flames lit the sky as rebel ships burned at Timber Creek. The Americans had finally evacuated Fort Mercer.[31]

On the 21st, drums woke the Crown's troops at 5 a.m. At six, the British and German soldiers began marching towards the Mantua Creek bridge—the jägers in front, followed by English guards, then 20 light dragoons, two light 6-pounders, the grenadiers, the 17th Light Dragoons, three battalions (with their light 3-pounder battalion guns), the other two 6-pounders, five more battalions, the baggage, and then an infantry and dragoon rear guard.[32] At the Mantua Creek bridge, Engineer Robertson noted that the crossing easily could have been defended. There, Cornwallis posted the 7th and 63rd Regiments to "keep up the Communication with Billingsport and to Collect Cattle." The rest of the army marched north on the Kings Highway to Woodbury, where most camped in a defensive arc around the village. Part of the light infantry reconnoitered the ruins of Fort Mercer and then the Big Timber Creek bridge. They found the ruins of the fort deserted and the bridge "Broke up." At Woodbury, the troops were warned not to wander because of rebels."[33]

The British occupation brought chaos to Woodbury as soldiers plundered and the army foraged. Job Whitall, a Woodbury farmer, butcher, and meat packer, recorded his family's losses in his diary. As the soldiers marched in, they took two of his horses and ransacked their home, taking:

> Bread, pies, milk, cheese, meat, dishes, cups, spoons & then took shirts, sheets, Blankets, coverlets, stockings, Breeches, a light Broadax and drove our cattle [most of the cattle escaped and came back].[34]

On November 22, the Whitalls remained alone most of the day, except for soldiers returning to take milk and potatoes, steal a pig, and a quartermaster or engineer taking the gears [wheels and undercarriage] of a wagon. The

Research into the Battle of Gloucester

following day, Whitall visited an uncle's home and found another ransacked house—doors broken down and desk drawers forced. In the cellar, the British soldiers had broken open a cask of Job Whitall's sugar and taken most of its contents. While Job was there, soldiers came and took ten of his father's sheep and four from a neighbor. Returning home, he found soldiers loading as much hay as they could on horses. On the 24th, the army left and Whitall checked his smoke house on the other side of Woodbury. Not only had the bacon disappeared, but "near a thousand feet of Boards" and all of his barrel staves were burned in camp fires.[35]

It appears Cornwallis' foraging comprised more of a corporate plundering than a well-conducted forage. The Whitalls embraced Quaker pacifism and endured fines for not joining the militia. But no British officer offered to pay for their cattle, wagon gears, or hay. In December, a German officer noted that a Cornwallis forage in Chester County, Pennsylvania, had "done infinitely more to maintain the rebellion than to smother it."[36]

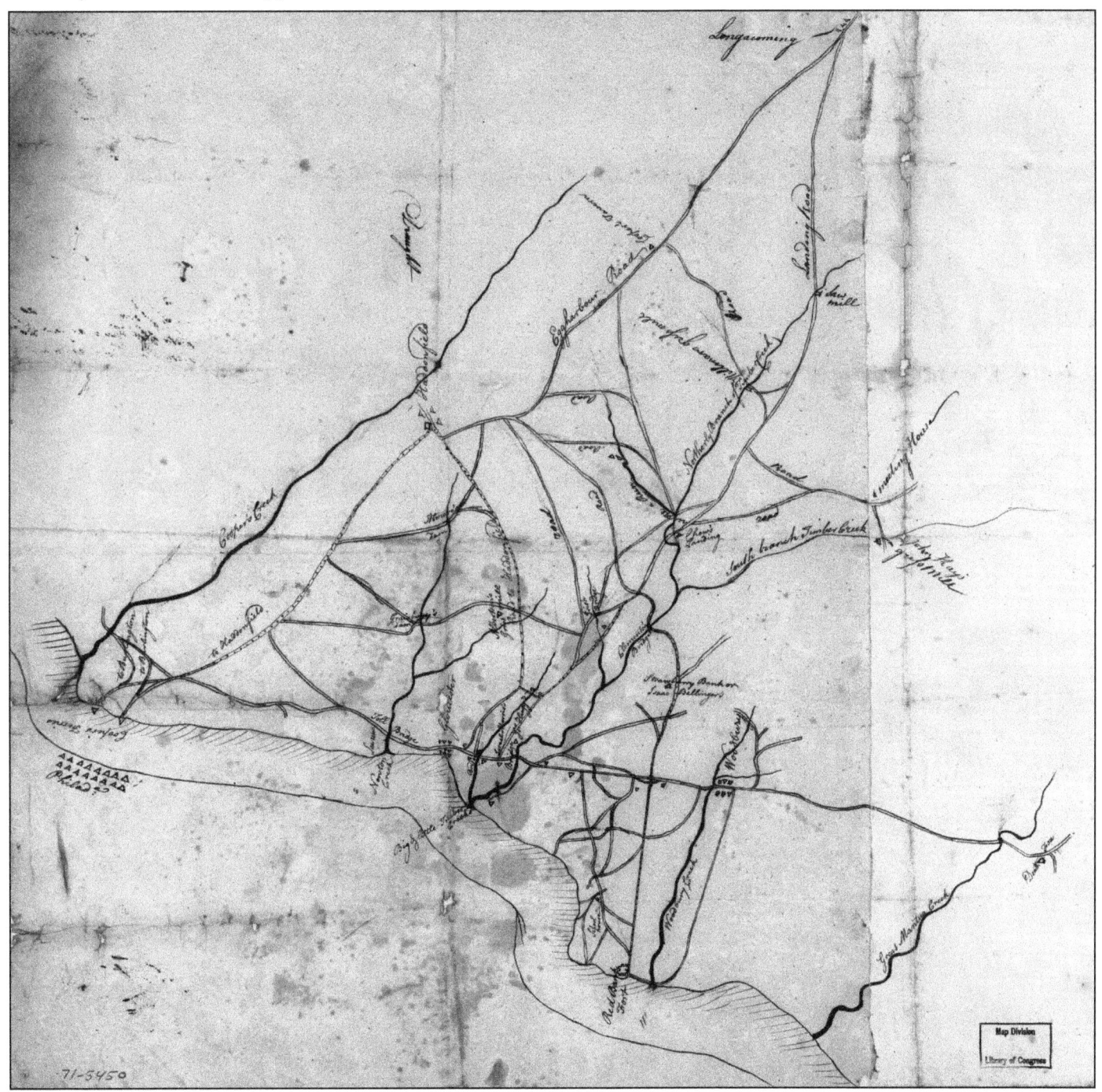

Sketch of roads in present-day Camden County, New Jersey, c. 1777, which historian Ed Fox has tentatively identified as the work of Colonel John Cadwalader. The map depicts the march route for the Hessians from Haddonfield to Red Bank. *Courtesy of the Library of Congress.*

While some soldiers plundered, others worked. The Fort Mercer garrison, having retreated to Haddonfield, on the 22nd, allowed Cornwallis to bring up the 7th and 63rd Regiments from Mantua Bridge. He dispatched the 26th and 63rd Regiments to Fort Mercer to demolish the earthen fortifications, while the 7th Regiment replaced the 1st Light Infantry in maintaining the Woodbury perimeter. The light infantry returned to the broken bridge at Big Timber Creek. Five of its thirteen companies crossed the creek in two small boats to

> Cover the Workmen employ'd in repairing it. In the Evening small party's of the Rebels appear'd and begun to be troublesome firing on us from a railing on the Other side of a small swamp, from which we soon drove them, but with the loss of 2 men of the 5th light Company kill'd, and a man of ye 4th Company Wounded.[37]

The dead men were Privates Stephen Sutton and John Hay [or Key?]. The "rebels" driven back included militia from Burlington, Cumberland, and Gloucester counties. A Burlington County man, Samuel Asay, received wounds from the exchange of musket fire.[38] At Woodbury, a rebel scouting party alarmed the camp. After driving the scouts back, British troops burned buildings that had obstructed their fields of fire.[39]

November 23, the demolition of the works at Red Bank continued. Leveling the massive earthworks—the ramparts were 18 feet high—was a prodigious job. In the afternoon, Cornwallis sent the 33rd Regiment to assist with the work. Besides shoveling the ramparts back into the ditches, the British spiked any artillery too heavy to move and pushed it over the high bank, where it tumbled into the Delaware. Provisions discovered in underground magazines were salvaged and loaded onto wagons. At Woodbury, by the end of the day, foragers had collected 400 head of cattle. On the Delaware River, Admiral Howe began organizing the boats and shipping needed to evacuate the troops and carry the forage.[40]

The following day, Cornwallis' troops at Woodbury began their return to Philadelphia. At daybreak, they broke camp and marched north on the Kings Highway. After crossing the rebuilt bridge over Big Timber Creek, they camped on high ground between Big and Little Timber Creeks—their flanks protected by the creeks and the Delaware River. At Red Bank, the three regiments continued working to level the earthworks.[41]

At daybreak on the 25th, the three regiments at Red Bank rejoined the other troops with Cornwallis, and the reunited army crossed Little Timber Creek and marched into Gloucester Town, arriving at 10:30 a.m. Then began the tedious work of embarking the cattle and the dragoon's horses on sloops and schooners. With only one wharf, the work of embarking the animals, baggage, and artillery would not be completed until noon on the 27th. Simultaneously, troops embarked from the beach on flatboats and sailors rowed vessels across the river. Officers from the vessels that had sent boats and H.M. Schooner Viper assisted with the embarkation process. A 6 p.m., the 10-gun Viper moved in towards shore and anchored. There, its 3-pounder guns joined the massive 24-pounders of the Vigilant in protecting the embarkation from attack.[42]

Lafayette's "little event:" the Skirmish with the Jäger Picket

The nearest Continental force was in Haddonfield, the headquarters of the South Jersey militia. During the 24th and 25th, reports on the enemy's activities at Gloucester Town flowed in from reconnaissance and also from interrogations of prisoners; the details were then carried to Major General Greene at Mount Holly. There was no shortage of prisoners. Despite warnings, some English and German soldiers could not resist slipping away from their units to plunder. During the 24th, Captain Henry Lee's detachment of the 1st Continental Light Dragoons brought in nine. Midday on the 25th, the militia brought in two groups. The first consisted of three members from the 33rd Regiment and four members from the 1st Battalion of British Artillery. The artillerists were a good catch, as they had brought three artillery horses (branded "GR") on which to pack their plunder. Just before 3 p.m., militia arrived with seven jägers—green-jacketed riflemen—several accompanied by their wives.[43]

Lafayette had gathered some of Greene's intelligence. The marquis arrived in Haddonfield late on the 24th. On the 25th, Lafayette—with his aides, three French officers, and some of Morgan's riflemen—spent the morning and early afternoon reconnoitering the British at Gloucester Town. They studied the roads and ground from Little Timber Creek to Newton Creek, even crossing Newton Creek to look into Gloucester Town from the "Sand-Point" at the creek's confluence with the Delaware. From the shore, Lafayette could plainly see the enemy vessels crossing the river. From prisoners, he learned that the nearest enemy outpost contained 350 jäger riflemen with two pieces of artillery. Back in Haddonfield, Lafayette wrote out his reconnaissance report and gave it to General Weedon to forward to Greene. Then, Lafayette headed west on the King's Highway to "annoy" the enemy.[44]

The marquis left Haddonfield with several militia groups and, as he marched, he gained more support until

Research into the Battle of Gloucester

he had a detachment of 300 to 400 men including more militia, riflemen, light dragoons, and his own entourage. Lafayette's entourage included his two aides—Majors Edmund Brice and Jean-Joseph de Gimat—and three French officers: Captain du Plessis, Colonel Armand, and the chevalier de Laumoy. Lieutenant William Lindsay, 1st Continental Light Dragoons, along with ten mounted troopers also accompanied Lafayette.

The footmen with Lafayette included almost 150 of Morgan's riflemen. These sharpshooters, members of Pennsylvania and Virginia rifle companies, were detached from their regiments and assigned to the rifle corps. As Colonel Morgan had fallen ill, Colonel Richard Butler, 8th Pa., and a Major Morris, led the detachment.[45] Lafayette's other men included 150 or more New Jersey militia under the command of Colonel Joseph Ellis, Sheriff of Gloucester County. Lieutenant Colonel Joseph Haight of Burlington County and Lieutenant Colonel Derrick Middagh from Somerset County served under Ellis. Their men comprised detachments from at least six counties—from Morris in the north to Cumberland in the south. While the ranks may have included some youngsters, many of these men were experienced irregulars—some serving intermittently since December 1775. They had been drilled, some under veterans of the Seven Years War like Colonel Ellis. Some company officers and sergeants were distinguishable by uniforms or other symbols of rank, and their men marched to the beat of the drum. More importantly, many or most of the men carried bayonets for their muskets. These were not amateur units.

How the militia deployed during the ensuing skirmish is not known. In his account of the battle, Lafayette describes them as two pickets (outposts) of militia under Colonels Ellis and Haight, but this may be simply a reflection of how Greene had proposed to organize the militia in the projected attack on Cornwallis. From the scant information in the militia pension declarations, it is clear that Lieutenant Colonel Haight led at the front while Lieutenant Colonel Middagh commanded at the rear. Ellis is stated as commander, but without any details. Ellis knew the area intimately. He lived in Gloucester Town, had farmland close to the Kings Highway, and was regimental commander of the men from the townships that the battle would cross. He likely supervised collecting intelligence—keeping in touch with the militia that watched the side roads for any sign of an enemy flanking party.[46] As Lafayette departed Haddonfield, he sent Captain du Plessis ahead on the "Gloucester Road" to locate the German riflemen. About two and a half miles from Haddonfield, du Plessis encountered the jägers.[47]

Captain Carl August von Wrede's 350-man detachment of the Jäger Corps was posted as a large "picket" (outpost) on the Kings Highway east of Gloucester Town. Further east, in the woods above the Kings Run bridge, Captain Wrede had established a smaller picket of Lieutenant Friedrich Kellerhausen and 26 men. When, about 2 p.m., the militia began harassing Kellerhausen's men, Captain Wrede immediately marched with the entire detachment to the outpost's relief. After crossing the Kings Run bridge, Wrede posted a reserve to cover the bridge and the outpost. This reserve consisted of a third of the recruits under Lieutenant von Bodungen. Wrede then carefully arrayed his men to reconnoiter the road and the woods—30 experienced men of his own company in the center, a third of the recruits to the left and a third to the right. With each group, Wrede posted an experienced officer: Lieutenant George Hermann Heppe on the left and Lieutenant Erich Carl von Hagen to the right. In the center with Captain Wrede was Ensign Wilhelm Freyenhagen, whose diary preserves the only detailed description of the skirmish.

> We barely advanced 100 paces when the enemy advanced on us in the best order with overwhelming superior numbers. He attacked with the heaviest musket fire and he was able on the flanks to mortally wound both Lts. Heppe and v. Hagen and force their commands back. Then with force and bravery he stormed the remainder. As we were outflanked on all sides Capt v. Wrede began a retreat.

The first men to strike the jägers were Morgan's riflemen—they had jogged into battle—but, the militia followed right behind them. The hill west of the bridge would have been a good place for the jägers to make a stand, but the detachment—90 percent composed of raw recruits—had collapsed. Had Wrede only been faced with Morgan's riflemen, he might have ordered his men to draw their hunting swords and charge. But he could not. Musket-armed infantry then advancing on him were, "in fine spirits," firing, loading, advancing with leveled bayonets, and then firing again—firing from behind trees wherever possible. While the militia contributed the volume of fire, the sharpshooting riflemen probably caused most of the casualties.[48]

Lieutenant Lindsay's ten dragoons played a role in making the Hessians "run very fast." Michel Capitaine's map of the battle confirms the obvious—when the action arrived at the farms of Isaac Burroughs and militia Captain William Harrison's farm fields, the troopers

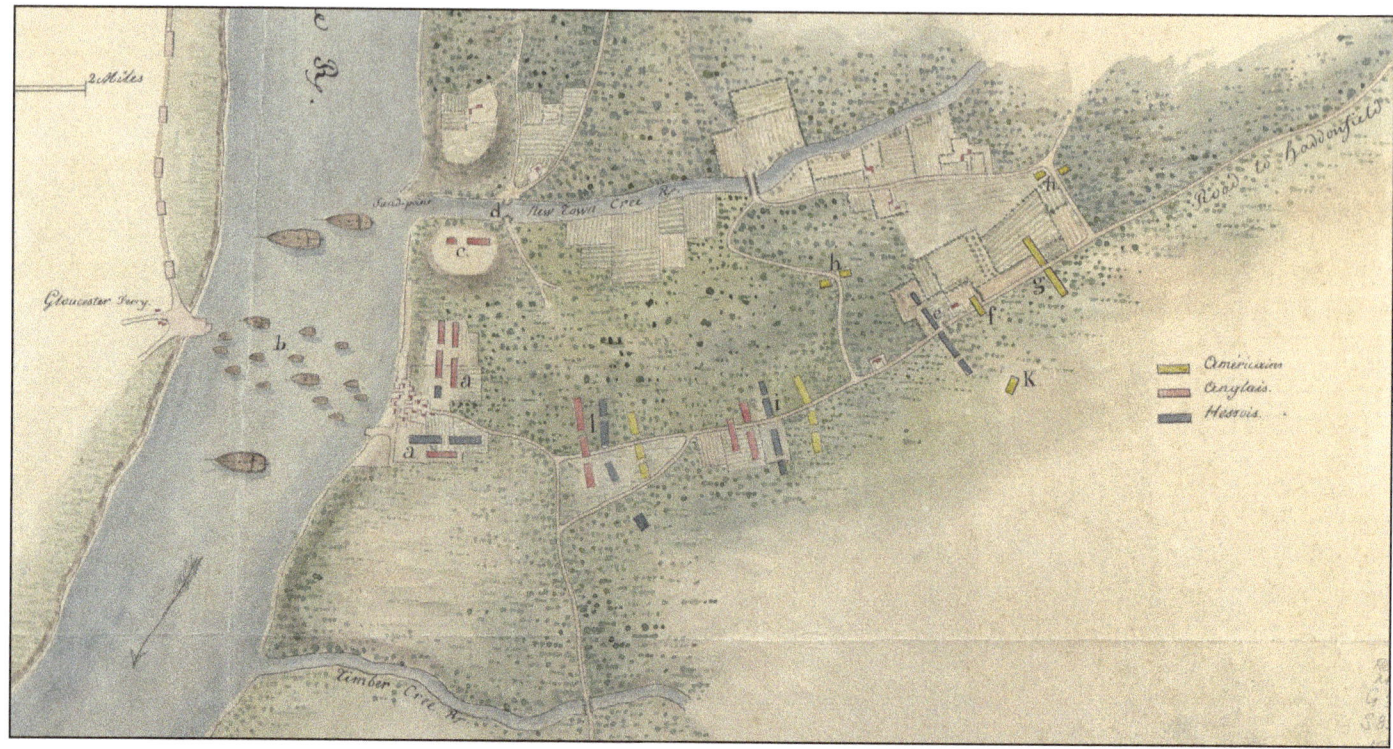

Detail from Michel Capitaine du Chesnoy, "Carte de l'action de Gloucester." Captain Harrison's and Burrough's fields are in the center of the detail immediately east of the triangular road intersection and below "i." In this beautifully rendered sketch map, the "American" troops are shown as yellow rectangles, the Hessian as blue, and the English as red. The map's legend identifies "f" as American riflemen, "g" as militia that supported them, and "k" as "Light dragoons sent on the enemy flanks." Translation by William T. Lawrence. Capitaine was a geographical engineer and cartographer and part of Lafayette's entourage as an aide-de-camp. *Courtesy of Cornell University.*

rode through the fields to outflank the enemy. Where the mounted officers with Lafayette served is unknown, but they participated. The horses of Major Brice, the chevalier du Plessis, and Colonel Armand all suffered wounds. Cavalryman Armand likely rode with Lindsay's troopers.

Wrede's military experience can be credited for keeping his detachment more-or-less together as they fled west on the Kings Highway. They had to leave their wounded behind, but Wrede had only two men captured. A half mile to the west, at Captain Harrison's fields, a British light infantry company came to the jägers' relief, intensifying the fighting and pausing the retreat. However, as soon as the light infantry and jägers resumed withdrawing, Lafayette's small force surged forward. As the fighting approached the Salem Road, a second British light infantry company joined—bringing with it the artillery company and two field pieces that had been stationed at the jägers' picket. The Continentals, however, continued pushing until it became dangerously dark. The skirmish had begun about 4 p.m. and sunset occurred at 4:41. With the light fast disappearing. Lafayette broke off, and began a slow march back to Haddonfield.

> The enemy knowing perhaps by our drums that we were not so near came again to fire at us—but the brave Major Moriss with a part of his riflemen sent them back and pushed them very fast [Lafayette].[49]

The skirmish had cost the Continentals only a few casualties—two fatalities and four or five wounded. The jägers had not been as fortunate. After darkness fell, the jägers made the long trek—almost 2.5 miles—to where the fighting had begun

> in order to collect and rescue our wounded as they had been left behind before. When all were found and brought in to the nearest house, we returned to camp at 7:45 p.m. Lt Heppe died of his wounds at 9 p.m. In all, there were two officers wounded, one dead, and eight foot Jägers dead and buried, 19 severely wounded and two missing [Ensign Freyenhagen].

Although the Continentals suffered far fewer casualties, the fatalities were still remembered in the 1830s when aged militia men submitted pension applications. The militia company officers had led from the front and they paid the price. Lieutenant John Lucas died instantly—a rifle or musket ball struck him "below the left nipple and went through his body." Lieutenant David Mulford of Captain Baker's company was mortally

Research into the Battle of Gloucester

Gilbert Motier the Marquis De La Fayette as a Lieutenant General, 1791. Portrait by Joseph-Désiré Court. *Courtesy of Wikipedia.*

wounded. Helped to the back, he died two hours later. Ensign John Tilton—acting as a lieutenant in Lucas's detachment—endured a shoulder wound. Writing to Washington the next day, the marquis de Lafayette reported five men wounded. The militia wounded included Hugh Jones and Thomas Harris—Harris had his arm broken by a rifle or musket ball.[50]

Withdrawing in the dark, the men of Captain Payne's Eggharbor company did not realize that their acting commander was missing until they arrived back in Haddonfield. Early the next morning, James Murphy and Patrick McCollum returned to the battleground to find him. They located Lieutenant Lucas' body in "a ditch and covered over with some rubbish and was pretty much stripped of his clothes." Murphy and McCollum took the body back to Haddonfield. Probably Lucas, Mulford, and any other Continental fatalities were buried in Haddonfield.[51] In Greenwich, Mulford's family erected a memorial stone.

The next morning, British sailors resumed ferrying animals, baggage, and troops back to Philadelphia.[52] Later in the day, the Continental regulars began arriving in Haddonfield. The general officers and their aides—horse mounted—were the first to arrive. What the generals learned from Weedon, Lafayette, and others proved disappointing. Greene wrote Washington at 4 p.m.

> I am sorry our march will prove a fruitless one. The enemy have drawn themselves down upon the Peninsula of Gloucester: the ships are drawn up to cover the troops. There is but one road that leads down to the point, on each side the ground is swampy and full of thick underbrush that it makes the approaches impracticable almost.... I proposed to the Gentlemen drawing up in front of the enemy and to attack their Picquet and endeavour to draw them out but they were all against it, from the improbability of the enemies coming out. The Marquis with about 400 militia and the rifle Corps attacked the enemies Picquet last evening, kill'd about 20 and wounded many more and took about 20 prisoners. The marquis is charmed with the spirited behaviour of the militia and Rifle Corps.[53]

Another part of Greene's letter included a response to Washington's letter of 8 p.m. from the previous night. Washington expressed concern that with Cornwallis returning to Philadelphia and with two and a half divisions of the Continental Army in New Jersey, Sir William Howe would attack the Continental Army encampment at Whitemarsh. (Howe did, nine days later.) Therefore, Washington ordered the Continental troops back to Pennsylvania. Greene immediately halted those troops that had not reached Haddonfield, and the next day they marched back to the Burlington-Bristol ferry. All of Greene's detachment arrived at Whitemarsh before Sir William Howe attacked on December 4, 1777.[54]

During the evening of November 26, British sailors burned a Gloucester Town tenement belonging to the local militia commander, Captain William Harrison, "for the part he took against them."[55]

During the morning of the 27th, remaining animals, baggage, and artillery were transported across the river. At noon, the seamen began loading the rear guard onto flat boats. First to depart were the British and German grenadiers. Last to leave was the 1st Battalion of British Light Infantry. As the flat boats left the beach, 200 or so rebels appeared at the edge of the adjacent woods and opened fire, wounding an officer, several soldiers, and a seaman.[56] Jäger Freyenhagen was impressed:

> The Rebels followed us to the water where they had to withstand musket fire from the boats and a strong cannonade from HMS VIGILANT

"In Memory of DAVID MULFORD, Lieutenant of the Greenwich Militia, who fell in a skirmish with the Hessians near Haddonfield in the *State* of *New Jersey* in the Year 1777, Aged 29 Years." *Photograph by Eric Stephenson.*

The Harrison Farmhouse, Bellmawr, New Jersey. The two-story portion was constructed in 1764 for William Harrison Jr., captain of the Gloucestertown Township militia. The New Jersey Department of Transportation staff refused to let members of the Camden County Historical Society examine this National Register eligible building prior to its demolition, March 6, 2017. Photograph by Nathaniel R. Ewan for the Historic American Building Survey, March 18, 1937. *Courtesy of the Library of Congress.*

plus a frigate [schooner VIPER] and a row-galley [CORNWALLIS]. The enemy withstood this with the greatest courage and resistance which the troops already ferried over could see clearly from the other side.[57]

By evening, Cornwallis' troops had returned to their barracks. The Continentals had lost control of the Delaware River. However, Lafayette's skirmish on the Haddonfield-Gloucester road would have enduring political significance.

THE PROMOTION OF MAJOR GENERAL THE MARQUIS DE LAFAYETTE

Since shortly after the marquis' arrival in late June, 1777, Commander in Chief Washington had been concerned about the gap between Lafayette's commission from the Continental Congress and Lafayette's understanding of his commission. Lafayette received a commission as a major general on July 31, "because of his zeal, illustrious family and connexions," but it was widely understood that the commission was honorific and "without pay or command." However, the written commission failed to so state the lack of a command, and the young man wanted a command. In August, Washington wrote Congress for clarification, but did not receive the response Lafayette wanted. October 14, from the hospital at Bethlehem, Pennsylvania (Lafayette had suffered a leg wound at Brandywine), Lafayette wrote Washington "with the confidence of a son, of a friend" that he "would deserve the reproaches of my friends and family if I would leave the advantages of mine to stay in a country where I could not find the occasions of distinguishing myself."[58] November 1, Washington wrote Henry Laurens, President of the Continental Congress:

> I feel myself in a delicate situation with respect to the Marquis Le Fayette. He is extremely solicitous of having a Command equal to his rank, & professes very different ideas as to

the purposes of his appointment from those Congress have mentioned to me.... it appears to me, from a consideration of his illustrious and important connections—the attachment which he has manifested to our cause, and the consequences, which his return in disgust might produce, that it will be adviseable to gratify him in his wishes.[59]

Again, Washington did not obtain the response that he and Lafayette desired. During the afternoon of November 26, Washington received two letters that encouraged him to ask again. The first, from an elated marquis, contained a long description of the skirmish, admitting that it was a "very trifling" affair, but that it would please Washington "on the account of bravery and alacrity" of the Continental soldiers. The second letter was from Major General Greene, who complimented Lafayette, noting "The Marquis is determined to be in the way of danger." That evening, Washington wrote Henry Laurens, recommending that Lafayette be given command of a Continental Army division.[60] This time, the members of Congress agreed, and on December 1, Laurens wrote Washington that it was "highly agreeable to Congress" that Lafayette command a division. In his general orders for December 4, 1777, Washington wrote:

> Major General The Marquis La Fayette is to take the command of the division lately commanded by General Stephen.[61]

Future Research

This article is a preliminary report to the David Library of the American Revolution, in Washington Crossing, Pennsylvania, on research conducted there during four, week-long visits, October 2017 to January 2018. More work will be required to complete it, especially among records of the Continental Army rifle corps. We have yet to identify the "brave Major Moriss" who led the push against the enemy counter attack at the end of the skirmish.

This research will have a second life. On February 1, 2018, Garry Stone and Paul W. Schopp began a study of the cultural landscape across which the battle was fought. Our work will be for the Camden County (NJ) Historical Society, a grantee of the American Battlefield Protection Program, National Park Service. Our task is to recreate the physical and human landscape of the battlefield. Where were the woods, fields, brush-choked swamps, and creeks that shaped how the skirmish was fought and persuaded Major General Greene not to attack the British at Gloucester Town? Who were the families being plundered by enemy marauders? Can we locate the site of the farmhouse to which the jägers took their wounded? We will search for answers in deeds and mortgages, old maps, tax lists, probate records, and the meeting minutes of the Society of Friends. Some of this research will take place at Stockton University, including delving into the Munn and Leap collections in the Bjork Library's Special Collections and Archives facilities. Now both deceased, David C. Munn and William W. Leap, long time Camden County local historians, donated their collections to Stockton to assure their meticulous research will live on beyond their own lives.

Acknowledgments

The authors are profoundly grateful to the compilers, translators, and editors who have assembled and published the Revolutionary War papers that have made this essay possible. We are especially grateful to the individuals who have made the German records accessible, particularly Bruce E. Burgoyne and Colonel Donald M. Londahl-Smidt. Stephen Gilbert provided the names of the two British light infantry men killed at the skirmish at the Big Timber Creek bridge, Matt White provided a copy of Eric Stephenson's photograph of David Mulford's memorial, and William T. Lawrence translated the Capitaine map legend. Librarians Kathie Ludwig (David Library) and Bonny Beth Elwell (Camden County Historical Society) and archivist Bette Epstein (NJ State Archives) all provided great assistance. Much of the information in this essay was gathered during the residential fellowship at the David Library of the American Revolution.

About the Authors

Garry Wheeler Stone is a retired archaeological historian living in a Quaker retirement community adjacent to Brandywine Battlefield. Before retiring, he worked 45 years in outdoor history museums, most notably at Monmouth Battlefield State Park and Historic St. Mary's City, Maryland. He is co-author (with Mark E. Lender) of *Fatal Sunday: George Washington, the Monmouth Campaign, and the Politics of Battle* (Oklahoma University Press, 2016).

Paul W. Schopp is the Assistant Director of the South Jersey Culture & History Center at Stockton University. He is a professional historian with over 44 years of experience working in the local history field. He is a well-known authority in the New Jersey history realm for his many reports, published articles, and books on state and Delaware Valley history. He is a member in long-standing of the West Jersey History Roundtable.

Research into the Battle of Gloucester

The American War for Independence in New Jersey is a special interest for Paul.

Jason R. Wickersty is a National Park Service Ranger at Gateway National Recreation Area. His research work specializes in the soldiers' pensions and damage claims of New Jersey during the Revolutionary War. He has written for the Company of Military Historians, American Battlefield Trust, and the *Journal of the American Revolution*. He lives in North Brunswick, New Jersey, with his wife Annie, daughter Abigail, and cat Síle.

Endnotes

1. David Hackett Fischer, *Washington's Crossing* (NY: Oxford University Press, 2004), 31–33, 66–73, 90–350; David McCullough, *1776* (NY: Simon & Schuster, 2005), 138–294; Arthur S. Lefkowitz, *The Long Retreat: The Calamitous American Defense of New Jersey, 1776* (Metuchen, NJ: Upland Press, 1998).
2. William James Morgan, ed., *Naval Documents of the American Revolution* (Washington, D.C.: Naval Historical Center, Department of the Navy, 1986), 8:408, 10: 239; David McConnell, *British Smooth-Bore Artillery: A Technological Study* (Ottawa: Environment Canada, 1988), 72–73.
3. Ira D. Gruber, *The Howe Brothers and the American Revolution* (Chapel Hill: University of North Carolina Press, 1972), 224–34.
4. Ambrose Serle, *The Journal of Ambrose Serle, Secretary to Lord Howe*, ed. Edward H. Tatam Jr. (San Marino, CA: 1940), 240–46.
5. Thomas J. McGuire, *The Philadelphia Campaign: Volume 1, Brandywine and the Fall of Philadelphia* (Mechanicsburg, PA: Stackpole 2006), 263–329.
6. Friedrich von Muenchhausen, *At General Howe's Side, 1776–1779*, trans. Ernst Kipping, ed. Samuel Stelle Smith (Monmouth Beach, NJ: Philip Freneau Press, 1974), 36–41; John Montresor, "The Montresor Journals," *Collections of the New York Historical Society for the Year 1882*, ed. G. D. Scull (New York: New York Historical Society, 1882), 462–72.
7. Montresor, "The Montresor Journals," 474.
8. Worthington Chauncey Ford, "The Defences of Philadelphia in 1777," *Pennsylvania Magazine of History and Biography* 19 (1935): 85–86, 236–38, 241–48, 361–71; Naval Documents, 10:467, 472, 478, 489, 492–93; Montresor, "The Montresor Journals," 474–76.
9. Francis Downman, *The Services of Lieut.-Colonel Francis Downman, R.A.*, ed. Colonel F. A. Whinyates (Woolwich, London: Royal Artillery Institution, 1898), 51–52.
10. George Washington, *The Papers of George Washington: Revolutionary War Series*, vols. 24–, ed. Philander D. Chase et al. (Charlottesville: University of Virginia, 1985–), 12: 295–96.
11. Washington, 11:227-31, 311-12; Israel Angell, *The Diary of Colonel Israel Angell Commanding Officer, 2nd Rhode Island Regiment, Continental Army* (Providence, RI: Preston and Rounds Company, 1899), ed. Norman Desmarais, Providence College's digital archives: http://digitalcommons.providence.edu/primary/2/, entries for October 1777.
12. Washington, 11:310–11, 392–93, 531–32; 12:19,
13. Ibid., 12:46–49, 59–64.
14. Ibid., 12:93, 94–95; see also 12:70–71.
15. Ibid., 12:142–43, 154–55; Johann Conrad Döhla, *A Hessian Diary of the American Revolution*, trans. and ed. Bruce E. Burgoyne (Norman, OK: University of Oklahoma Press, 1990), 57.
16. Washington, 12:70–71, 80, 140, 223, 248, 275, 309, 312–13; Angell, entries for October 1–18.
17. Washington, 12:292–96. For army officers' belief that the Delaware froze in the winter (it would), see *Huntington Papers: Correspondence of the Brothers Joshua and Jedediah Huntington during the Period of the American Revolution* (Hartford: Connecticut Historical Society, 1923), 379.
18. Washington, 12:286–87, 304–307, 313, 322–23; *Naval Documents*, 10:522.
19. Washington, 12:316–17, 321–23; Stanley J. Idzerda, editor, *Lafayette in the Age of the American Revolution. Selected Letters and Papers, Vol. I, December 7, 1776-March 30, 1778* (Ithaca, NY: Cornell University Press, 1977), 155. Troop strengths are from Charles H. Lesser, ed., *The Sinews of Independence: Monthly Strength Reports of the Continental Army* (Chicago: University of Chicago Press, 1976), 53. Most are from December 3, 1777, while the report for Huntington's Brigade is from November 16, 1777.
20. Nathaniel Greene, *The Papers of General Nathanael Greene*, 13 vols., ed. Richard K. Showman et al. (Chapel Hill: University of North Carolina Press, 1976–2015), 2:200.
21. Greene, 2:200–205; Angell, November 20, 1777.
22. Greene, 2:203, 205; Lafayette, 1:156, 159.
23. Greene, 2:208–11; Washington, 12:307, 337.
24. Brice: Lafayette, 1:19n, 85n; National Archives, Founders Online [https://founders.archives.gov/documents/Washington/03-11-02-0004; Gimat: National Park Service https://www.nps.gov/york/learn/historyculture/gimatbio.htm, and National Archives, Founders Online: https://founders.archives.gov/documents/Washington/05-10-02-0255; du Plessis: Wikipedia https://en.wikipedia.org/wiki/Thomas-Antoine_de_Mauduit_du_Plessis, Armand: https://en.wikipedia.org/wiki/Charles_Armand_Tuffin,_marquis_de_la_Rouerie, de Laumoy: https://en.wikipedia.org/wiki/Jean_Baptiste_Joseph,_chevalier_de_Laumoy; black servant: Lafayette, 1: 76, 84n. Departure and arrival: Lafayette, 1:156.
25. Greene, 2:212–17; Washington, 12:410.
26. Sir Henry Clinton, *The American Rebellion: Sir Henry Clinton's Narrative of his Campaigns, 1775–1782*, ed. William B. Willcox (New Haven, CT: Yale University Press, 1954), 72–81; Stephen Kemble, *Journals of Lieut. Col. Stephen Kemble, 1773–1789*; and British Army orders: Gen. Sir William Howe, 1775–1778; Gen. Sir Henry

Clinton, 1778; and Gen. Daniel Jones, 1778 (Boston: Greg Press, 1972), 139, 142; Döhla, 57–58; Johann Ernst Prechtel, *A Hessian Officer's Diary*, trans. Bruce E. Burgoyne (Westminster, MD: Heritage Books, 1994), 12–13; Stephan Popp, *A Hessian Soldier in the American Revolution*, trans. Reinhart J. Pope. (self-pub., 1953), 7.

27. Kemble, 544; *Naval Documents*, 10:522; Pattison, 13; subsequently, wives of jägers were captured while plundering in Newton Township. Wives and children were with some of the German troops already garrisoning Philadelphia including among the jägers—see the Church Book of Georg Christoph Coester, in Bruce E. Burgoyne, trans., *The Diary of Lieutenant von Bardeleben and Other von Donop Documents* (Westminster, MD: Heritage Books, 1998), 115–31.

28. Archibald Robertson, *His Diaries and Sketches in America, 1762–1780* (NY: New York Public Library, 1930; reprint ed., Arno Press, 1971), 155; *Naval Documents*, 10:534; Freyenhagen, "Journal of Ensign/Lt. Wilhelm Ernst Freyenhagen Jr., 1776–1778," Part 2, ed. Donald M. Londahl-Smidt, *Hessians: Journal of the Johannes Schwalm Historical Association* 14 (2011): 70.

29. *Naval Documents*, 10:146–47, 472–78, 514–15; Freyenhagen, 70.

30. Robertson, 156; Pattison, 15; Washington, 12:324; Frank H. Stewart, *History of the Battle of Red Bank* (Woodbury, NJ: Gloucester County Freeholders, 1927), 21; the Mantua Creek skirmish probably is the one remembered by David Somers of the Eggharbor Township militia (National Archives, Washington, D.C.: Revolutionary War Pension and Bounty-Land-Warrant Application Files [Record Group 15, Microfilm 804], Pension declaration S 4868).

31. Robertson, 156; Henry Stirke, "A British Officer's Revolutionary War Journal," ed. S. Sydney Bradford, *Maryland Historical Magazine* 54 (1961): 150–75; John W. Jackson, *The Pennsylvania Navy, 1775–1781: The Defense of the Delaware* (New Brunswick: Rutgers Univ. Press, 1965), 272–74.

32. Pattison, 25–26; Freyenhagen, 70.

33. Robertson, 156; Stephan Popp, *A Hessian Soldier in the American Revolution*, trans. Reinhart J. Pope (Privately printed, 1953), 8.

34. Job Whitall, *The Diary of Job Whitall of Gloucester County, New Jersey: 1775–1779*, ed. Florence DeHuff Friel (Woodbury, NJ: Gloucester County Historical Society, 1992), 85 [spellings modernized].

35. Whitall, 85–86.

36. Carl Leopold Baurmeister, *Revolution in America: Confidential letters and Journals 1776–1784 of Adjutant General Major Baurmeister of the Hessian Forces*, trans. and ed. Bernard A. Uhlendorf (New Brunswick: Rutgers University Press, 1957), 139.

37. Robertson, 157; Stirke 175; Stephen Gilbert, *British Light Infantry, Chapter 3: Light Infantry in NJ, PA, and NY, 1777–1778* (2002 draft provided to Garry Stone), n.p.

38. Samuel Asay (R 273); Robert Leeds, Capt. Payne's Coy., Eggharbor Township, Gloucester County (S.18489); and from Cumberland County, Charle Simpkins (R.9588), and Jeremiah Towser (S.6254).

39. Gilbert, n.p.; Robertson, 157.

40. Robertson, 157; Döhla, 59–60; Freyenhagen, 71; *Naval Documents*, 10:582–83, 602.

41. Robertson, 157; Freyenhagen, 71.

42. Freyenhagen, 71; *Naval Documents*, 10:595; Rif Winfield, *British Warships in the Age of Sail, 1714–1792* (Barnsley, Great Britain: Seaforth Publishing, 2007), 334.

43. Greene, 2:207–217; Pattison, 15.

44. Lafayette, 1:156; Michel Capitaine du Chesnoy, *Carte de l'action de Gloucester* (Cornell University Library, Division of Rare and Manuscript Collections), Greene, 2:214.

45. Possibly Anthony James Morris, major, 1st Continental Infantry, January 1, 1776; lieutenant colonel, 2 PA, October 25, 1776; retired June 1777[?] (Francis B. Heitman, *Historical Register of Officers of the Continental Army during the War of the Revolution, April 1775 to December 1783* [Baltimore, MD: Genealogical Publishing, 1982], 402).

46. Greene, 2:219; Lafayette, 1:156–58; Pension declaration of John A. Auten (S.945). The 150 riflemen are presumed to be all that were fit to march. The footsore and sick would have remained in camp to guard their baggage.

47. Freyenhagen indicates a location just east of the Kings Run or about 2.5 miles from Haddonfield. Today, the location is in Haddon Township near the intersection of the Kings Highway and Dallas Avenue.

48. Pension declaration of Richard Sayres (S.4660). September 3, 1777, von Wrede's and Ewald's jäger companies had driven rifle-armed Continental light infantry from Iron Hill, DE, with rifle and hunting sword (Johann Ewald, *Diary of the American War: A Hessian Journal*, trans. and ed. Joseph P. Tustin (New Haven: Yale University Press, 1979), 78; McGuire, 1:149–56.

49. Lafayette, 1:156; for militia musicians who served at Haddonfield, see pension files of Richard Tice (S.28912) and Levi Price (S.3733).

50. Pensions Richard Sayers (S.4660), Robert Leeds (S.18489), Joshua Reeves (S.29404), and Patrick McCollum (S.2768); Lafayette, 1:156–57.

51. Pension Patrick McCollum (S.2768). Warm clothes were wasted on a corpse. After the failed October attack on Fort Mercer, the Continentals stripped the bodies of the enemy and Continental rank & file, as did the British grenadiers after occupying Fort Mifflin.

52. Pension Jadock Bowen (S.960).

53. Greene, 2:218–19.

54. Greene, 2:217–25.

55. Prechtel, 14; Döhla, 60; Paul W. Schopp, "Historic Cultural Context" in New Jersey Department of Transportation, I-295/I-76/Route 42 Direct Connection, Phase I/II Archaeological Investigation Technical Environmental Study (Volume I), March 2006, http://www.state.nj.us/transportation/commuter/roads/rt295/pdf/PhaseI-IIArchaeoInvestTESVol_I.pdf, Part 4:4–34

56 John André, *Major André's Journal*, ed. Henry Cabot Lodge (Tarrytown, NY: William Abbatt, 1930), 66; Montresor, 479; Stirke, 175; pension John A. Auten (S.945).
57 Freyenhagen, 71.
58 Lafayette, 1:86n17, 88, 121–24, 146, 152–55; Washington, 11:4–5.
59 Washington, 12:81.
60 Lafayette, 1:156–61, 65; Washington, 12:408–411, 417–22.
61 Washington, 12:534.

Pencil sketch of Monument on the banks of the Delaware River. Drawing shows an obelisk monument to Lieutenant Colonel Christopher Greene, commemorating the Battle of Red Bank, on the banks of the Delaware River, near Red Bank, New Jersey; also shows a steamboat and sailboats on the river. Inscribed in pencil on upper left: "This monument was erected on the 22d Oct 1829 to transmit to posterity a grateful remembrance of the patriotism and gallantry of Lieut. Colonel Christopher Creenl [i.e., Greene] who with 400 men conquered the Hessian Army of 2000 troops (then in the British Service) at Red Bank on the 22d Oct 1777. Among the slain was found thier [sic] commander Count Donop whose body lies intered [sic] near the spot where he fell." Drawn by James Fuller Queen, dated between 1840 and 1870. *Courtesy of the Library of Congress.*

The Battle of the Kegs

Francis Hopkinson (1737–1791)

Of the five New Jersey signatories to the Declaration of Independence, only Francis Hopkinson resided in South Jersey. Born in Philadelphia, he was the son of Thomas Hopkinson and Mary Johnson. He attended the College of Philadelphia (now the University of Pennsylvania), matriculating in 1751—its first class.

During the 1760s in Philadelphia, Hopkinson sold dry goods, offered his services as conveyancer, and served as secretary of the Library Company of Philadelphia. A talented man, he was noted as both an author and composer. Siding with the Patriots during the Revolution, Hopkinson not only signed the Declaration of Independence, but served in various roles

Advertisement in *The Pennsylvania Gazette*, May 19, 1768.

in the nascent United States government, including as a member of the Second Continental Congress and chairman of the Navy Board. Hopkinson designed the first official American flag, Continental paper money, the first U.S. coin and had a hand in designing the Great Seal of the United States. It is to Hopkinson, not Betsy Ross, that credit must go for the design of a national emblem featuring stars and stripes. His first compensation request for designing the U.S. flag and the Great Seal was for a quarter cask of wine. After the states ratified the federal Constitution, he served as a federal district judge in Pennsylvania.

Hopkinson penned his famous piece of doggerel, "The Battle of the Kegs," as a propaganda ballad that describes an attack upon the British Fleet in the Delaware River at Philadelphia on January 6, 1778. At the direction of David Bushnell, inventor of the TURTLE, fabrication of the world's first waterborne mines started with Colonel Joseph Borden's cooperage supplying the wooden kegs. Bushnell constructed the contact fuzes for the kegs, ordered the kegs to be filled with black powder and then inserted the fuzes. Bushnell released the kegs from Bordentown at the change of tide and the slackening tide carried the kegs downriver. Bushnell and company hoped that they would collide with anchored British warships and explode as river mines. Few of the kegs struck their targets, however, as the British had hauled their ships into positions that protected them from floating river ice, and, therefore, avoided the exploding kegs. The fleet received minor damage, and the only casualties were two curious young boys who were killed by an exploding keg.

Hopkinson, in fact, conflates the ineffectual attack of 1778 with an earlier event in 1777, when a floating keg sank a small British tender to the HMS CERBERUS, killing four sailors and wounding an unknown number. Alerted by the sudden explosion, British soldiers converged on the riverside wharves and were ordered to shoot at any piece of wood in the water. The ensuing defense on the Philadelphia riverfront forms the basis of the poem, which sarcastically praises the courage and enduring heroism of the British army.

Lines 33–36 refer to General William Howe, commander of British forces who occupied Philadelphia from September 26, 1777, until June 18, 1778, and his scandalously reputed mistress Elizabeth Lloyd Warren, wife to Boston Loyalist Joshua Loring Jr. The "Erskine" first mentioned at line 41 is Sir William Erskine, Quartermaster General under Howe.

The Battle of the Kegs

Francis Hopkinson, from Ellis Paxson Oberholtzer's *The Literary History of Philadelphia* (Philadelphia: George W. Jacobs & Co., 1906).

THE BATTLE OF THE KEGS

Gallants attend, and hear a friend,
    Trill forth harmonious ditty,
Strange things I'll tell which late befell
    In Philadelphia city.

'Twas early day, as poets say,   5
    Just when the sun was rising,
A soldier stood on a log of wood,
    And saw a thing surprising.

As in amaze he stood to gaze,
    The truth can't be denied, sir,   10
He spied a score of kegs or more
    Come floating down the tide, sir.

A sailor too, in jerkin blue,
    This strange appearance viewing,
First damn'd his eyes, in great surprise,   15
    Then said, "Some mischief's brewing.

"These kegs, I'm told, the rebels bold,
    Pack'd up like pickled herring;
And they're come down t' attack the town
    In this new way of ferrying."   20

The soldier flew, the sailor too,
    And scared almost to death, sir,
Wore out their shoes, to spread the news,
    And ran till out of breath, sir.

Now up and down, throughout the town   25
    Most frantic scenes were acted;
And some ran here, and others there,
    Like men almost distracted.

Some "Fire" cried, which some denied,
    But said the earth had quaked;   30
And girls and boys, with hideous noise,
    Ran through the streets half naked.

Sir William he, snug as a flea,
   Lay all this time a snoring,
Nor dream'd of harm, as he lay warm,   35
   In bed with Mrs L——g.

Now in a fright he starts upright,
   Awaked by such a clatter;
He rubs both eyes, and boldly cries,
   "For God's sake, what's the matter?"   40

At his bedside he then espied
   Sir Erskine at command, sir,
Upon one foot he had one boot,
   And the other in his hand, sir.

"Arise, arise," Sir Erskine cries,   45
   "The rebels—more's the pity,
Without a boat are all afloat,
   And ranged before the city.

"The motly crew, in vessels new,
   With Satan for their guide, sir.   50
Pack'd up in bags, or wooden kegs,
   Come driving down the tide, sir.

"Therefore prepare for bloody war,—
   These kegs must all be routed,
Or surely we despised shall be,   55
   And British courage doubted."

The royal band now ready stand,
   All ranged in dread array, sir,
With stomach stout to see it out,
   And make a bloody day, sir.   60

The cannons roar from shore to shore,
   The small arms make a rattle;
Since wars began I'm sure no man
   E'er saw so strange a battle.

The rebel dales, the rebel vales,   65
   With rebel trees surrounded;
The distant wood, the hills and floods,
   With rebel echoes sounded.

The fish below swam to and fro,
   Attack'd from every quarter;   70
Why sure, thought they, the devil's to pay,
   'Mongst folks above the water.

The kegs, 'tis said, though strongly made,
   Of rebel staves and hoops, sir,
Could not oppose their powerful foes,   75
   The conquering British troops, sir.

From morn to night these men of might
   Display'd amazing courage;
And when the sun was fairly down,
   Retired to sup their porridge.   80

An hundred men with each a pen,
   Or more, upon my word, sir.
It is most true, would be too few,
   Their valor, to record, sir.

Such feats did they perform that day,   85
   Against these wicked kegs, sir,
That years to come, if they get home,
   They'll make their boasts and brags, sir.

The text of "The Battle of the Kegs" is taken from Samuel Kettell's *Specimens of American Poetry* (Boston: S. G. Goodrich and Co., 1829).

Should New Jersey Be Considered the Crossroads of the American Revolution?
A Project to Incorporate Local History in the Classroom

Zachary T. Baer

Introduction

In a survey distributed to each class on the first day of school, I include a question in an effort to learn more about the interests of my 100-plus students. "What historical topic or area would you like to learn more about?"

As many history teachers would expect, topics that overwhelmingly receive the most interest are the Civil War and World War II. Yet, some of my students surprise me. They have responded, "I would like to learn more about where I live." Or, as another simply stated, "Medford history."

Admittedly, the New Jersey-themed wall art in my room may prod these responses. Nevertheless, I am quite pleased with the interest they express. While teaching "provincial" history may seem counterintuitive in our modern "global" world, research reveals that assignments pertaining to local history provide students with opportunities that connect them to their personal world in ways the grand narrative of history does not.

One of the first areas in which I envision incorporating New Jersey history is our unit on the American Revolution. All too often, high school students enter class possessing enough knowledge to launch into the familiar tales related to the Revolution: they know about a massacre in Boston, they know the colonists loathed the imposition of taxes without representation, and they know about George Washington crossing some river around Christmas.

Despite this cursory knowledge, however, the students lack context and, even more so, an understanding of just how "revolutionary" the revolution was to New Jerseyans. What better way to demonstrate the widespread impact of the Revolution on the lives of American citizens than to research the numerous events that occurred in South Jersey during the Revolution?

What follows is a lesson plan for a four-day project entitled, "A Pop-Up Museum of the American Revolution." The project—designed in the spirit of the "new" Museum of the American Revolution in Philadelphia—asks students to create an exhibit on a selected topic to be included in our classroom museum. I introduce the project following a traditional review and assessment of the American Revolution, ensuring students have adequate background knowledge. The students are asked to transfer their learning into an argumentative essay that explains whether they agree with the posit that New Jersey should be considered the "Crossroads of the American Revolution."

Overall, my students have a very enjoyable time with this project. They stay engaged the entire time and remain eager to learn about their topic. The pedagogy underpinning this project is to challenge students centered on the following five elements, which are based on Shawnee High School's long-term goals for students:

- Research: choosing and analyzing appropriate sources.
- Synthesis: connecting information from prior knowledge and multiple sources.
- Collaboration: understanding others' ideas and opinions while completing a project.
- Argument: Independently formulating and effectively defending/articulating the importance of their topic via writing an essay.
- Presentation: oral presentation that asks students to defend and present their topic.

Time Frame

Four classes, 55-minute each (This could increase to five classes or decrease based on students' level).

Students also complete a take-home essay (which could also be done in class if time permitted).

Standards

Literacy in Social Studies / History:

CCSS.ELA-LITERACY.RH.9-10.1: Cite specific textual evidence to support analysis of primary and secondary sources, attending to such features as the date and origin of the information.

CCSS.ELA-LITERACY.RH.9-10.2: Determine the central ideas or information of a primary or secondary source; provide an accurate summary of how key events or ideas develop over the course of the text.

New Jersey Standards:

6.1.12.D.2.a: Analyze contributions and perspectives of African Americans, Native Americans, and women during the American Revolution.

6.1.12.D.2.d: Analyze arguments for new women's roles and rights, and explain why 18th-century society limited women's aspirations.

Objectives

Day 1: You will be able to research your topic and begin to analyze why New Jersey is considered the "Crossroads of the American Revolution" by using library and online sources.

Day 2: You will be able to research and analyze why New Jersey is considered the "Crossroads of the

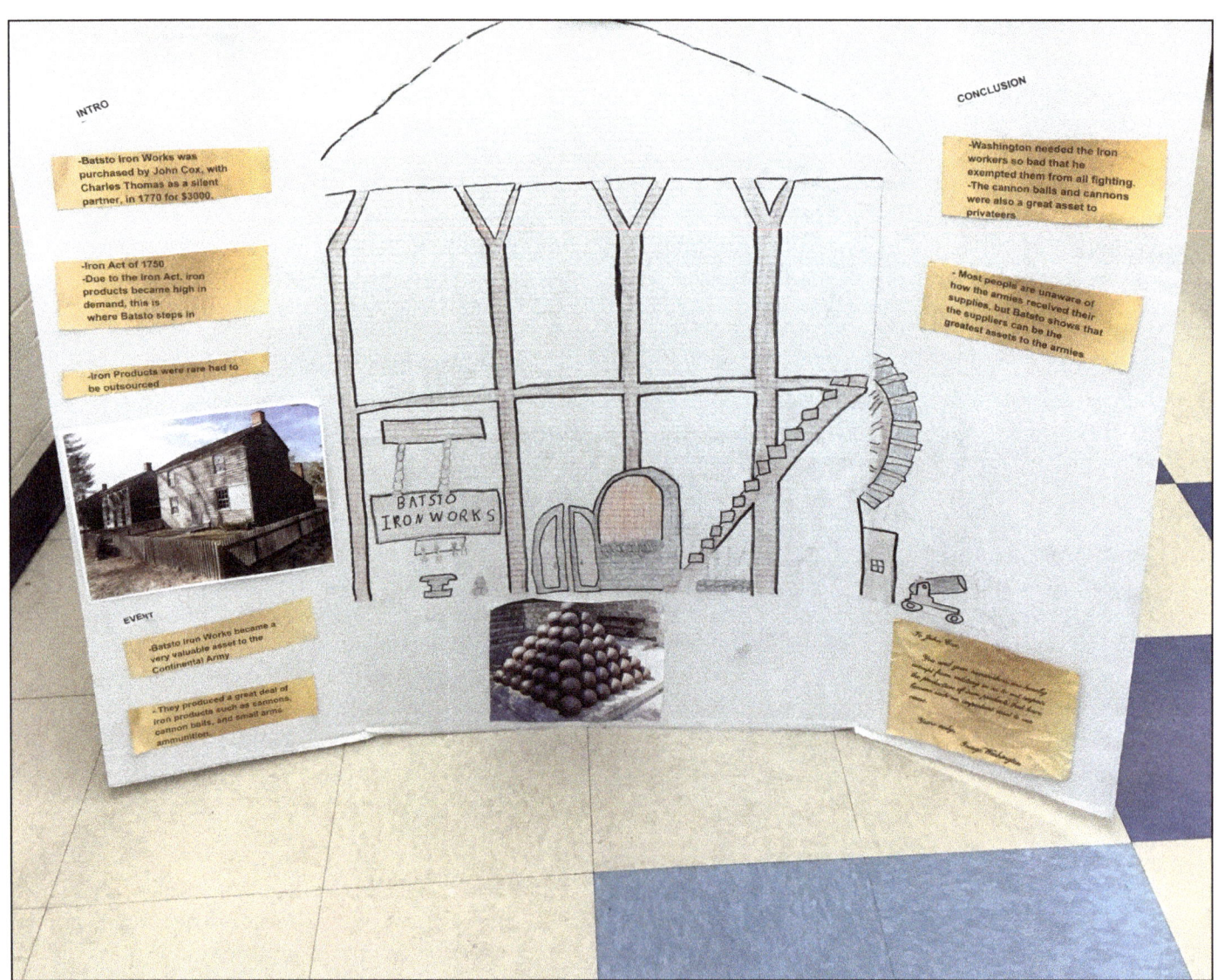

Student display panel depicting the Batsto Iron Works. *Photograph by the author.*

The Crossroads of the American Revolution?

American Revolution" by creating an outline for your poster.

Day 3: You will be able to create a tri-fold poster that effectively displays your exhibit and its relation to New Jersey being considered the "Crossroads of the American Revolution."

Day 4: You will be able to present, view and listen to each group's "exhibit" and synthesize information to demonstrate why New Jersey is considered the "Crossroads of the American Revolution."

Materials

Any material listed below with an asterisk next to it can be provided by emailing, zbaer@lrhsd.org.
- *Article, "New Jersey: The Crossroads of the American Revolution"
- *Project handout
- Computer access with printer capabilities
- Tri-fold poster boards (Students purchase and bring to class)
- *Research sources packet (Or, you could use this issue of *SoJourn*)

Progression of Activities / Teaching (abbreviated for this article)

Day 1 + 2:

To introduce students to the project, I typically begin by asking students if they have ever visited Independence Hall or if they know about the new Museum of the American Revolution. I then explain that we will be engaged in a project that will have them create exhibits about New Jersey's role in the American Revolution.

As a class, we then read the article, "New Jersey: The Crossroads of the American Revolution."

I distribute the "Project handout" and provide my expectations, including the rubric.

I allow students to gather in groups. You may also consider assigning groups, depending on your class.

Students are urged to select topics from the project handout sheet (first come, first serve)—Again, you may consider pre-assigning topics, based on your class.

At the time, this issue of *SoJourn* was not available. In the future, I will include topics based on what is presented in this issue and have copies on hand for the students to use.

Students begin to research topics, using the research guide. In the research guide, I provide a number of links to each topic to assist students in their research.

Students work at this for the remainder of Day 1 and Day 2.

I inquire frequently with each group and create checkpoints to ensure work is complete and that the students understand the material.

Day 3:

Students should have completed tri-fold poster and work on presentation.

Day 4:

Students are told that they will be divided into two groups.

Half the class presents first, while the other half serves as the audience.

Students receive peer-grade sheets that ask them to grade each presentation. These are collected at the class end. This helps students remain on task while circulating the room.

Each group serves as a station with which another group is matched. After each group has spent four minutes, each group rotates.

After each group listens to all the presentations, the other half of the class presents. Step three is then repeated.

The presentations should consume most of the class time. You can adjust the schedule to best fit your class to make sure each group has enough time to present.

Collect peer-grade sheets.

Explain essay in project handout (to be completed for homework).

Be sure to emphasize that students should incorporate elements from the presentations into their essay explaining why New Jersey is considered the crossroads of the American Revolution.

About the Author

Zachary Baer is a history teacher at Shawnee High School. He is a member of the West Jersey History Roundtable and holds a deep, abiding interest in local history. Zachary resides in Gibbsboro, New Jersey, and looks forward to receiving feedback and comments from *SoJourn* readers. Comments can be sent directly to the author at zbaer@lrhsd.org.

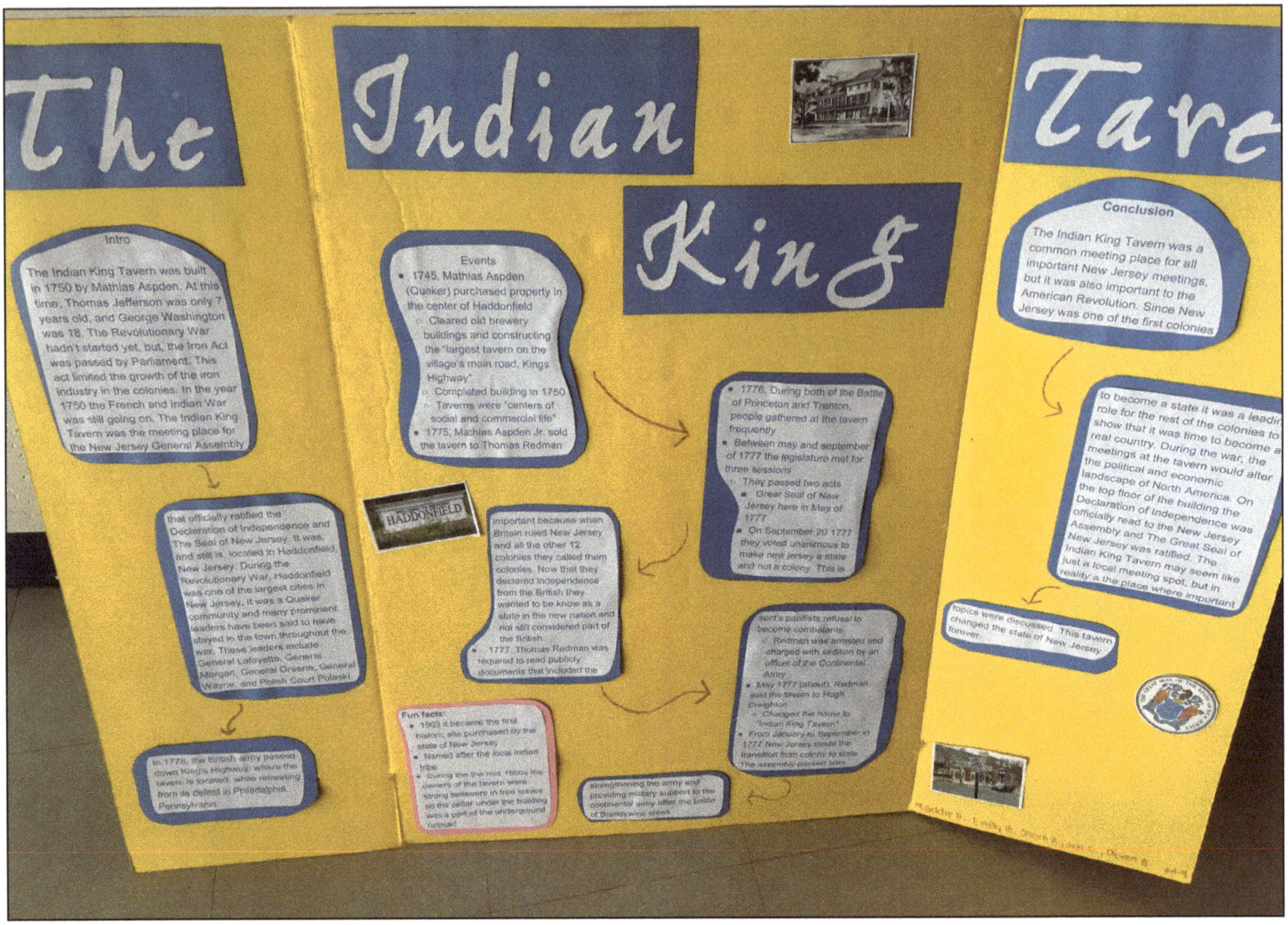

Student pop-up museum display about the Indian King Tavern in Haddonfield. *Photograph by the author.*

Monument at Chestnut Neck, Port Republic, New Jersey. The inscription on this, the earliest of several monuments at Chestnut Neck, reads: "In honor of the brave patriots of the Revolutionary War who defended their liberties and their homes in a battle fought near this site October 6, 1778. Dedicated October 6, 1911." The soldier atop the monument faces the Mullica river, standing watch for the enemy. *Photo courtesy of the South Jersey Culture & History Center, July 26, 2018.*

When Mad Anthony Came to South Jersey:
Civilian Experience during the American Revolution

Claude M. Epstein

Squalor and misery. Anyone watching the news from Syria in the last several years has witnessed from afar the tragedies of war. Alongside civilians being killed or maimed—businesses, schools, hospitals and public buildings have been turned into piles of rubble. Civil authority has become chaotic and millions of people have been dislocated, fleeing to places of safety; trade has come to a near standstill. This is life in a war zone.[1]

New Jersey was once a war zone, too. Fortunately, that was a long time ago during the American Revolution. No one alive can possibly remember the events of those times; yet we are able to read about the major battles and military operations and political events which occurred throughout South Jersey. What was it like for ordinary citizens living through this period of disruption and disorder? Their civilian experiences are rarely mentioned despite the fact that there were military operations in New Jersey during every year of the Revolution (Table 2, see next page).

The South Jersey Social Environment

Far fewer people resided in South Jersey during the colonial period than today. They also lived farther away from one another (Table 1). A few small towns existed, such as Burlington, Haddonfield and Salem, but most people lived on isolated farms. Many living in South Jersey made their living as farmers, wood cutters, trappers, and fishermen.

For those colonists who *did* reside in towns, an analysis of eighteenth-century ledger books provides some clues about how they made their living before, during and after the Revolution.[1] These ledgers list the types of items being bought and sold in South Jersey towns and villages. Tables 3A and 3B show the items sold in Toms River & Forked River from 1751 to 1760, Barnegat Bay from 1766 to 1767, Somers Point from 1773 to 1781, and Cape May Court House from 1778 to 1790.[2,3] Table 4A and 4B lists the items sold in the Delaware Valley, specifically in Salem, from 1764 to 1770, Woodbury from 1779 to 1789, and Bordentown from 1790 to 1797.[4] Agricultural products were similar between these two regions, but industrial products differed. Near the shore, wood products tended to be of the less finished variety (e.g., bark, bolts, rough pine, and cedar), since the forests of the Pine Barrens were more accessible. Those sold within the Delaware Valley were of the more finished variety, for example coffins and chairs.

Poverty was a noteworthy aspect of the 1770s economy in South Jersey. The poorer classes included slaves

Counties	1726	1810	2010
Atlantic (formed from Gloucester in 1837)			494
Burlington	5	30	562
Camden (formed from Gloucester in 1844)			2322
Cape May	3	16	387
Cumberland (formed from Salem in 1748)		26	324
Gloucester (incl. Atlantic & Camden)	2	20	895
Monmouth (incl. Ocean)	5	21	1345
Ocean (formed from Monmouth in 1850)			917
Salem	5	42	288

Table 1. Population Density of South Jersey Counties (population per square mile).

and indentured servants, as well as unskilled laborers on farms, households, businesses, in lumbering and along the waterfront. Almshouses and jails had existed in many South Jersey counties for some time. A distinct segment of the South Jersey population struggled financially, placing an additional financial burden on the rest of the community.

The people of New Jersey embraced various Protestant denominations. The schisms that created these denominations resulted in some tensions between, and competition for, congregants. Table 5 lists the various denominations and their numerical strengths[1,5] Methodists, missing from the list, were ordained as Anglicans and did not split from them until after the Revolution. The Quakers, Methodist segment of the Anglican Church, Moravians and Mennonites were pacifists. Once the Revolution began, this became a cause of tension.

Nature of the Problem

The American Revolution, like most wars, created misery for many and opportunity for some. This occurred in different ways. Some localities endured military operations, where whole armies encamped in and around local communities. The logistical support for such military movements had a major impact on these communities with respect to food, shelter and other supplies. Both armies sent out foragers to gather supplies from the surrounding countryside. On a smaller scale, individuals, or small groups of soldiers, gathered what they needed from the surrounding countryside when they were dispatched to forage or gather intelligence. Furthermore, soldiers without specific orders plundered local farms and towns for their own greed and benefit.

William Stryker provides a general description of the impact of these military and quasi-military operations on the civilian population:

> The condition of the State of New Jersey during the passage of these hostile armies across its territory was most deplorable. Situated between two powerful States, close to two great cities, one under British rule and the other the objective point of the march of the English army, the people living on the highway between these centers of interest had to undergo all the suffering which follow in the track of war. Their farms were devastated, their houses ransacked, their barns consumed, their money and valuables stolen, their cattle and horses, their forage, crops, and merchandise carried off, their bridges and their churches damaged and despoiled. Society was thoroughly disorganized, quarrels were engendered, and families were subject to every indignity or else obliged to flee for their lives.[6]

County	1776	1777	1778	1779	1780	1781	1782	1783	Total
Delaware River	2		6						8
Atlantic		1	3	1		1	1	1	8
Burlington	4	1	7						12
Camden			9						9
Cape May	3								3
Cumberland	1					1			2
Gloucester			6						6
Ocean	1		3	4	2		4		14
Salem			7	1	1				9
Mercer	10	5	4						19
Middlesex	7	14	2	7	4	2	2		38
Monmouth	14	2	2	12	10	8	5		53
Bergen	16	22	7	17	16	8	5	1	92
Essex	1	1	1	1	6	5	2	1	18
Hudson	7		2	5	6				20
Hunterdon	1								1
Morris		2		1			1		4
Passaic	1		1		1				3
Somerset	2	5	1	2					10
Sussex					1				1
Union	7	5	4	4	19	9	2		50

Table 2. Battles and Skirmishes of the American Revolution in New Jersey.[3]

When Mad Anthony Came to South Jersey

Industry & Trade	Toms & Forked River	Barnegat Bay	Somers Point	Cape May Court House	Industry & Trade	Toms & Forked River	Barnegat Bay	Somers Point	Cape May Court House
Tailoring			X	X	Hides	X			X
Rope			X		Leather	X			
Stockings			X		Feathers	X		X	X
Linen				X	Skins			X	
Baskets				X	Bricks	X			
Spinning				X	Shoemaking			X	X
Cooperage	X		X		Harness Making			X	
Cordwood	X			X	Carpentry			X	X
Lumber	X			X	Blacksmithing			X	X
Bark	X				Salt			X	
Bolts	X				Work	X		X	
Rails		X	X	X	Carting			X	X
Shingles		X	X		Scow Transport				X
Rough Pine/ Cedar		X			Cash	X			X
Cedar bolts	X								
Lumber			X						
Tar			X						

Table 3A. Jersey Shore Industrial Ledger Items.

Agriculture	Toms & Forked River	Barnegat Bay	Somers Point	Cape May Court House	Agriculture	Toms & Forked River	Barnegat Bay	Somers Point	Cape May Court House
Butter	X				Cranberries		X		
Eggs	X			X	Apples				X
Cheese	X				Apples Trees				X
Tallow				X	Cows				X
Corn	X		X	X	Geese			X	
Wheat	X		X	X	Fowl			X	X
Hay	X				Cattle			X	X
Flour		X		X	Fish			X	X
Hay			X		Turkeys			X	
Clover Seed				X	Oysters			X	
Oats				X	Venison				X
Flaxseed	X		X		Pork & Hams	X		X	X
Potatoes				X	Beef	X			X

Table 3B. Jersey Shore Agricultural Ledger Items.

83

Stryker continues his description by highlighting the fear residents experienced from the presence of Hessian troops:

> These Hessian soldiers, whose services had been purchased, who were fighting for hire, were uncouth in manners, low in morals, but well trained in military duties, and familiar with war and violence.
>
> ... the Germans were the first to commence a pillage upon the inhabitants, friend and foe alike. They took possession of every article they desired, under the spirit of the orders which Von Donop had received from Howe.[7]

Large Scale Military Operations

Large Scale operations crossed New Jersey several times. Those effecting South Jersey include the following:

- Washington retreats from New York through New Jersey to Pennsylvania with the British in pursuit (November 20 to December 7, 1776)
- Washington re-crosses the Delaware, Battles of Trenton and Princeton and advances across Jersey to Morristown (December 25, 1776 to January 6, 1777)
- British Occupation of Philadelphia and Washington at Valley Forge (September 26, 1777 to June 18, 1778)
- British Retreat from Philadelphia to New York, Battle of Monmouth Court House and Washington's encampment at Somerville (June 18 to December 11, 1778)
- Punitive Naval Raid on the Mullica River (October 5 to October 22, 1778)

Americans Cross the Delaware River with the British in Pursuit (1776)

The governmental institutions that guaranteed local law and order weakened and even disappeared with the movement of troops and the shifting perception of who was winning the war. Such institutions as loyalist or patriot government, the clergy, or military commands lost authoritative control over large parts of New Jersey.

Slaves and indentured servants often ran away from their owners. They frequently hid in wilderness areas such as the Pine Barrens. They, too, needed food, housing, and other supplies and stole these items from local residents. Yet, some people managed to benefit from the Revolution. Privateers received permission from either the rebel or the English government to capture each other's shipped goods. Privateers would own, rent, or a buy a ship, equip it with a crew and military hardware, and derive profits from the sale of the captured ships and cargo. Harbor and overland transport had to be established to bring the captured goods to Philadelphia or New York, thereby employing dock workers and teamsters. This stimulated the establishment of support industries such as taverns, inns, stables, wheelwrights, and farriers. Local farmers, in turn, would profit from supplying all these supportive institutions with food, houses, and fodder.

The British Occupation of Philadelphia

British and Hessian troops, totaling 17,000, occupied Philadelphia beginning on September 26, 1777. American forces largely encircled the Crown's military; Washington's army occupied the Pennsylvania highlands surrounding Philadelphia while the various American county militias remained active on the Jersey side of the

Industry & Trade	Salem	Woodbury	Bordentown	Industry & Trade	Salem	Woodbury	Bordentown
Spinning	X	X	X	Cooperage	X		
Wool	X	X		Sleighs	X		
Linen	X			Scythe			X
Cordwood		X		Tailoring		X	
Lumber	X			Shoemaking	X	X	
Coffins	X			Leatherwork	X	X	
Fences	X			Carpentry	X		
Chairs	X			Cooperage			X
Rails			X	Labor	X	X	X
Shingles			X	Carting	X		
Logs			X	Cash	X	X	X
Bricks	X						

Table 4A. Delaware Valley Industrial Ledger Items.

When Mad Anthony Came to South Jersey

Agriculture	Salem	Woodbury	Bordentown	Agriculture	Salem	Woodbury	Bordentown
Butter	X	X		Peaches		X	
Cheese	X			Turnips	X		
Eggs	X	X		Beans	X		
Honey		X		Potatoes		X	
Dung		X		Cabbage	X		
Tallow	X		X	Onions	X		
Vinegar	X		X	Fowl	X	X	
Cider	X			Geese	X		
Hay	X	X		Horses	X		
Straw		X		Cows	X		
Wheat	X			Sheep			X
Corn	X	X	X	Shad		X	
Rye			X	Pork & Hams	X	X	X
Oats	X			Beef & Veal	X	X	X
Timothy Seed			X	Venison			X
Buckwheat			X				
Flaxseed	X						

Table 4B. Delaware Valley Agricultural Ledger Items.

Delaware. Two major events affected the residents of South Jersey. First, the British attempted to secure their eastern flank along the Delaware River once they occupied Philadelphia. Second, American forces embarked on a major foraging operation in South Jersey with British forces in pursuit during the early months of 1778.

Battle of Red Bank

The Battle of Red Bank is well described online by the Friends of Red Bank, a local support group for the historic battlefield and fort; other essays in this issue also take up its history.[8] The British needed to maintain an open Delaware River in order to resupply their forces in Philadelphia. They had to vanquish the American forces manning Fort Mifflin on Mud Island, just off the Pennsylvania mainland, and Fort Mercer on the east bank of the Delaware at Red Bank. In addition, they had to breach the *chevaux-de-frise*, a defensive array of iron-tipped stake clusters, providing impediments to naval craft sailing up the Delaware, extending from Fort Billingsport (now Paulsboro) downstream of Philadelphia to Red Bank. The British navy also had to contend with the Pennsylvania navy's armed galleys near the mouth of Woodbury Creek.

The British dispatched Colonel Carl von Donop's Hessian brigade to take Fort Mercer. The brigade crossed the Delaware River at Cooper's Ferry (now Camden) north of the fort on October 21, 1777. They marched through Newton Township and encamped at Haddonfield. The next day, Tory guides led them to Big Timber Creek at Westville, but found the bridge there dismantled. The Hessians were forced on a four-mile detour in order to cross Big Timber Creek upstream, using Clement's Bridge at Westcottville. They finally reached Fort Mercer later in the afternoon. There the Hessians suffered a crushing defeat at the hands of the 1st and 2nd Rhode Island Regiments of the Continental army, then manning the fort.

The civilian population endured what we would now call *collateral damage*. Congress usurped the apple orchard of Job Whitall, had it cut down, and replaced it with Fort Mercer. Once the Hessians reached Haddonfield, the Tories identified local Patriots, who were then guarded to prevent them from alerting the continental forces at Fort Mercer. In addition, some Haddonfield residents voluntarily quartered Hessians in their homes to

Group	Estimate	Group	Estimate
Presbyterians	36,000	Anglicans	10,000
Quakers	24,000	Mennonites	2,000
Dutch Reformed	24,000	Moravians	200
Calvinists	15,000	Roman Catholics	200
Lutherans	12,000	No Affiliation	14,600
Baptists	12,000		

Table 5. Religious Affiliations in New Jersey in 1786.

Figure 1. Colonel Carl Emil Ulrich von Donop (1732–1777). *Courtesy of Wikipedia.*

preclude other Hessian soldiers from looting their dwellings. Still other residents transported their valuables and livestock to localities out of town, where they would be safe from either side's troops.

The Hessians held the wife of militia major Samuel Hugg in custody while on their march from Haddonfield to Fort Mercer. She, in turn, noted the local Tories that served as guides leading the Hessians through the countryside. This whole operation exacerbated the local conflicts between Jersey Tories and Patriots living near one another.

Anthony Wayne's Foraging Expedition in South Jersey

It is well known that the winter of 1777–1778 was severe and that Washington's army, encamped at Valley Forge, was starved for supplies by the inaction of the Continental Congress. The British in Philadelphia had their own difficulties obtaining supplies from New York due to the American naval blockade of the Delaware. As the winter dragged on, the situation grew worse, especially for the Americans at Valley Forge.

General Anthony Wayne (Figure 3) and a detachment of Washington's army crossed from Wilmington, Delaware, to Salem, New Jersey, on February 19, 1778.[9] Washington sent Wayne with orders to gather horses and cattle and bring them back to Valley Forge, paying the owners a reasonable price for the supplies commandeered, and depriving the English of the same supplies.[10] Wayne's foragers encountered great difficulty in South Jersey. Owners hid livestock in local swamps and the continental troops lacked familiarity with these places. Even so, Wayne ultimately managed to collect large numbers of cattle and horses. On February 22, he had them herded and driven to Wrangletown, then Mount Holly, and finally to Trenton. On February 23, Wayne ordered the hay available from Salem to Billingsport burned so that it could not be taken by the British. He ordered the same for the hay collected at the mouth of Raccoon Creek and Mantua Creek.[11]

The British sent 2000 troops across the Delaware from Philadelphia on February 20 to thwart Wayne's efforts.[12] They disembarked at Billingsport, where 1500 men marched toward Salem, while the remaining 500 marched toward Haddonfield. Wayne, informed of the British movements, abandoned Haddonfield on the 26th, but returned around the 28th, joining with General Casimir Pulaski and his horsemen. They moved to attack a British column, marching adjacent to the Cooper River on March 1. After several skirmishes, the British fell back to Cooper's Ferry and withdrew to Philadelphia. The British had abandoned most of the cattle, horses, and wagons they had stolen from local residents.[13]

The journal of British Officer John Graves Simcoe (Figure 4) describes what happened around Salem.[14] The 27th and 46th regiments of the British army, under the command of Colonel Charles Mawhood, and Major Simcoe's Queen's Rangers sailed down the Delaware, landing in Salem on March 17. At Salem, they met 300 New Jersey Volunteers (Tory), who told them that 300 American militia were at Quinton's Bridge and Hancock's Bridge on Alloways Creek, south of Salem.

Mawhood and Simcoe led their troops towards Quinton's Bridge on the 18th, south of Alloways Creek, where they laid a trap for the American militia who approached from the north. The Queen's Rangers, wearing their green uniforms, occupied a house on the north side of the bridge while others lay in the fields nearby. The British regiments, wearing their red uniforms, showed themselves down the road south of the bridge. The militia gave chase and soon found themselves trapped between the Queen's Rangers and the British Regiments. The Crown's forces killed and captured many militiamen. Two days later, Major Simcoe and the Queen's Rangers landed at the mouth of Alloways Creek, marched through two miles of swamp/marshland, and finally reached the south bank of Alloways Creek at Hancock's Bridge. There, in a surprise attack, they took the Hancock House and all of its out buildings (Figure 2). Most of the militia had already evacuated the area, so the British bayoneted the remaining 20–30 troops to prevent alerting the American militia with gun fire. The Queen's Rangers finally did fire their muskets at escaping militia, alerting the remaining Patriots of the British presence. Simcoe then thought it prudent to withdraw and return to Salem. Two days later, he received orders to seize Thompson's Bridge, but the militia fled at their arrival. Mahwood feared that increasing numbers of American militia occupied the area. Since the British had achieved their foraging goals, Mahwood withdrew his forces to Philadelphia.

Local residents suffered greatly during these operations. Two civilians—both Tories—suffered bayoneting by the Queen's Rangers at Hancock's Bridge. Simcoe observed two houses burned to the ground near Haddonfield. Both Hessian and English soldiers pillaged many houses. The British also held people in detention. Finally, both sides commandeered horses and cattle, while the troops burned much of the hay available for livestock.

Figure 2. The British Surround Hancock House, from *Simcoe's Military Journal: a History of the Operations of a Partisan Corps, Called the Queen's Rangers, Commanded by Lieut Col. J. G. Simcoe, during the War of the American Revolution* (New York: Bartlett & Welford, 1844).

Figure 3. General Anthony Wayne.

Figure 4. Major John Graves Simcoe.

Naval Punitive Operation against Little Egg Harbor

Both sides of the conflict engaged in privateering as a potent form of economic warfare. A privateer simply needed to hire or purchase a ship and assemble a crew, receive authorization from the government—called a letter of marque—avoid capture by the other side, then sell the goods taken at a vast profit. Little Egg Harbor, and, to a lesser extent, Mays Landing and Toms River, became safe centers for American privateers, where they could offload cargo and put captured ships up for sale. The captured cargo or, "prizes," could then be sold or shipped by wagon through the Pine Barrens to Philadelphia. This occurred with even greater frequency once the British began blockading the coast and Delaware Bay.[15]

American privateering had a serious impact on the British economy. Trade losses reached £1,800,000 sterling and insurance costs soared. South Jersey Tories informed the British that Little Egg Harbor was a major center for American privateering and the British gave orders for an attack.[16] Captain John Knight, RN, sailed from the Delaware Bay with a complement of three ships. They *acquired* a pilot who could navigate up the Mullica River, passing over bars and avoiding running aground, and unsuccessfully attempted to gain a pilot for the Great Egg Harbor River. On June 12, 1777, the British flotilla sailed across the bar at the mouth of the Mullica River. They soon arrived at Fox Burrows, where they seized two American brigs: one a privateer vessel and the other a merchant man with its cargo of timber and tar.

The Patriots Colonel John Cox, owner of the Batsto Ironworks, Lieutenant Colonial Elijah Clark, a local mill owner, and Major Richard Wescoat, a tavern owner who was in charge of the government stores at "The Forks" near Batsto, recognized the vulnerability of the Mullica River and its privateering operation to attack by the British Navy.[17] They petitioned the New Jersey Council of Safety to fortify the area. Eventually, Clark and Wescoat built a fortification with eight to ten cannons at Fox Burrows that could protect the approach to Little Egg Harbor. They received payment from the General Assembly of New Jersey for their out-of-pocket expenses.[18]

But these preparations did not stop the British. William Stryker describes in detail the British punitive raid on the Mullica River and Little Egg Harbor.[19] Nine British warships left New York Harbor and arrived at the mouth of the Little Egg Harbor Inlet on October 5, 1778. In order to protect the shore communities, Washington, alerted to the British plans, dispatched troops from Trenton on October 4, under the command of Brigadier General Casimir Pulaski. Contrary winds delayed the British sloops at the inlet, but on the 6th, the British navigated up the Mullica in smaller vessels. Local Tories informed them that Chestnut Ridge, twenty miles upstream, provided moorings for privateer vessels. They proceeded to Chestnut Neck, forced the local militia to flee, and then destroyed the town. They burned two previously scuttled prize ships, eight sloops and schooners, a large whale boat and some piraguas. They also plundered—and then burned—twelve houses and several barns. They looted the storehouse, then burned it and destroyed the town's protective breastworks. Chestnut Neck was thoroughly razed.

The British soldiers then proceeded to Bass River, where they dined with a local Tory, who thereby prevented the British from pillaging his farm. Crown forces destroyed the house and barn of Eli Mathis, along with the local salt works, a saw mill, and the houses of twelve Patriots. By October 8, the larger warships, HMS Zebra and HMS Vigilant, cleared the bar at Little Egg Harbor Inlet.

Pulaski's American forces reached Little Egg Harbor on October 8 and encamped on James Willets' farm. A detachment under Lieutenant Colonel Carl de Bosen was sent to a forward position at Thomas Osborn's farm, a short distance away. Informed by an American deserter of de Bosen's location, on October 15, a British raiding party surrounded the Osborn farm and killed or captured the entire detachment. With the Americans in hot pursuit, the British returned to the fleet and prepared their departure. Exiting the Mullica, the HMS Zebra ran aground. Her crew transferred to other ships in the fleet and the British then torched the Zebra.

In a later incident, Boyd Porterfield and his 71st Regiments of Highlanders raided Squan Inlet and the Shark River on the Monmouth County shore. This was a less ambitious raid than that of Chestnut Neck, but they managed to destroy a valuable salt works including eight to ten salt kettles and boilers, as well as a great deal of beef and bacon, and a sloop loaded with grain. They had planned more destruction but did not pursue it because the winds endangered their retreat back to their Staten Island base.[20]

Paramilitary Operations

The war situation in New Jersey was more of a local civil war with multiple sides. Many New Jersey residents were Tories and either aided the British army with supplies, shelter, and intelligence, or joined the British militia, called the New Jersey Volunteers. Others were Patriots and joined the American army or served in county militias. Jersey Quakers and Moravians, however, as well as individuals of other denominations, were pacifists and refrained from any military activity. Others benefited financially, changing sides from one to the other as the economics dictated.

Major military activity ceased in the nine Coastal Plain counties by the end of 1778. However, major actions continued in North Jersey, due to its proximity to New York City, which the British occupied until the last British transports left New York harbor on December 4, 1783. The war in South Jersey, after the end of 1778, consisted of raids by the various militias. These raids involved kidnapping, killing and the destruction of property.

Both sides had militias in New Jersey. Six regiments of the New Jersey Loyalists fought for the British. Some members of the First and Third Regiments participated in the raid on Chestnut Neck. The Second Regiment participated in the skirmishes at Quinton's Bridge and Hancock's Bridge, the Battle of Monmouth, and in the capture of Captain Joshua Huddy.[21] Other regiments remained active in northern New Jersey. County militias fought with the American army.

Two particular units are worthy of special consideration. The Queen's Rangers, drawn from several colonies, under the command of Lieutenant Colonel John Graves Simcoe, were highly active in the skirmishes at Quinton's and Hancock's Bridges as well as the Battle of Monmouth. This unit was particularly daring and served as a kind of guerrilla unit for the British Army, but departed for the southern conflicts at the end of 1778.

The Black Brigade was made up primarily of freed and escaped slaves. Unlike African Americans in New England who fought for the Patriots, those in the Black Brigade fought for the British.[22] They were stationed at Refugee Town on Sandy Hook after a runaway slave named Titus, also called Captain Tye, organized the brigade. When the Governor of Virginia, the Earl of Dunmore, promised to free any slave who joined the British Army on November 7, 1775, many slaves either escaped to Virginia or conspired to gain their freedom in the other colonies. John Corlies, a Monmouth County Quaker, refused to free his slaves, so his local Quaker congregation read him out of meeting. His slaves included the above mentioned Captain Tye, whose regiment undertook reconnaissance missions as well as joined with white refugees, called "Cow Boys," and the Queen's Rangers while raiding New Jersey Patriots. Colonel Tye and his unit of black and white Refugees undertook many raids between 1779 and 1780.[23] They are listed below:

1. The capture of militia Captain Elisha Stewart
2. The plundering of 80 head of cattle, 20 horses, wearing apparel, and household furniture from houses near Shrewsbury
3. The murder of John Russell and his son after looting and burning his home
4. The kidnapping of Matthias Halsted and the plundering of his furniture, wearing apparel, and eight head of cattle
5. The attack on the home of Captain Barnes Smock, called the, "Hornet's Nest," a patriots' meeting place
6. The retaliatory murder of Joseph Murray at Colt's Neck
7. The capture of many of the top militia officers
8. The initial capture of Captain Joshua Huddy at Colt's Neck and the burning of his house

Tye died of a wound in 1780, but his black and white refugee unit continued activities into 1782, when they plundered Patriot homes from Forked River through Barnegat Bay and went on a robbery spree near Mount Holly.[24]

The Pine Robbers mark the limit of paramilitary activity in South Jersey. They were bandits who provided support and intelligence for the New Jersey Loyalists. They tended to be young thugs from the poorer segment of the South Jersey population, especially those who held no property. Henry Ward characterizes the reason why this condition arose in the Pine Barrens:

> Outlaw gangs flourished briefly in certain parts of the Pine Barrens region of New Jersey. Locale and wartime conditions blended perfectly for the encouragement of brigandage. The thinly distributed population and civil authorities, the wilderness refuge, the isolated farm households on the fringes of the Pine Barrens, and the carting inland of goods brought off privateer vessels all invited depredations. Individual travelers on the few roads could be waylaid. Some stolen goods could be assigned to Loyalist refugees for transportation and sale in New York City.[25]

Many such gangs of banditti formed to burn and plunder Patriot houses, as well as to carry out highway robberies and assaults of tax collectors, smugglers and cargo thieves. Some even went so far as to assault and murder their victims (Table 6).

Gang Name	Area of Operation
Woodward Gang	Upper Freehold
An unnamed gang	Monmouth County
Jacob Fagan Gang	Manasquan River
Lewis Fenton Gang	Manasquan River
John Bacon Gang	Eastern Burlington/Ocean Counties
Joseph Mulliner	Mullica River Basin
Jonathan West	Toms River
Henry Sellers	Freehold
William Giberson Jr.	Little Egg Harbor
Richard "Dick" Bird	Bayville

Table 6. Pine Robbers and their Locations of Operation.

Property Losses Claimed by New Jersey Citizens

The material losses encountered by New Jersey residents during the Revolution are reported in several data sources that describe the kinds of property losses experienced. These data sets are available at the *Battles, Raids, and Skirmishes of the American Revolution* website,[26] David Munn's map of the *Battles, Raids, and Skirmishes in New Jersey*,[27] and the New Jersey State Archives.[28]

The *Skirmishes* website provides a temporal sequence of military activity that occurred in each New Jersey County (Table 2). Counties closer to New York City received more activity. The intensity decreased in South Jersey after 1778. Munn's geographical survey map provides information on the location and kind of property losses experienced by South Jersey residents during the Revolution (Table 7). The New Jersey State Archives contains a database of damage claims that New Jersey citizens filed against British forces, the Continental Army, the New Jersey Militia, and the militias of neighboring states.[29] The New Jersey Legislative Council and General Assembly passed an act on December 20, 1781 (Chapter V. Laws of 1781, p.6, and amended on December 27), authorizing appraisers to make an inventory and file it with the legislature. These inventories were registered as late as 1786. There were no inventories filed for Cape May, Cumberland, Gloucester, Salem, or Sussex Counties and only one for Monmouth County. Burlington County residents filed the overwhelming bulk of the inventories for the counties of the Coastal Plain. Though the State authorized the inventories, they never approved any compensation for these claims.

Some conclusions can be drawn from this imperfect dataset, primarily from the Burlington County entries.[30] Citizens filed 298 inventories: 44 against American forces, while 254 were against the British forces. A total of 133 claims resulted from the activities occurring during Washington's retreat from New York to Pennsylvania and return to Morristown (November 20, 1776, to

When Mad Anthony Came to South Jersey

January 6, 1777). Property owners filed 218 claims for damages that occurred during the time the British occupied Philadelphia and their subsequent retreat through New Jersey (June 18, 1778, through December 11, 1778). An additional five claims were made for damages occurring during the British punitive expedition against Chestnut Neck (October 5–22, 1778). See Table 8 for damages claimed by South Jersey citizens.

The South Jerseyan's Experience of the Revolution

What did it feel like to live in South Jersey during the American Revolution? Certainly the primary emotions experienced would have been fear and anger; fear of what might happen and anger at what did happen. If today the impact of national or international events is shared over a wide area and with great immediacy, thanks to modern media outlets, violence and disturbance experienced locally in South Jersey during the Revolution was no less bewildering and was, perhaps, heightened because generated by the civil war between Tory and Patriot neighbors. When your locality becomes a battle ground, conflict among neighbors is unavoidable.

Many journals and diaries exist in which local residents describe life in South Jersey during the American Revolution; that of Nicholas Collin will be discussed in detail. Aside from living through the Revolution in South Jersey, he knew many people living in Gloucester and Salem counties, since he served as a Lutheran minister for two congregations: one in Swedesboro and the other in Penn's Neck. In addition, he was not aligned with either side, since he was a pacifist and a citizen of Sweden. He had no political stake in the outcome. He witnessed numerous events, ranging from the retreat of Washington's Army out of New York to the withdrawal of the British from Philadelphia. What follows are extracts from his journal.

> Already this year [1776] there was much anxiety here about the war. In the spring some warships came up into the river and fought against the American galleys a quarter of a [Swedish] mile from the Pennsneck Church. After the English army had defeated the American, capture N[ew] York and spread itself over [New] Jersey, there was constant alarm. Formerly nearly all had been eager [to take part], but now as the fire came closer, many drew away, and there was much dissension among the people. Many concealed themselves in the woods, or within their houses, other people were forced to carry arms, others offered opposition and refused to go. The people were afraid to visit the church, because the authorities took the opportunity to get both horses and men.[31]

Collin, as a pacifist, endured harassment. The American militia took him into custody on February 4, 1777, and forced him to sign an Oath of Allegiance to the new government, even though he was a citizen of a foreign country. He endured false accusations of expressing unpatriotic sentiments in one of his sermons, but did not face prosecution. The day after the Battle of Red Bank, Collin and some friends viewed the battle site, for which action he was accused of being a spy. Patriots arrested him and threatened to immediately hang him. Fortunately, a Patriot, who escaped with his family from Philadelphia and obtained shelter from Collin, cleared the matter up and he was released once again.

When General Anthony Wayne and 300 soldiers passed through Swedesboro in February 1778, Wayne was billeted at Collin's house and treated Collin with great respect. At that time, Collin noticed that the continental soldiers were poorly dressed. With the British in pursuit, the Continentals departed Swedesboro, which the British then occupied. Collin records nearly being shot by British sentries because he did not hear their order to stop; they thought he was attempting to escape. Collin developed a low opinion of British soldiers.

> The English soldiers are undisciplined and cannot always be controlled. This was one of the main reasons for their slight success because often both friend and foe were robbed in the most despicable manner, and sometimes with the permission of the officers.[32]

Conditions in South Jersey were in a wretched state after the British left Philadelphia. The American army looked like it was losing, Continental currency floundered, and the economy deteriorated. Although goods were still being smuggled into the area from other colonies and from abroad, many community members began trading with the English; they needed the English currency to buy sugar, tea, syrup, and liquor. Collin vividly describes the insecurity of people at that time:

> Everywhere distrust, fear, hatred, and abominable selfishness were met with. Parent and children, brothers and sisters, wife and husband were enemies to one another. The militia and some regular troops on one side and refugees with the English men on the other were constantly roving about in smaller or greater numbers, plundering

Location	Village	House	Barn	School	Mills	Salt Works	Iron Works	Wagons	Boat/Ship	Livestock	Horses	Plunder	Robbery	Murder	Kidnap
Alloway Br.		1													
Bordentown					1										
Burlington Co.												1			
Chestnut Neck	1	1							1					1	
Delaware Bay									1						
Egg Harbor		1	1		1				11			1			
Elsinboro							1				1	1			
Forked River						1									
Freehold												1			
Gloucester							1				1				
Hancock's Br.														1	
L. Penn's Neck												1			
Manasquan						2			1			1			
Mantua												1			
Maurice River									2						
Middletown		1	1									2	1		1
Shrewsbury									1						
Penn's Neck															x
Red Bank		1	1									2			1
Salem												3			
Sandy Hook		1							2	1	1	1	1		
Shark River						1									
Shrewsbury						1					1	1	1		1
Swedesboro		2		1				1			1	2			2
Toms River						1									
Tuckerton													1		
Woodbury												1			

Table 7. Types of War-related Damages.

Claims	No.	Claims	No.
Goods & Chattels	275	Damaged Buildings	2
Horses	6	Wagons	2
Cows	1	Chocolate	1
Slaves	4	Rum	1
Indentured Servant	1	Tobacco	1
Imprisonment	1	Books & Papers	1
Troop Provisions	1	Iron Mill & Inventory	1

Table 8. Type and Number of Items Claimed in South Jersey.

and destroying everything in a barbarous manner, cattle, furniture, clothing and food; they smashed mirrors, tables, and china, etc., and plundered women and children of their most necessary clothing, cut up the bolsters and scattered the feathers to the winds, burned houses, whipped and imprisoned each other, and surprised people when they were deep asleep.[33]

The American militia arrested fifteen people for trading with the English and marched them off to prison. On Easter 1777, militiamen tied a man to a pine tree near Collin's church and whipped him so severely that he soon died. There were atrocities committed on both sides. The British burned a schoolhouse in the course of a skirmish with the American militia.

The Refugees (pro-British) caused much misery. Their actions are listed in Table 9 while those inflicted by the American militia are listed in Table 10.

The property of many Tories was subsequently confiscated. Collin concludes the following:

> From all this it is apparent how terrible this Civil war raged, although during the whole time only one man was shot because both parties fought not like real men with sword and gun, but like robbers and incendiaries. The fact that no important detachments were stationed here contributed greatly toward such barbaric license, as the province was too wild and of less importance, so that straggling parties under lesser and poor officers were allowed to proceed according to pleasure.[34]

As the war was coming to an end and it was becoming apparent that the British would lose, wealthy Tories, as well as soldiers in the British army, its Loyalist Regiments, and miscellaneous banditti, attempted to avoid retribution from the conquering Americans. South Jersey residents left their homes and businesses. Tories from many colonies made their way to safety in New York City, the last British stronghold. Between 1782 and 1784, 60,000 Loyalists left from New York, of whom 11,500 had formerly been slaves in the colonies. Most went to the Maritime Provinces and eastern Canada, though a smaller number went to England, Florida, and other British colonies.[35] Many subsequently returned, discontented with life abroad. However, 80–90% of the Loyalists did not leave, but remained resident in the colonies.

Conclusions

This article began by mentioning the misery, squalor, civil disorder, and forced migrations of the Syrian people caused by their prolonged civil war. Like Syria, New Jersey was once a war zone. By way of contrast, however, the Syrian population is much larger and more concentrated in cities and towns. Today's advanced lethal weaponry makes Syria's destruction far more pervasive than that during the Revolution. Nevertheless, misery, squalor, civil disorder, and forced migration did occur in South Jer-

Name	Action	Name	Action
James Stillman	Cattle Stolen	R. Otto	House Burned
Peter Lock	Harassed	Southerland	Imprisoned
Widow Hendicison	Harassed	Hendricson	Imprisoned
Thomas Batton	Harassed	Widow Dalbo	Lost Livestock
Mrs. Biddle	House Burned		

Table 9. People Impacted by Refugee Activity.

Name	Action	Name	Action
Jan Dericson	House Pillaged	John Halton	Cattle/Household Goods Stolen
Jacob Jones	House Pillaged	Mrs. Halton	Apparel Stolen
Anders Jones	House Pillaged	Robert Clark	Fined
John Cox	Furniture Smashed	James Clark	Fined
Isac Jöstason	House Pillaged	Thomas Clark	Fined
Captain Brown	House Pillaged		

Table 10. People Impacted by the American Militia.

sey. The war brought destruction to area houses, public buildings, churches, schools, and farm buildings. People's incomes suffered with the loss of their livestock and trade items. Civil disorder allowed banditry to flourish where civil authority was lacking. Consequently, felonious behavior occurred such as murder, kidnapping, assault, arson, rape, theft, and burglary. People hear a great deal about the battles and the heroes of the American Revolution, but the experience of the people in South Jersey, having to live through these times, is rarely described and remains unappreciated.

About the Author

Claude Epstein is a founding faculty member of Stockton University and co-founder of the Environmental Studies Program and the Professional Master's Degree in Environmental Science. He received his Ph.D. from Brown University in Geology and taught at Stockton from 1971 to 2011. He was instrumental in studying the impact of Stockton's experimental sprayfields, the University's first sewage treatment system, in use from 1972 through 1982. He was also part of the team that examined the impact of Stockton's geothermal well field. As a hydrogeologist he worked on the aquifers, streams and wetlands of South Jersey. His book-length study of the environmental and cultural history of South Jersey rivers is being prepared for publication by the South Jersey Culture & History Center.

Endnotes

1. Peter O. Wacker & Paul G. E. Clemens, *Land Use in Early New Jersey: A Historical Geography* (Newark: New Jersey Historical Society, 1995), 205–206.
2. Wacker & Clemens, *Land Use in Early New Jersey*, 205.
3. John K. Robertson, Patrick O'Kelley & Norm Demarais, "Battles Raids & Skirmishes of the American Revolution," (2000-2002, 2010), www.revwar75.com/battles/index.htm.
4. Wacker & Clemens, *Land Use in Early New Jersey*, 206.
5. Wacker & Clemens, *Land Use in Early New Jersey*, 164.
6. William S. Stryker, *The Battles of Trenton and Princeton*, (Boston: Houghton & Mifflin and Co., 1898), 22–23.
7. Stryker, *The Battles of Trenton and Princeton*, 39, 47.
8. Friends of Red Bank, The Fort at Red Bank, http://friendsofredbank.weebly.com/the-battle-of-red-bank.html. For two other detailed accounts of the Battle of Red Bank in this issue of *SoJourn*, see Jeffrey M. Dorward, "Forgotten Victories," 41–52, and Stone, Schopp, and Wickersty, "Research into the Battle of Gloucester," 55–73.
9. Frank H. Stewart, "Foraging for Valley Forge by General Anthony Wayne in Salem and Gloucester Counties, New Jersey," *History Quarterly*, 33, no. 2 (April 1995): 78.
10. Letter from Brigadier General Anthony Wayne to George Washington, February, 25, 1778.
11. Thomas Cushing and Charles E. Sheppard, *History of Gloucester, Salem, and Cumberland Counties, New Jersey* (Philadelphia: Everts & Peck, 1883), 28.
12. Letter from Brigadier General Anthony Wayne to George Washington, February, 25, 1778.
13. Stewart, "Foraging for Valley Forge," 81–82.
14. John Graves Simcoe, *A Journal of the Operations of the Queens Rangers* (London: Printed for the author, 1789), not paginated.
15. Donald Grady Shomette, *Privateers of the Revolution: War on the New Jersey Coast, 1775–1783* (Anglen PA: Schiffer Publishing Ltd, 2016), 50–59.
16. For more a more detailed account of this first raid on Little Egg Harbor, see J. Anthony Harness, "Knight at Egg Harbor," in this issue of *SoJourn*, 31–40.
17. Shomette, *Privateers of the Revolution*, 96–97.
18. Shomette, *Privateers of the Revolution*, 97.
19. William S. Stryker, *The Affair at Egg Harbor New Jersey October 15, 1778* (Trenton: Naar, Dan & Naar, 1894). For another detailed account of the raid on Chestnut Neck, see J. Anthony Harness, "The Lord's Orders," in this issue of *SoJourn*, 95–106.
20. "New Jersey Volunteers: Porterfield to Clinton, Raids on Squan & Shark River, NJ," *The Online Institute for Advanced Loyalist Studies*, http://www.royalprovincial,com/history/battles/vrep5.shtml.
21. The Online Institute for Advanced Loyalist Studies, http://www.royalprovincial.com/military/rhist/njv/njvlist.htm.
22. Graham Russell Hodges, *Slavery: Freedom in the Rural North: African Americans in Monmouth County New Jersey, 1665–1865* (Lanham, MD: A Madison House Book, 1997), 91–112.
23. Harry M. Ward, *Between the Lines: Banditti of the American Revolution* (Westport, CT: Praeger Publishers, 2002), 61–64.
24. Ibid.
25. Ward, *Between the Lines*, 103.
26. John K. Robertson, Patrick O'Kelley, & Norm Demarais, *Battles, Raids & Skirmishes of the American Revolution*, http://www.revwar75.com/battles/index.htm.
27. David C. Munn, *Battles and Skirmishes in New Jersey of the American Revolution* (Trenton: New Jersey Geological Survey, 1976).
28. New Jersey State Archine Searchable Databases and Records, https://wwwnet-dos.state.nj.us/DOS_ArchivesDBPortal/RevWarDamages.aspx.
29. Ibid.
30. Ibid.
31. Amandus Johnson, *The Journal and Biography of Nicholas Collin* (Philadelphia: The New Jersey Society of Pennsylvania, 1936), 236–51.
32. *Journal and Biography of Nicholas Collin*, 244.
33. *Journal and Biography of Nicholas Collin*, 245.
34. *Journal and Biography of Nicholas Collin*, 249.
35. Maya Jasanoff, *Liberty's Exiles: Loyalists in the Revolutionary World* (New York: Random House, 2012), 357.

The Lord's Orders

J. Anthony Harness

In the late summer of 1778, Major General George Washington's chief concerns were the defense of the vital Hudson Highlands and the security of the storm damaged French fleet at Boston. To realize these two goals, he had formed his main army in a line running from West Point to Danbury, Connecticut, choosing Fredericksburg, New York, as his headquarters.[1]

On September 18, 1778, Washington received the first warning of a possible British movement into New Jersey from Brigadier General William Maxwell, stationed at Elizabeth, New Jersey.[2] This alarm was followed on September 23 by intelligence reports from Colonel George Baylor and Brigadier General Charles Scott that told of a 5,000 man British force landed at Paulus Hook and loose in northern New Jersey, and another 3,000 enemy troops advancing from Kingsbridge, New York.[3] These columns were led by Lieutenant General Lord Charles Cornwallis and Lieutenant General Wilhelm von Knyphausen, respectively.

On September 24, 1778, Washington warned Major General William Alexander, Lord Stirling, of these British maneuvers and ordered him to detach Brigadier General James Clinton's brigade from his division, and send it to Peekskill, New York, with orders to defend that area if the British advanced on it. Also, Stirling and his other two brigades were to join Washington at Fredericksburg.[4]

But four days later, on September 28, Washington, feeling that he needed to bolster his troops in New Jersey, put his faith once again in the man whom he would trust over and over throughout the war for "important and quasi-independent service outside of his main lines."[5] He gave the defense of the state to Lord Stirling, with these instructions:

You will proceed forthwith into the State of New Jersey and take the command of the Troops there. These will consist of two continental Brigades under Brigadier Generals Maxwell and Woodford, and such of the Militia of the State as shall be collected on the occasion . . . You will make such a disposition of your whole force as shall appear to you best calculated to cover the Country—check the incursions of the enemy, and give them annoyance, if any opportunity should offer which may be, with prudence, embraced. It seems most probable the enemy have nothing more in contemplation than a Forage; but it is possible they may have some design against the Forts in the Highlands, you will take such a position as will have an eye to their security, that your Continental troops at least may have an easy communication with, and be able to succour them should the Enemy make an attempt that way . . . Genl Pulaski's Legion is on the March from Trenton. They may be hastened forward to join you.[6]

General Washington also wrote a letter to Lord Stirling on this date that explained his confidence in appointing Stirling to this post: ". . . there should be some officer of higher rank than any now there to take the direction of the whole. Your knowledge of the country will give you a peculiar advantage for this purpose. . . ."[7]

Lord Stirling rode south the next morning.[8] He moved through the Highlands toward Kakiat, New York, as rumors were that the British were marching toward that area.[9] When he arrived at Kakiat, about five miles above Mahwah, New Jersey, on September 30, he reported to Washington that Cornwallis' force had formed a line above Hackensack from New Bridge to the English Neighborhood, protecting nearly fifty vessels that were loading forage on the Hackensack River. He also confessed that he could not ascertain the location of American Brigadier General William Woodford's Brigade. Stirling had heard three tales of where they might be, all of which, in his opinion, left them in jeopardy.[10] And lastly, Stirling gave the commander in chief news of what he had learned of British Major General Charles Grey's bayonet attack on Colonel George Baylor's 3rd Continental Light Dragoons at Old Tappan on the night of September 27.[11]

For the next several days, Stirling collected his forces and shuffled them across northern New Jersey to get the situation under control. On October 1, he ordered Woodford forward to Paramus.[12] Stirling followed him with his command later that afternoon and reconnoitered the enemy for the next two days from "Hackensack Bridge to Tapan," determining their lines, and uncovering an enemy force of 600 men and two redoubts west of New Bridge, New Jersey.[13] On the morning of October 3, Stirling ordered Woodford, along with Colonel Oliver Spencer's Regiment, the Goshen Militia, and part of his light horse, to remain at Paramus, while he advanced to Aquakanock on the Passaic River. There he expected to meet Maxwell and two regiments of his brigade that he had ordered to march from Elizabeth with Brigadier General Nathaniel Heard's 1,000 militia and Brigadier General William Winds' 600 men.[14]

Though Stirling could report the small success his whaleboats had had against the enemy on Newark Bay, having burnt two of the twenty-three forage vessels going down the Hackensack River that morning,[15] the larger part of his October 4 dispatch to Washington was glum. He could not see any way for his force to be proactive, "... from the position of the Enemy it is Vain to Attempt anything more than to watch them well." Count Pulaski had not arrived: "I forwarded the letter to Count Poulasky by Express but I have heard Nothing of him or the Messenger, I have sent another this Morning to find him out."[16]

At Aquakanock, he found the militia "all home Sick" and constantly seeking to return to their families.[17] He complained to Washington that

> ... General Heard informs me that out of 1,000 he Marched here yesterday he has not 400 left, It is the Same with Genl Winds & at New Ark and Elizabeth Town. The Spirit of going home is universal under the pretence of having been Called out on a Sudden Alarm for two or three day's only....[18]

Stirling had written that morning to New Jersey Governor William Livingston, his double brother-in-law and long-time friend, before he wrote to Washington, asking for aid with the militia desertions.[19] Livingston quickly directed Winds and Heard to call up another two classes of militia, and ordered out an additional two classes from Burlington County himself.[20]

With these actions between September 30 and October 4, Stirling labored to contain the British forage in Bergen County, while still having his troops positioned so that they could fall back and hold the passes to the Highlands according to Washington's ultimate command.

And though Stirling's boyhood friend,[21] British Lieutenant General Sir Henry Clinton, would be very happy if his army's incursion into Bergen County lured Washington down from his strong defensive positions, he had no intention of attacking the Hudson Highlands.

Clinton hoped, however, to use the activity of Cornwallis and von Knyphausen to draw American forces in New Jersey away from an amphibious raid he had planned for Egg Harbor.[22] His targets were a base for American privateers at the Fox Burrows anchorage at Egg Harbor Inlet, an associated privateering center on the Mullica River at Chestnut Neck, the large number of salt works in these sections,[23] and the area of the Forks, situated even further up the river, where Batsto Ironworks stood as a source of American munitions and other war matériel.[24] In fact, as Stirling arrived to the confused state of affairs at Kakiat, New York, on September 30, that evening,[25] the British expedition under Commander Henry Collins, Royal Navy, sailed from New York toward Egg Harbor with Captain Patrick Ferguson's embarked force, composed of Regulars from the 5th Regiment and Provincials from the 3rd Battalion, New Jersey Volunteers.[26]

Franklin W. Kemp's *A Nest of Rebel Pirates*, the definitive work on the Egg Harbor foray, states that Governor Livingston was warned on September 29 of the enemy's preparations for a raid on the Jersey seaboard by General Maxwell at Elizabeth, though the target itself was not known. In the predawn hours of September 30, Livingston met with his Council of Safety, and that body decided to dispatch warnings to the shore villages under possible threat, and to General Washington at Fishkill, New York.[27]

Most of Maxwell's intelligence on this British movement came from Major Richard Howell,[28] a coast

The Lord's Orders

watcher who ran an observation post at Black Point, New Jersey, on the Shrewsbury mainland near the Sandy Hook Peninsula. As well as observing British shipping, Howell also ran spies into New York City to gather information on the enemy.[29] His communiques were sent to Maxwell, who forwarded the reports to Stirling, and through both Generals, as a redundancy measure, they were sent ultimately to Washington.[30]

Maxwell forwarded intelligence to Washington on October 8, that summarized Howell:

> ...I recd a Letter from Major Howell dated the 4th Inst. says that on the 1st Inst. a Fleet of four Ships & eight Brigs Schooners & Sloops sailed to the Southward, designed as they imagined for Egg harbour; ....[31]

Thus, American officers had discerned Egg Harbor as the likely target of Collins, and they pushed that information down the long, meandering intelligence webs that stretched across the chaotic New Jersey landscape by sometime between the October 1 and October 4.

Collins suffered bad weather and unfavorable winds, and was delayed in reaching Egg Harbor until October 5[32] and then could not get his larger ships across the bar for fear of grounding. By that time, the area had been put on the alert. Livingston's warning had reached the local militia at the Fox Burrows outpost, which commanded the Little Egg Inlet, on October 2,[33] and the four privateersmen there had escaped to sea.[34] Major George Payne,[35] a tavern-keeper at Chestnut Neck, and an experienced Company Commander, who had fought in the Battle of Iron Works Hill that drew Hessian forces away from Trenton prior to Washington's attack, maintained observation of the enemy until Collins' galleys and smaller armed vessels entered the inlet.[36] Then the Fox Burrows detachment withdrew.

The British reports mention no armed opposition in the advance of their reduced task force up the Mullica River, but their progress was hindered by a lack of pilots, shoal water, and continual groundings, throughout October 6.[37] So much so, that by that afternoon, when the shrinking flotilla of flatboats, tenders, and galleys carrying Ferguson's men finally reached the breastworks at Chestnut Neck, Collins could employ only his shallowest draft vessels for fire support.[38]

Engraving of William Alexander, Lord Stirling, Major General in the American Revolutionary army. *Courtesy of The New York Public Library Digital Collections.*

That would have been good news for the defense of Chestnut Neck, if the Americans there had been reinforced. But the men of Colonel Richard Somers' 3rd Battalion, Gloucester County Militia, stood alone. There were only about 150 of them,[39] in artillery works that had no guns,[40] standing against those cannon that the British *had* been able to bring up the river. They faced the famed "Captain Rifle Ferguson,"[41] and his 300 Regulars,[42] veterans of Bunker Hill, Long Island, White Plains, Forts Washington and Lee, Brandywine, Germantown, and Monmouth,[43] and a hundred experienced Loyalist raiders.[44] They faced nearly as many Jack tars as soldiers, from Collins' puddle-fleet, that could be pressed into use as auxiliary troops.[45]

At 4 p.m. the British attacked. The 3rd Gloucester held firm against the enemy's close-in shore bombardment, but Collins' gunfire, such as it was, was still too much for them. It effectively suppressed the Jersey musketry, and with no vigorous American return fire, the British transports easily navigated past the militia's emplacements and landed Ferguson's force on Somers' left. Once ashore, Ferguson's flanking attack forced the disrupted Jerseymen from their works and drove them into the woods.[46] The British then razed Chestnut Neck to the ground.[47]

But the Americans had been trying to brace Somers' men. Major General Benedict Arnold received word of the impending attack on Egg Harbor on October 3 in Philadelphia.[48] It is unknown through whom Arnold learned of the danger approaching Egg Harbor. Either Stirling, Maxwell, or Livingston may have informed him. Howell may even have taken such an unorthodox step on his own. Three months before, the Major had reported vital intelligence to Maxwell, prior to the Battle of Monmouth Courthouse, by way of Arnold.[49] Or, Arnold may have been informed of the developing situation by his commercial partners in the CHARMING NANCY, a trading vessel stranded at Little Egg Harbor while the New Jersey Court of Admiralty adjudicated her legal standing.[50]

In any event, the warning was passed to him, and Arnold ordered Colonel Thomas Proctor's under-strength[51] artillery to proceed immediately for the defense of Egg Harbor.[52] The next day, Arnold sent a reinforcement of 100 militiamen to follow Proctor.[53]

However, another day passed in Philadelphia before Congress, now also aware of the destination of Collins' naval force, issued orders to reinforce Egg Harbor on Oct. 5.[54] They chose the problematic Brigadier General Count Casimir Pulaski for the task.

For the prior two weeks, Pulaski's Legion had received a series of conflicting orders, due to overlapping authority and the Army's long lines of communication. Pulaski had been waiting in Philadelphia for transit to South Carolina, when on September 17, because of the British incursion into Bergen County, Congress gave him orders to march for Trenton.[55] Then, on September 19, Washington ordered him instead to Fredericksburg, New York, subject to Congress and the Board of War's confirmation.[56] Unaware of that order, Henry Laurens, the President of Congress, wrote to Washington on the 20th informing him of Congress' orders of the 17th for the Count to proceed to Trenton.[57] As noted earlier, Washington passed on the information that "... Genl Pulaski's Legion is on the March from Trenton. They may be hastened forward to join you...." on the 28th when he gave the command of the Jerseys to Lord Stirling.

Then, on September 29, unaware that Pulaski was yet still in Philadelphia, Washington ordered the Polish General to Paramus and put him directly under the command of Stirling.[58] Congress, unaware of Washington's new orders, the next day directed Pulaski to Princeton, along with the rest of the available Continental troops in Philadelphia, to await Washington's possible directions.[59]

Washington most likely did not hear of Congress' last orders to Pulaski until October 7, when he wrote to Lord Stirling to inform him of it.[60]

Notwithstanding these perplexing orders, Pulaski had remained in Philadelphia until October 3, dealing with his Legion's fiscal and legal troubles with Pennsylvania's civil authorities, his subsequent arrest by the County Sheriff, the interjection of the Board of War into these affairs, and the resulting official rebuke of his conduct by Congress.[61]

Unfortunately, by October 5, when Congress acted to defend Little Egg Harbor, Pulaski had at last left Philadelphia. He was in Trenton, en route to Princeton, and his orders from Congress, to instead proceed to Egg Harbor, would take many more hours to reach him, as he marched further away from his newest destination.[62]

But Lord Stirling had also acted on Major Howell's intelligence. He sent orders to deploy troops and vessels to the Egg Harbor region to Livingston at Princeton, as can be deduced from Livingston's letters to Stirling of the 6th and 11th.

Livingston wrote to Stirling on October 11, 1778:

> I informed your Lordship last night, that I had preferred your orders for the Troops in the vicinity of Trentown or Princeton marching to Egg Harbor to those of their march to Camp on account of the advice I had of the Enemy's motions in the former region.[63]

Livingston explains in this letter that he had previously neglected to deliver further intelligence that he had on the situation at Egg Harbor, and was writing to rectify that. Luckily, for the historical record, his preface repeated the news of the delivery of Stirling's orders to those troops, because his letter of October 10 cannot now be found.[64]

Indeed, most of Stirling's correspondence concerning the Revolutionary War has disappeared. His grandson and biographer, William Alexander Duer, said it was gathered for preservation and later lost.[65]

But a recent search of the Library of Congress's web site has revealed these orders from Lord Stirling that Governor Livingston mentions, and that Lord Stirling informed Washington of on October 9:

> ...Count Poulasky is gone down to Eggharbour, I have sent such orders to Princetown as If there be occasion the troops fit for Service there may march to the Same place, ...[66]

These orders were sometime in the past hand-labeled in ink:

> Lord Stirling,
> plan for (illegible)
> (illegible) the Refugees
> of Egg Harbor[67]

The Lord's Orders

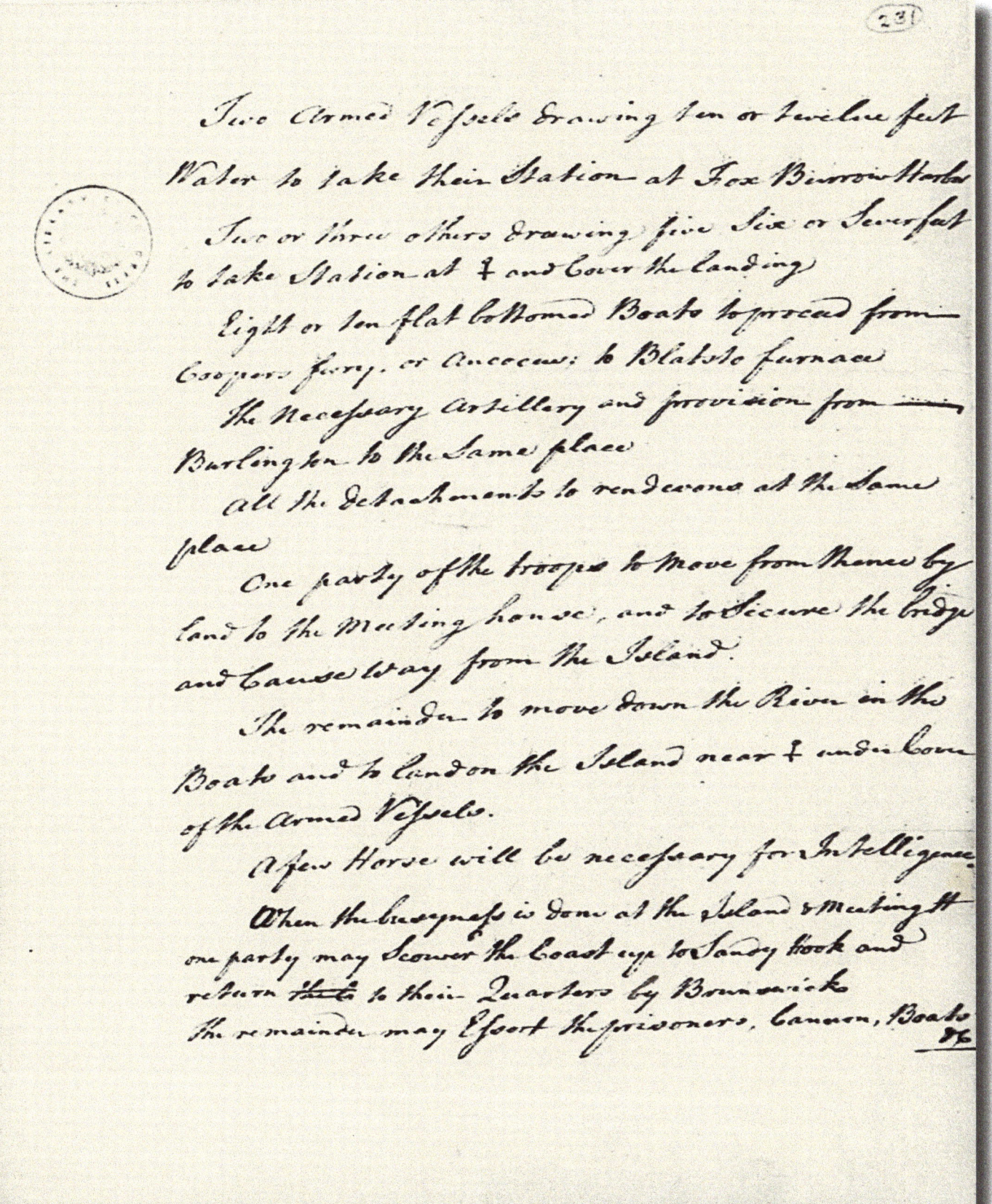

George Washington Papers at the Library of Congress, 1741–1799: Series 4. General Correspondence, 1697–1799, William Alexander, Lord Stirling, October 1778, Plan for Attack on Egg Harbor, New Jersey. *Courtesy of the Library of Congress.*

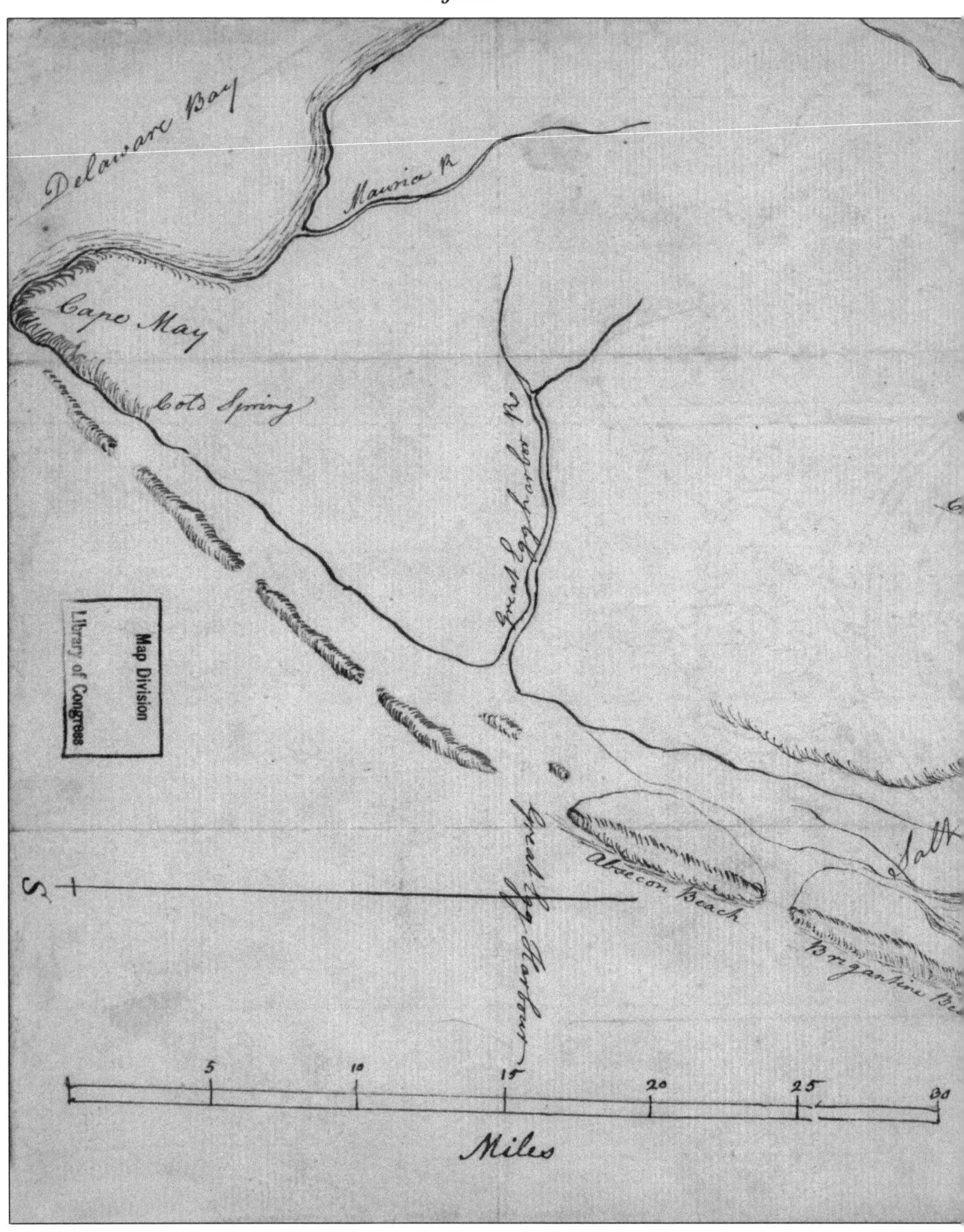

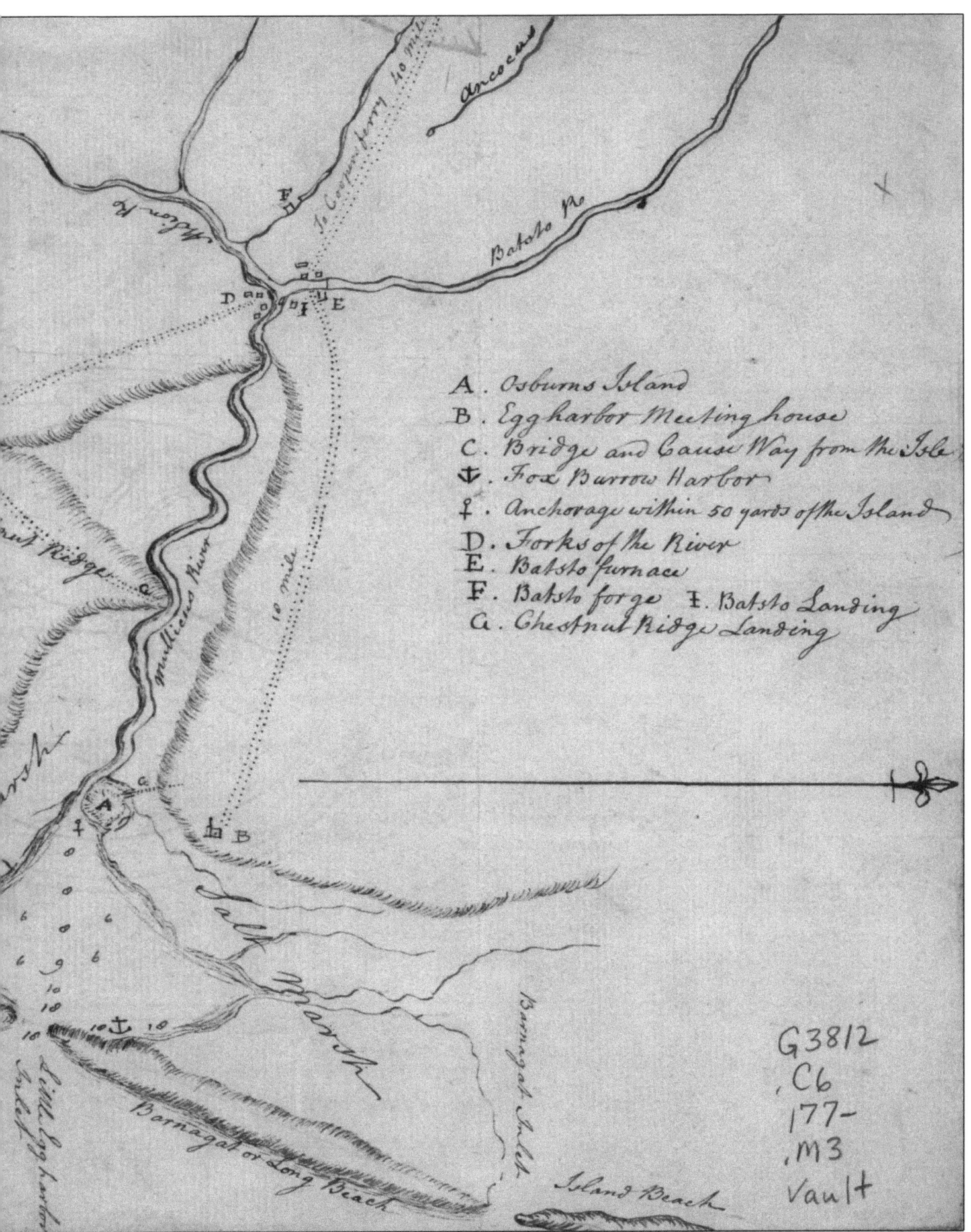

The orders are now designated by the Library of Congress website as:

> William Alexander, Lord Stirling, October 1778, Plan for Attack on Egg Harbor, New Jersey.[68]

The orders describe the deployment of troops for operations at Egg Harbor. Stirling's soldiers would be advancing into a fluid environment, and he had very little tactical intelligence to impart to them. The orders seem solid and deliberate, meant to avoid enemy ambush. And though vague by modern standards, they suggest the general idea for his ground units to make a two-pronged movement on Osborne Island and Egg Harbor Meeting House, coordinated with naval activity at the area of the inlet.

The dispositions he ordered should have allowed his local commanders to facilitate any counterattacks they saw fit to dislodge the enemy if they were still ashore. But if the British had reembarked to their ships, his forces would also be positioned for a quick and sure reestablishment of American control over the region.

Lord Stirling's Orders read:

> Two Armed Vessels drawing ten or twelve feet Water to take their Station at Fox Burrow Harbor
>
> Two or three others drawing five Six or Seven feet to take Station at [ANCHORAGE SYMBOL] and Cover the landing
>
> Eight or ten flat bottomed Boats to proceed from Coopers ferry or Ancocus to Blatsto [sic] furnace
>
> The Necessary Artillery and provision from Burlington to the Same place All the detachments to rendevous at the Same place
>
> One party of the troops to move from thence by land to the Meeting house and to Scoure the bridge and causeway from the Island.
>
> The remainder to move down the River in the Boats and to land on the Island near [ANCHORAGE SYMBOL, as before] under Cover of the Armed Vessels. A few Horse will be necessary for Intelligence.

Previous page: Little Egg Harbor Area. Map of the coast of New Jersey from Barnegat Inlet to Cape May. 1770s. *Courtesy of Library of Congress Geography and Map Division.*

> When the business is done at the Island + Meeting H one party may Scourer the Coast up to Sandy Hook and return to their Quarters by Brunswick. The remainder may Escort the prisoners, Cannon, Boats.[69]

None of Lord Stirling's subordinate commanders or their units are named. Is this because Lord Stirling was not sure which units Governor Livingston would be able to deliver the orders to, or—after all of the back-and-forth and delay with the various movement orders—which would actually be available? Or are there pages missing? Is there a lost preface to these orders which designates the officers/units assigned to this mission?

In spite of the unspecified recipients, if we look at the American units involved in the relief of Egg Harbor, it appears that Stirling's orders for the advancing land forces were followed. What is known is that American troops had arrived at the Forks near Batsto by October 7 and discouraged the British from attempting to press farther up the river.[70] Collins mentioned the American Colonel Proctor by name in this regard, in his report of his actions up to October 9.[71] Proctor was even in the area before his troops, having reconnoitered his avenue of approach to Egg Harbor, and observing the British arrival from Fox Burrows with Major Payne.[72] Lord Stirling reported to Washington on October 11 that General Pulaski had stopped the enemy's advance by his presence near the Forks.[73]

Pulaski deployed near Osborne Island, where his outpost was successfully surprised on the night of October 14 by Ferguson.[74]

Proctor, with less than half of the militia that was ordered to accompany him from Philadelphia,[75] encamped about two miles away from Pulaski[76] which would put him near the Meeting House at Egg Harbor.

American vessels saw action at the inlet on October 15 and 16 when two small privateers were taken by the British,[77] and on October 19 when Pulaski reports hearing an all day naval engagement[78] that resulted in the capture of an American sloop by Collins' armed boats.[79]

However, the local Egg Harbor area militia are not mentioned in Stirling's orders. Part of Somers' 3rd Gloucester withdrew to Leeds Point,[80] after the fight at Chestnut Neck, and kept the enemy's actions on the Mullica under observation with small unit reconnaissance patrols,[81] while the rest fell back to Somers Point to defend the Great Egg Harbor area from possible British sea raid.[82] The company of Batsto workmen, originally organized as specially exempt militia by

Colonel John Cox in 1777,[83] must have added its weight to Pulaski's and Proctor's forces as they arrived at the threatened ironworks, but there is no evidence that they advanced toward the enemy with the relief forces. There is also Pulaski's report to Congress of October 16 that complains that his aid, Major Julius Count de Montfort, who had been sent to the Forks to bring the militia forward, received no support from them, had been threatened with mutiny, and ". . . that even the colonel, who commanded and lives at the Forks, wanted to use him in a cruel manner."[84]

Nor were 300 militiamen from Monmouth County under Colonel Samuel Forman mentioned by Lord Stirling in these orders. They would not start for Egg Harbor to reinforce Pulaski until sometime between October 10 and 12 according to Major Howell's intelligence journal.[85]

In the midst of Collins' venture, a fast sloop from New York brought a message from Admiral James Gambier RN, the new commander in chief, North American Station. His orders, received on October 10, were for Collins to end the raid and return immediately.[86] But again contrary winds and shoals were against Collins, and his departure was delayed until the 20th.[87] Ferguson took this opportunity to strike Pulaski's outpost near Osborn Island on October 14. It worked as a diversion, consuming American attention,[88] and protecting Collins' floundering fleet. But in the end, HMS Zebra, an armed sloop, was hopelessly grounded and with American strength increasing at Little Egg Harbor, she was scuttled and burned, and Collins at last withdrew his expedition.[89]

Lord Stirling was nearly a hundred miles away from the scene of the action, but his cursory orders for the defense of Egg Harbor greatly influenced the outcome of nearly two weeks of fighting. Most notably, in saving Batsto from the enemy.

And though the British were able to level Chestnut Neck, wreck the captured British vessels anchored there, destroy the salt works on the Bass River, overpower three American privateers, and punish General Pulaski's force in a daring night raid, Clinton may have neglected to mention in his later writings the importance of the Batsto Ironworks in the purpose behind Collins' expedition. Indeed, Lieutenant Colonel Stephen Kemble, Clinton's chief of intelligence at the time, would give the Army's part in the venture precedence over the Royal Navy's when he wrote:

> Monday, Oct. 19th. Reported that Captain Rifle Ferguson had failed in his attempt upon Egg Harbor.[90]

Postscript

An interesting item in the document itself is Lord Stirling's use of an unmistakable map symbol to refer to an anchorage. It is the same symbol used on a long-known map of the Egg Harbor area that indicated an anchorage within fifty yards of Osborne's Island (see map on pages 100–101). Charles Boyer used the map in his 1931 work *Early Forges & Furnaces in New Jersey*, though not in direct reference to the Battle of Chestnut Neck. Franklin W. Kemp included it in his *A Nest of Rebel Pirates*, believing that the "untitled and anonymous," map probably dated from the time of the battle.[91] It can be found today in the on-line collections of the Library of Congress.[92]

Along with the landing near Osborne's Island, four other sites—of the nine denoted in the map key—are mentioned in Stirling's orders. They include Fox Burrows Harbor, Batsto Furnace, Egg Harbor Meeting House, and the Bridge and Causeway from the Island (the wording of this last location is identical in both the orders and the map key.)

It begs one to presume that this schematic did, in fact, accompany Lord Stirling's orders for the defense of Egg Harbor in October of 1778.

Endnotes

1. *The Papers of George Washington Digital Edition,* ed. Theodore J. Crackel, et al., Revolutionary War Series 17, no. 15, September–31 October 1778 (Charlottesville: University of Virginia Press, Rotunda, 2007–), http://gwpapers.virginia.edu/editions/letterpress/revolutionary-war-series/volume-17-15-September-31-October- 1778/.
2. "To George Washington from Brigadier General William Maxwell, 9 September 1778," Founders Online, National Archives, http://founders.archives.gov; source: *The Papers of George Washington*, Revolutionary War Series, vol. 16, 1 July–14 September 1778, ed. David R. Hoth (Charlottesville: University of Virginia Press, 2006) and "From George Washington to Brigadier General William Maxwell, 19 September 1778," Founders Online, National Archives, http://founders.archives.gov; source: *The Papers of George Washington*, Revolutionary War Series, vol. 17, 15 September–31 October 1778, ed. Philander D. Chase (Charlottesville: University of Virginia Press, 2008). Further notes from this digital source will be marked †.
3. "To George Washington from Colonel George Baylor, 23 September 1778"†; and "To George Washington from Brigadier General Charles Scott, 23 September 1778."†
4. "From George Washington to Major General Stirling, 24 September 1778."†
5. "From George Washington to Major General Stirling, 28

September 1778."†
6 "Instructions to Major General Stirling, 28 September 1778."†
7 "To George Washington from Major General Stirling, 28 September 1778."†
8 "To George Washington from Major General Stirling, 29 September 1778."†
9 "From George Washington to Major General Horatio Gates, 30 September 1778."†
10 "To George Washington from Major General Stirling, 30 September 1778."†
11 Ibid.
12 "To George Washington from Major General Stirling, 1 October 1778"†; and "To George Washington from Major General Stirling, 3 October 1778," first letter†.
13 "To George Washington from Major General Stirling, 3 October 1778," first letter †.
14 Ibid.
15 "To George Washington from Major General Stirling, 4 October 1778."†
16 Ibid.
17 Ibid.
18 Ibid.
19 Ibid.
20 This mobilization of Burlington militia is almost definitely for the defense of (then) Burlington County's Atlantic shoreline that, along with Old Gloucester County's, comprised the Egg Harbor Region. "To Major General Stirling from Governor William Livingston, 5 October 1778," Carl E. Prince and Dennis P. Ryan, ed., *The Papers of William Livingston*, vol. 2, July 1777–December 1778 (Trenton: New Jersey Historical Commission, 1980), 455.
21 Alan Valentine, *Lord Stirling* (New York: Oxford University Press, 1969), 29.
22 The descriptor "Egg Harbor" or "Eggharbor," when used in eighteenth-century correspondence and newspaper descriptions, refers to today's "Little Egg Harbor," the inlet to the Mullica River and surrounding area. Maps from the period typically distinguish between Little Egg Harbor and Great Egg Harbor, the inlet to the Great Egg Harbor River, eighteen miles southwest of the Mullica. Throughout this article, Egg Harbor, mirroring common eighteenth-century usage, refers to Little Egg Harbor. Franklin W. Kemp, *A Nest of Rebel Pirates*, 2nd edition (Egg Harbor City, NJ: The Laureate Press, 1966, 1993), 24; "To Lord George Germain from Lieut. General Sir Henry Clinton, 8 October 1778," *The Remembrancer* (London: J. Almon, 1779), 151–52; and "To Lord George Germain from Lieut. General Sir Henry Clinton, 25 October 1778," *The Remembrancer* (London: J. Almon, 1779), 151.
23 "To Rear-Admiral James Gambier RN from Commander Henry Colins RN, 9 October 1778," *The Remembrancer* (London: J. Almon, 1779), 154–56; and "Report of Capt. Ferguson, of the 70th Regiment, to his Excellency Sir Henry Clinton from, dated Little Egg-harbour, Oct. 10, 1778," *The Remembrancer* (London: J. Almon, 1779), 151–52.
24 "To Rear-Admiral James Gambier RN from Commander Henry Colins RN, 9 October 1778," *The Remembrancer* (London: J. Almon, 1779), 155.
25 Ibid., 154; and "To George Washington from Brigadier General William Maxwell, 8 October 1778"†—in which Maxwell delivers Major Richard Howell's intelligence reports.
26 "Report of Capt. Ferguson, of the 70th Regiment, to his Excellency Sir Henry Clinton from, dated Little Egg-harbour, Oct. 15, 1778," *The Remembrancer* (London: J. Almon, 1779), 153.
27 Kemp, *A Nest of Rebel Pirates*, 22.
28 Richard Howell would become New Jersey's third Governor, serving in that office from 1793 to 1801.
29 "From George Washington to Brigadier General William Maxwell, 8 October 1778"†; and "From George Washington to Major Richard Howell, 5 October 1778."†
30 "To George Washington from Major General Stirling, 20 October 1778."† The system of duplicate messages is well seen in this letter and the corresponding editor's notes.
31 "To George Washington from Brigadier General William Maxwell, 8 October 1778."†
32 "To Rear-Admiral James Gambier RN from Commander Henry Colins RN, 9 October 1778," *The Remembrancer* (London: J. Almon, 1779), 154.
33 "Report of Capt. Ferguson, of the 70th Regiment, to his Excellency Sir Henry Clinton from, dated Little Egg-harbour, Oct. 10, 1778," *The Remembrancer* (London: J. Almon, 1779), 151.
34 "To Rear-Admiral James Gambier RN from Commander Henry Colins RN, 9 October 1778," *The Remembrancer* (London: J. Almon, 1779), 154.
35 Rev. Norman Goos, "Carefully Planned Distractions Create Opportunities for Surprise Victories: The 3rd "Atlantic County" Battalion and the Famous Battles at Trenton and Princeton," *Atlantic Heritage Center, 2010–2011, Sixty Third Yearbook with Historical and Genealogical Journal* 16, no. 3 (December 2010), 22.
36 "Richard Somers (I), Letter, To: 'Colonel Richard Somers' From: 'Major George Payne,' [1778?]," Digital Library@ Villanova University, Series LII, *http://digital.library.villanova.edu/Item/vudl:262289#?c=0&m=0&s=0&cv=0&z=-1.3536%2C-0.0661%2C3.7073%2C1.3214*.
37 "To Rear-Admiral James Gambier RN from Commander Henry Colins RN, 9 October 1778," *The Remembrancer* (London: J. Almon, 1779), 154–55.
38 Ibid. 155.
39 Kemp, *A Nest of Rebel Pirates*, 24.
40 "To Rear-Admiral James Gambier RN from Commander

The Lord's Orders

41 Henry Colins RN, 9 October 1778," *The Remembrancer* (London: J. Almon, 1779), 155; and "Report of Capt. Ferguson, of the 70th Regiment, to his Excellency Sir Henry Clinton from, dated Little Egg-harbour, Oct. 10, 1778," *The Remembrancer* (London: J. Almon, 1779), 152.

41 This British Army sobriquet for Captain Patrick Ferguson stems from his advancement of a breech-loading rifle of his own design. Lieut. Col. Stephen Kemble, "The Kemble Papers. Vol. I. 1773–1789," *Collections of the New York Historical Society for the Year 1883* (New York, 1884), 164.

42 Kemp, *A Nest of Rebel Pirates*, 10.

43 Richard Cannon, Esq., "Fifth Regiment of Foot or Northumberland Fusiliers," *Historical Records of the British Army* (London: William Clowes and Sons, 1836), 42–49.

44 Kemp, *A Nest of Rebel Pirates*, 13–14.

45 Ibid. Approximate number derived from Kemp's Order of Battle for British Forces, 14–15.

46 "To Rear-Admiral James Gambier RN from Commander Henry Colins RN, 9 October 1778," *The Remembrancer* (London: J. Almon, 1779), 155; and "Report of Capt. Ferguson, of the 70th Regiment, to his Excellency Sir Henry Clinton from, dated Little Egg-harbour, Oct. 10, 1778," *The Remembrancer* (London: J. Almon, 1779), 152.

47 Ibid.

48 "To George Washington from Major General Benedict Arnold, 11 October 1778."†

49 "To George Washington from Major General Benedict Arnold, 21 June 1778," and the corresponding editor's notes. Founders Online, National Archives, http://founders.archives.gov. Source: *The Papers of George Washington*, Revolutionary War Series, vol. 15, May–June 1778, ed. Edward G. Lengel (Charlottesville: University of Virginia Press, 2006).

50 Richard K. Murdoch, "Benedict Arnold and the Owners of the *Charming Nancy*," *Pennsylvania Magazine of History and Biography*, 84, no. 1 (January 1960) 39; https://journals.psu.edu/pmhb/article/download/41541/41262.

51 Kemp, *A Nest of Rebel Pirates*, 23; and as noted there, Joseph Reed, President of the Supreme Executive Council of Pennsylvania, in *Pennsylvania Archives*, vol. 7, 1778–79, 135.

52 "To George Washington from Major General Benedict Arnold, 11 October 1778."†

53 Ibid.

54 Leszek Szymanski, *Casimir Pulaski, A Hero of the American Revolution* (New York, NY: Hippocrene Books, 1979, 1994), 207; and "To Major General Stirling from Governor William Livingston, 6 October 1778," Carl E. Prince and Dennis P. Ryan, ed., *The Papers of William Livingston*, vol. 2, July 1777–December 1778 (Trenton: New Jersey Historical Commission, 1980), 457.

55 Szymanski, *Casimir Pulaski*, 200; and "To George Washington from Henry Laurens, 20 September 1778."†

56 "From George Washington to Brigadier General Casimir Pulaski, 19 September 1778"†; and "From George Washington to The Board of War, 19 September 1778."†

57 "To George Washington from Henry Laurens, 20 September 1778."†

58 "From George Washington to Brigadier General Casimir Pulaski, 29 September 1778."†

59 "To George Washington from Henry Laurens, 2 October 1778"†; and Szymanski, *Casimir Pulaski*, 201.

60 "From George Washington to Major General Stirling, 7 October 1778."†

61 Szymanski, *Casimir Pulaski*, 198–206.

62 Ibid., 206.

63 "To Major General Stirling from Governor William Livingston, 11 October 1778," Carl E. Prince and Dennis P. Ryan, ed., *The Papers of William Livingston*, vol. 2. July 1777–December 1778 (Trenton: New Jersey Historical Commission, 1980), 461.

64 Ibid.

65 George E. Helmke, *Lord Stirling, William Alexander, Country Gentleman and New Jersey's Military Leader in the War for Independence* (Basking Ridge, NJ: The Historical Society of Somerset Hills, 2000), 25.

66 "To George Washington from Major General Stirling, 9 October 1778."†

67 "William Alexander, Lord Stirling, October 1778, Plan for Attack on Egg Harbor, New Jersey," *George Washington Papers at the Library of Congress*, 1741–1799, series 4, General Correspondence, 1697–1799. http://memory.loc.gov/cgibin/ampagecollId=mgw4&fileName=gwpage053.db&recNum=997&tempFile=./temp/ ~ammem _ 4z0s& filecode=mgw&nextfilecode=mgw&itemnum=1&ndocs=100.

68 Ibid.

69 Ibid.

70 Ferguson's report of October 10, 1778, to Clinton gives the impression that both Proctor and Pulaski had coalesced their forces at the Forks/Batsto area. "Report of Capt. Ferguson, of the 70th Regiment, to his Excellency Sir Henry Clinton from, dated Little Egg-harbour, Oct. 10," *The Remembrancer* (London: J. Almon, 1779), 151–52; and Arnold gives an account of Proctor's and Pulaski's general movements of early October in his letter of October 11, 1778, to Washington. "To George Washington from Major General Benedict Arnold, 11 October 1778."†

71 To Rear-Admiral James Gambier RN from Commander Henry Colins RN, 9 October 1778," *The Remembrancer* (London: J. Almon, 1779), 154–56.

72 Richard Somers (I), "Letter, To: Colonel Richard Somers From: Major George Payne, [1778?]," Digital Library@Villanova University, Series LII, *http://digital.library.villanova.edu/Item/vudl:262289#?c=0&m=0&s=0&cv=0&z=- 1.3536%2C-0 .0661%2C3.7073%2C1.3214.*

73 Stirling's report on Egg Harbor is in his first letter to Wash-

ington dated October 11, 1778. "To George Washington from Major General Stirling, 11 October 1778."†

74 "To Rear-Admiral James Gambier RN from Commander Henry Colins RN, 15 October 1778," *The Remembrancer* (London: J. Almon, 1779), 156; and "Report of Capt. Ferguson, of the 70th Regiment, to his Excellency Sir Henry Clinton dated Little Egg-harbour, Oct. 15, 1778," *The Remembrancer* (London: J. Almon, 1779), 153–54; and Pulaski to Congress, Ex. Doc. No. 120 49th Congress (2nd session) Senate (Original: P.C.C. M247.181) quoted in Szymanski, *Casimir Pulaski*, 211; and Pulaski to President Laurens, October 19, 1778, and Pulaski to President Laurens, October 21, 1778, quoted in Szymanski, *Casimir Pulaski*, 213–15; and Paul Bentalou, *A Reply to Judge Johnson's Remarks* (Baltimore 1826), 36–37, quoted in Szymanski, *Casimir Pulaski*, 209–10; and Patrick Ferguson, writing as Egg-Shell, in an open letter to the President of Congress, countering Pulaski's report of the engagement, in *The Royal Gazette*, publ. by James Rivington, New York, no. 220, Saturday November 7, 1778, 3, as quoted at http://www.silverwhistle.co.uk/lobsters/ferguson.html.

75 "To George Washington from Major General Benedict Arnold, 11 October 1778."†

76 "Report of Capt. Ferguson, of the 70th Regiment, to his Excellency Sir Henry Clinton from, dated Little Egg-harbour, Oct. 15, 1778," *The Remembrancer* (London: J. Almon, 1779), 153.

77 Kemp, *A Nest of Rebel Pirates*.

78 Pulaski to President Laurens, October 19, 1778, quoted in Szymanski, *Casimir Pulaski*, 214.

79 Kemp, *A Nest of Rebel Pirates*, 50.

80 Richard Somers (I), "Military Order, To: Colonel Richard Somers From: Head Quarters, Leeds Point, N.J., October 17, 1778," Digital Library@Villanova University, Series LII, *http://digital.library.villanova.edu/Item/ vudl: 262297#c=0&m=0&s=0&cv=0&z=0.4052%2C0.0323%2C1.8104%2C0.643*.

81 Rev. Norman Goos, private collection of pension applications of Atlantic County soldiers (present-day) from the New Jersey State Archives.

82 Richard Somers (I), "Military Order, To: Colonel Richard Somers From: Colonel Thomas Proctor, October 23, 1778," Digital Library@Villanova University, Series LII, http://digital.library.villanova.edu/Item/vudl:262301#?c=0&m=0&s=0&cv=0&z=-0.0047%2C0.7847%2C1.1542%2C0.4114.

83 William S. Stryker, *Documents Relating to the Revolutionary History of the State of New Jersey* (Trenton, NJ: The John L. Murphy Publishing Co., 1901), 409, https://archive.org/details/ser2newjerseyrev01newjuoft.

84 This most likely refers to Lt. Colonel Elijah Clark. Szymanski, *Casimir Pulaski*, 212.

85 Howell's intelligence can be found in the editor's notes for "To George Washington from Major General Stirling, 16 October 1778."†

86 "Report of Capt. Ferguson, of the 70th Regiment, to his Excellency Sir Henry Clinton from, dated Little Egg-harbour, Oct. 15, 1778," *The Remembrancer* (London: J. Almon, 1779), 153; and "To Rear-Admiral James Gambier RN from Commander Henry Colins RN, 15 October 1778," *The Remembrancer* (London: J. Almon, 1779), 156.

87 Harry P. Folger 3rd, "The Battle at Chestnut Neck and The Affair at Little Egg Harbor, October 6, 1778–October 22, 1778," Col. Richard Somers Chapter, New Jersey Society, Sons of the American Revolution, http://www.colrichardsomers.com/Pages/SuggestedReading.aspx.

88 An illustration of this point are the stern orders Colonel Proctor sent out after Ferguson's raid on Pulaski's outpost. Proctor wrote to Somer's congregated militia that ". . . the Several Captains Commanding Company's will pay Suitable Attention to their duty, and the Conduct of their men, the Enemy laying so near this post as to give them every Advantage of Attacking at night if they think proper—And to prevent being Surprised the Soldiers are to lay on their arms during the night season and the Captains of the Day to Visit the outposts and to See the Continentals Alert on their Duty." Digital Library@Villanova University, "Military Order, To: Colonel Richard Somers From: Head Quarters, Leeds Point, N.J., October 17, 1778."

89 Neither Colins nor Ferguson mention the loss of the sloop H.M.S. Zebra in the reports to their superiors that were published. William S. Stryker, *The Affair at Egg Harbor New Jersey October 15, 1778*, Col. Richard Somers Chapter, New Jersey Society, Sons of the American Revolution, http://www.colrichardsomers.com/Pages/SuggestedReading.aspx, 7.

90 Lieut. Col. Stephen Kemble, "The Kemble Papers. Vol. I. 1773–1789," *Collections of the New York Historical Society for the Year 1883* (New York, 1884), 164.

91 Kemp, *A Nest of Rebel Pirates*, 43.

92 "Map of the coast of New Jersey from Barnegat Inlet to Cape May," *Library of Congress Geography and Map Division*, https://www.loc.gov/item/73691635/.

Born a Peacemaker, Became a Patriot:
1st Lieutenant Jeremiah Leeds, New Jersey's 3rd Battalion, Gloucester County Militia During the Revolutionary War, with Genealogical Notes on the Leeds Family

Norman Reeves Goos

Patriot Jeremiah Leeds served in New Jersey's 3rd Battalion, Gloucester County militia, under Colonel Richard Somers from 1776 through 1783, as stated in his federal Revolutionary War pension application.[1] In his application, he recounts that he served as an active militiaman during the Battle of Trenton (December 1776), the Second Battle of Trenton and Princeton (January 1777), Red Bank on the Delaware River (October–November 1777), and Chestnut Neck (October 1778), as well as in many other skirmishes and defensive actions during his seven years in the Gloucester County Militia. He marched as a private in various militia companies associated with Colonel Richard Somers' Battalion[2] before being commissioned as a 1st Lieutenant on September 18, 1777. An unsubstantiated family story places this company as temporarily stationed with General Maxwell's New Jersey Brigade in the Continental Army during the winter of 1777, where he met George Washington.[3] Jeremiah's federal pension application clearly leaves open this possibility, as Leeds spent the winter of January–February 1777 at Millstone, Middlesex County, where Washington encamped.

Jeremiah's Military Service

Eastern Gloucester County—today's Atlantic County—began gearing up for military conflict on December 12, 1774, when seven of the older, highly esteemed residents of the area were among 77 men chosen countywide to serve on the Gloucester County Committee of Observation. These seven included Elijah Clark, Richard Wescott, Richard Somers, Lemuel Sayre, Thomas Stites, Robert Morss, and John Somers.[4]

Like his ancestors before him, Jeremiah Leeds grew up in a Quaker home and upon reaching his majority was received into membership of the Religious Society of Friends' Great Egg Harbor Monthly Meeting. When the war began, Jeremiah lived the traditional peace witness of a Quaker with an agrarian-based lifestyle. After British sailors landed at Leeds Point and appropriated some of his prized livestock, however, he and his brother Vincent angrily converted from pacifistic Quakers to armed militants.[5] John F. Hall recounts the story in full:

> Jeremiah Leeds, in his old age, used to tell the story of the visit which his father, John Leeds, received one day from foraging redcoats, just before the Revolution. A British vessel entered Great Bay in full view from Leeds Point. Soldiers and sailors came ashore in barges for fresh meat. The captain ordered the Quaker farmer to drive up his cattle which were grazing in the Meadows nearby; this was done, whereupon two fat steers were selected from the herd and quickly knocked in the head, their bodies quartered, loaded on wagons and taken to the barges and to the ship. "All right. That's all," was the farewell greeting of the captain to the farmer, who considered himself lucky in losing so little by the uninvited visitors. The steers happened to be the personal property of Jeremiah and his brother Vincent and were worth perhaps at that time six or eight dollars per head. This event had its effect in making a soldier of the Quaker boy Jeremiah in the War of the Revolution which soon followed.[6]

His federal pension application states that Jeremiah Leeds entered Colonel Somers' 3rd Gloucester County Militia Battalion in September 1776 in Captain

Nehemiah Morss's company as a private; he was 22 years old.

This service was clearly not Jeremiah's first military experience, however, since the Great Egg Harbor Quaker Monthly Meeting minutes record that one Evi Smith indicted Jeremiah on February 5, 1776, for "... bearing of armes in the Military Way...."[7] The meeting overseers appointed Robert and Jesse Smith to visit Jeremiah Leeds "... and treat further with [him] and report their sense to next Meeting...."The men so appointed visited with Jeremiah and filed their report at the May 6, 1776, monthly meeting. Those present at the meeting reached a consensus that Jeremiah should be "... disowned and testified against..." and no longer welcome to worship with his fellow Quakers at the meetinghouse "... until he shall become sensable [sic] of his misconduct and make satisfaction to this Meeting...."[8] Jeremiah was advised of his right of appeal, as reported in the May 27 meeting minutes, but "... he signified he should not appeal..." and continued in his military service.[9] This earlier military service may be the direct result of the British actions relative to Jeremiah's cattle, but how he performed this early military service remains unclear.

After receiving orders to join with Capt. Morss, Jeremiah reported that the entire "... Company parraded at Wrangleborough on Little Egg Harbour River and went from there down the River in Boats to a place called the Fox Boroughs at which place a small fort had been built where we remained in the service one month and were discharged...."[10] Fox Burrows stood to the rear of the Little Egg Harbor Inlet at present-day Holgate. While there, Leeds and his fellow militiamen kept watch for British and Loyalist intruders. It appears that Atlantic County historian Alfred P. Heston first erroneously called the Chestnut Neck fort by the name of Fox Burrows.[11]

Jeremiah was recalled to active duty as a private during the latter part of November 1776, serving under

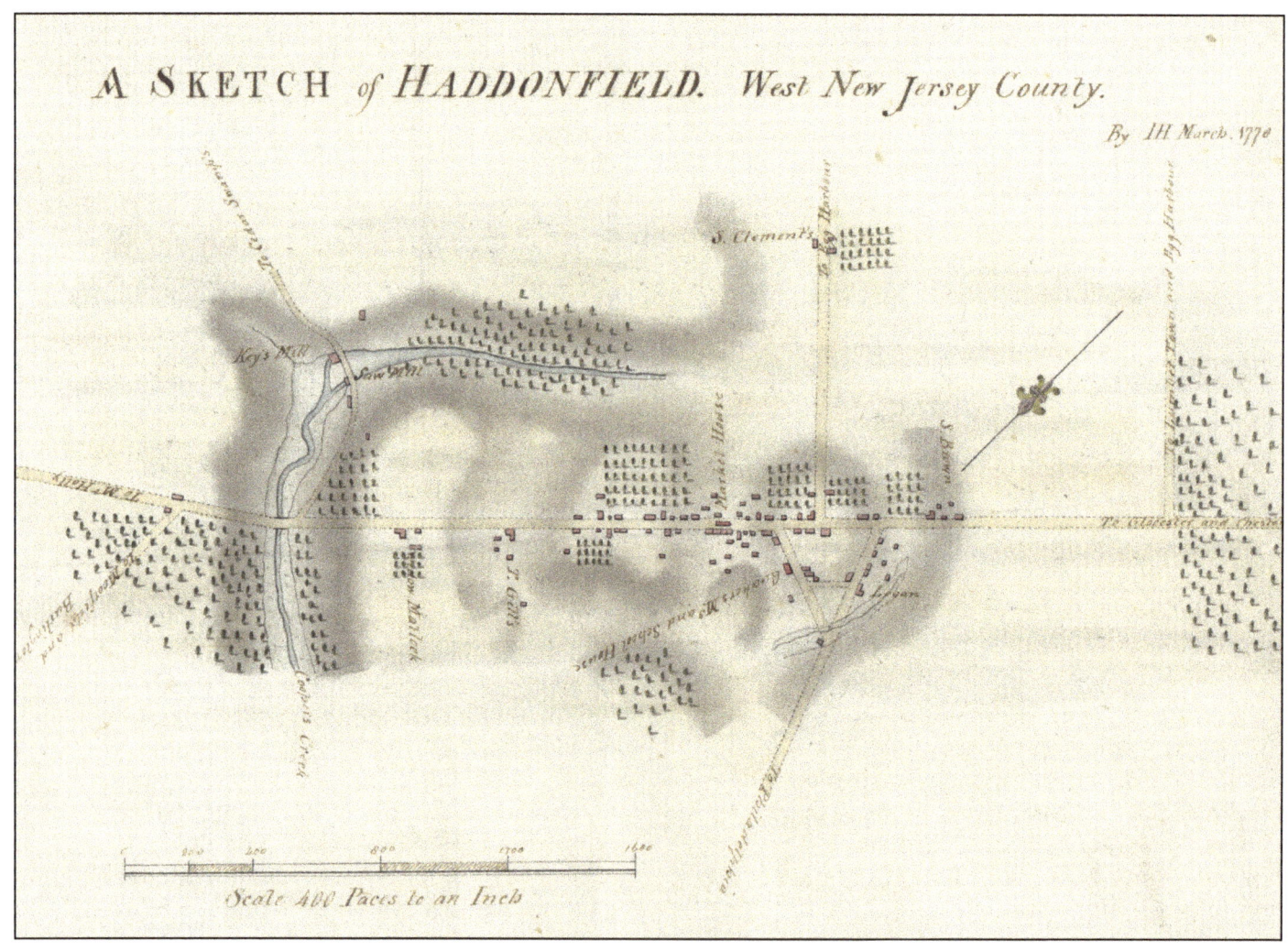

"A Sketch of Haddonfield: West New Jersey County," which John Hills, a British military engineer and cartographer, prepared in March 1778. This map illustrates the town that Jeremiah Leeds entered several times on orders. Interesting details on this map include the market house in the middle of Kings Highway and the rather sharp oxbow in Cooper's Creek, suggesting that a freshet had destroyed the dam constructed for the old Free Lodge Mill. *Used with permission, William L. Clements Library, Henry Clinton Papers.*

Born a Peacemaker, Became a Patriot

Captain Zephaniah Steelman in his company. Jeremiah records that the

> ...Company marched from Eggharbour by Blue Anchor to Haddonfield, where we quartered and remained a few days. From there we marched by Moorestown to Mount Holly, where we remained until driven out from that place by the Hessians [Battle of Ironworks Hill]. We retreated back to Haddonfield (staying one night at Moorestown), remained at Haddonfield but a very short time, then marched to Bordentown. Remained there until morning of the Battle of Trenton (being three or four days). That morning we marched to Trenton and was in the battle there on the 2d January 1777. Early the next morning we marched to Princeton, our company being in the rear of the army, we were not in the active part of the battle at that place. After the battle, we remained at Princeton a few days then marched back by Trenton and Burlington to Haddonfield, where we were discharged, after having served at least one month and a half.[12]

During the January 1777 Battle of Princeton, Jeremiah suffered a personal tragedy when he witnessed the death of his friend, Forrest Bellangy (or Bellangee), after a cannon ball took off his leg at the knee. Following the end of the battle at Princeton, Jeremiah's company established a winter bivouac at Millstone, although by sometime in March, Jeremiah had returned to Eggharbour. While at Millstone, superior orders may have attached Steelman's company to General Maxwell's New Jersey Brigade. This may be the source of Jeremiah's idea that he served in the New Jersey Continentals, although, in fact, he did not.

"Map of the environs of Camden, N.J." [1778?], showing the area around Cooper's Ferry. Relief shown by shading. See note in upper right-hand corner: "Proper advanced posts (as yet) unoccupied." Jeremiah Leeds received repeated orders to guard Coopers Ferry. *Courtesy of the Library of Congress.*

Jeremiah next served for the month of March 1777 as part of Captain George Payne's company. Jeremiah notes:

> In the month of March 1777 [I] entered as a private in a Company of Militia Commanded by Capt. George Payne in Col. Richard Somers' Regiment. The Company marched from Eggharbour aforesaid to Haddonfield and from there to Coopers Ferry opposite Philadelphia, where we were stationed as a guard and remained in the service one month and were discharged.[13]

The assigned guard duty at Coopers Ferry sought to prevent British and Loyalist marauders from creating mayhem in West New Jersey.

During the month of May 1777, Jeremiah was again called up for active duty and served as a private in Capt. Samuel Snell's militia company, which marched to Haddonfield, "... where we quartered and remained in the service one month, and were discharged."[14] In June or July, Jeremiah was again active in his military service, entering as a private in Captain William Rice's company. This troop "... marched from Eggharbour to Haddonfield aforesaid, where we quartered and remained in the service one month and were discharged."[15]

In August or September 1777, Jeremiah received activation orders and he joined the militia company of Captain Christopher Rape as a private. "The company marched to Haddonfield aforesaid and from there to Coopers Ferry, where we were stationed as a guard—and where we remained one month and were discharged."[16]

Upon his next activation, Jeremiah was no longer a private. He served as First Lieutenant in Captain Joseph Covenover's 6th Company in the Somers Regiment on September 18, 1777, and was listed as such in a surviving "list of officers" (reproduced on the following page). As with all of the other companies in which Jeremiah served, Covenover's company was attached to Colonel Richard Somers' Regiment. Jeremiah and his soldiers

> ... marched from Eggharbour aforesaid by Blue Anchor and Chewslanding to Red Bank. The Battle of Red Bank was fought the afternoon before we arrived. We were at Chewslanding at the time of the battle and heard the firing. This service commenced in October 1777 and ended in November 1777.[17]

It appears that Covenover's troops served in a collection of companies that performed the "mop up" following the battle at Fort Mercer in Red Bank, Gloucester County, on the Delaware.

Jeremiah reentered service in Captain Covenover's Company, retaining his rank as First Lieutenant. The company "... marched from Eggharbour to Haddonfield, where we quartered and remained in service one month and were discharged. This service commenced in December 1777 and ended in January 1778." Based on the narrative in his federal pension application, it appears Jeremiah did not receive another activation order until August 1778 and he presumably spent this extended period of "downtime" at home tending to his farm.

Jeremiah returned to active service in Captain Covenover's Company during August 1778 as First Lieutenant. Jeremiah notes,

> ... the company parraded at the forks of Little Eggharbour River, where we remained about 10 days or two weeks. From there we marched down to Chesnut Neck, where we remained till after the Battle at that place, in which the Town was burnt and the vessels &c. From there we marched down the River to Leeds Point, where we remained till the British Vessels left the Bay, which was about ten days. One of the largest vessels grounded in going over the bar and being unable to get her off, after several day's trial, they set fire to her and abandoned her. This is probably the reason why they remained in the Bay so long. After they left the Bay, we marched down to Somers Point, where we remained about two or three weeks, when we were discharged late in the month of October 1778 after having served at least two months, the service having commenced in August. Col. Proctor was at Eggharbour during a part of this term.

> This was the last service [Leeds] performed during the war, and the whole length of time that he served during the war—and whilst engaged in a regularly organized body was ten months and a half—six months and a half of which time he served as a private and four months a first Lieutenant of Captain Conovers Company— during all which time he was in actual service either in the field or the garrison and during which time he was not employed in any civil pursuit.

> ... [I] was drafted sometimes and sometimes volunteered. Once [I] hired as a substitute (but got the measles and could not go) when called to the service.[18]

Born a Peacemaker, Became a Patriot

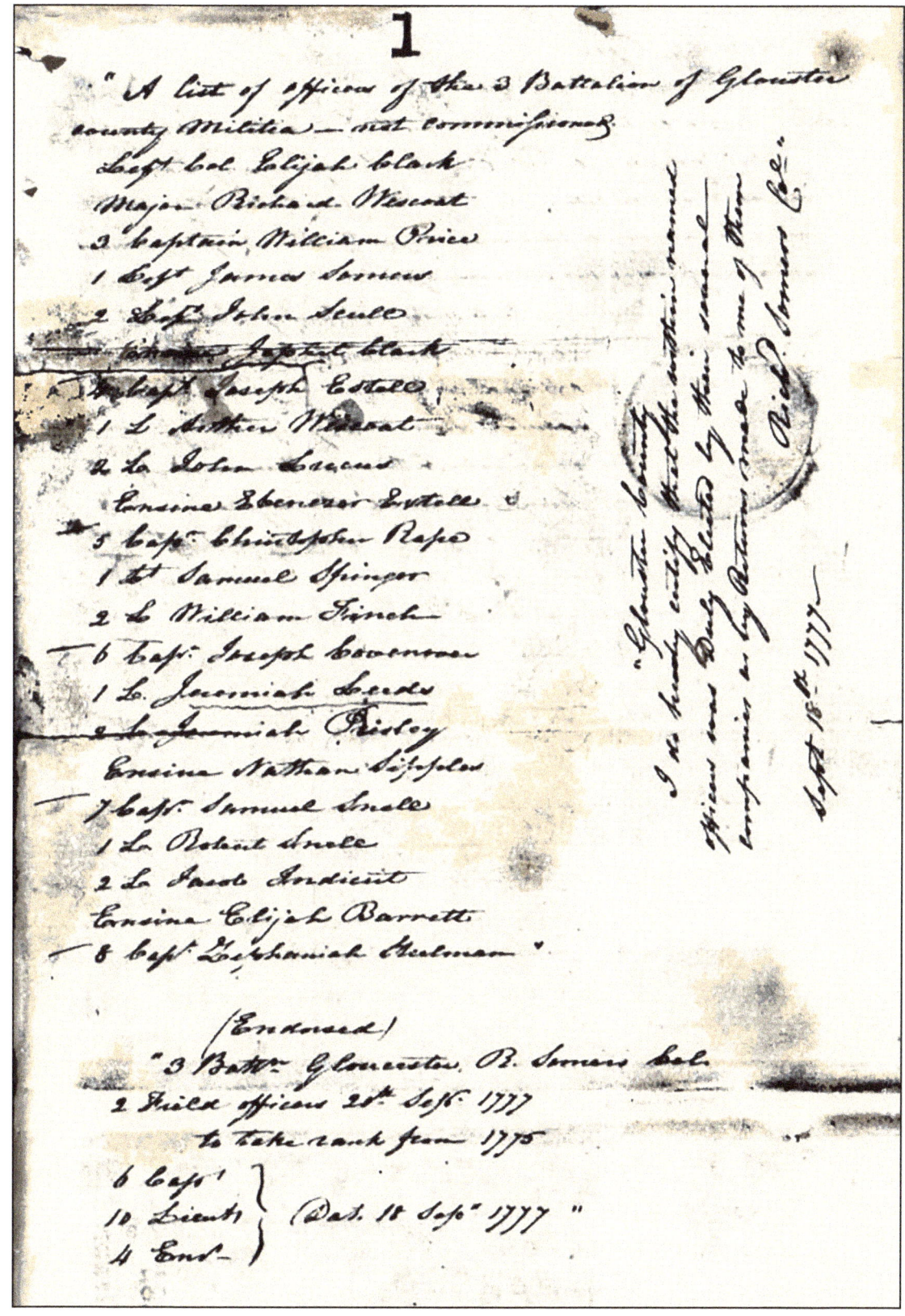

A list of officers of the 3rd Battalion of Gloucester county Militia—not commissioned, September 18, 1777. Lieutenant Colonel Elijah Clark, Major Richard Westcoat, Captain William Price, First Lieutenant James Somers, Second Lieutenant John Scull, Ensign Japhet Clark; Captain Joseph Estell, First Lieutenant Arthur Westcoat, Second Lieutenant John Lucas, Ensign Ebenezer Extell; Captain Christopher Rape, First Lieutenant Samuel Springer, Second Lieutenant William Finch; Captain Joseph Covenover, First Lieutenant Jeremiah Leeds, Second Lieutenant Jeremiah Risley, Ensign Nathaniel Sipple; Captain Samuel Snell, First Lieutenant Robert Snell, Second Lieutenant Jacob Endicott, Ensign Elijah Barrett, Captain Zephaniah Steelman.

Letter to Colonel Richard Somers from Major George Payne, [1778?]. "Sir The Enemy are much in the same state as they were this morning[.] two sloops are beating into the Inlet & one Frigate under sail—should be glad to see the Militia come in faster—Colonel Proctor has ?sent? of this moment for his artillery[.] they will be here in the Morning—he wants nothing but militia to support[.] there are none come but Capt. Wescott, with above 30 men[.] I am yours & George Payne Maj Monday 6 oclock evening." *Used with permission from the Barry-Hayes Collection, Independence Seaport Museum, Philadelphia.*

Born a Peacemaker, Became a Patriot

During this final round of his active service, Jeremiah, along with his company, prepared for the defense of Chestnut Neck against the pending British attack. The fort at Fox Burrows lay unarmed, serving at best as a lookout post to monitor activities at the inlet per Captain George Payne's October 5, 1778, letter (see previous page) to Colonel Richard Somers.[19] The outnumbered militia completed an orderly tactical retreat to Leeds Point while the British burned the thirteen buildings in the deserted Chestnut Neck village, including Payne's Tavern—the site of several privateering auctions. Despite the immediate rout at the hands of the British and Loyalists, the militia and the lack of British knowledge of navigating the Mullica River prevented the Crown's troops from proceeding upriver and destroying the Batsto ironworks, producer of munitions, and the warehouses at The Forks, built to store the goods captured by Privateers before the auctions.

Although Jeremiah indicates he did not serve again after the above last described military actions at Chestnut Neck and subsequent, there was one mention of him being listed for call up on August 28, 1780, but he could not be located to receive this notice.[20] Thirteen years later, Jeremiah's name appears on an activation list for Captain Richard Adams' company, but whether he served is unknown.[21] Jeremiah left his revolutionary militia duty unscathed as his federal pension application fails to mention any bodily injury from his military service that would qualify him for a larger pension.[22]

When Congress passed another in a string of Revolutionary War pension acts on June 7, 1832, it was more liberal in its coverage than all previous pension laws, allowing state militia officers and enlisted men with less than two years, but at least six months, of service to apply. The payments were retroactive to March 1, 1831, and not predicated on financial needs.[23] Jeremiah initially failed to apply as he could not locate his commission certificate as a First Lieutenant among his personal papers. This lack of submitting his application, following Congress passing the act, would prove deleterious to Jeremiah. After the Gloucester County Clerk, John C. Smallwood, located a list of the officers serving in Colonel Somers' regiment in the files of the New Jersey Secretary of State's office during 1833, Jeremiah filed his first federal pension application in 1834 with Smallwood's assistance. An extended period of jousting over Jeremiah's pension application ensued, with the federal pension commissioner expressing his disagreement with the application, and Smallwood going well beyond the call of duty to obtain the pension that Jeremiah deserved. He not only submitted documents and letters to Washington but also spoke to the federal powers that be in person.[24]

The federal pension commissioner finally relented and issued a certificate of pension on February 15, 1836, awarding Jeremiah $60 per annum. The pension office calculated the arrears from March 4, 1836, back to March 1, 1831, the date set for pensions to begin under the June 7, 1832, congressional act and the arrears totaled $330, although no voucher exists within the pension file for making payment of said arrears. The pension office issued a letter on May 16, 1837, to the pension agent and the order for the first pension payment was finally issued on March 1, 1838. It appears Jeremiah received his pension payment from March 4, 1838, until his death in October 1838.[25] Whether his pension payments began with the issuance of the pension certificate in February 1837 is unclear, based on the documents found in Jeremiah's pension file. Jeremiah's second wife, Millicent, continued to receive his pension until her death in 1873. She also applied for a bounty land certificate during the mid-1850s.[26]

A Summary Account of Jeremiah's Life

The Egg Harbor Quaker Meeting records Jeremiah Leeds' nativity as occurring on March 4, 1754,[27] at Leeds Point, Gloucester County, New Jersey, the son of John and Sarah (nee Mathis) Leeds.[28] Jeremiah's father and mother were lifelong active Quakers and both served as Public Friends or Quaker ministers from the meeting house located at Leeds Point. Jeremiah had nine siblings and he was probably the tallest of the family, measuring about 6'2" in height and weighing 250 pounds plus.[29] Although the local Quaker monthly meeting read Jeremiah out of meeting for his military activities, he later became a Methodist Church member.

He married Judith Steelman on December 8, 1776, and sired eight children; after Judith's death, at 63 years of age, Jeremiah married 24-year old Millicent Steelman Ingersoll on October 12, 1817, and fathered four more children.[30] As an interesting aside, Judith and Millicent were second cousins, twice removed, both sharing great-great-grandparents, Andrew and Judith Steelman.

The tax duplicates housed at the New Jersey Archives list Jeremiah as a landowner in both Galloway and Egg Harbor Township for at least the years between 1778 and 1802.[31] He began, at least on March 6, 1805, to acquire land on Absecon Beach per Gloucester and Atlantic county recorded deeds (paying about 40 cents an acre).[32] He acquired enough land on the island that it became known as Leeds Beach. His son, Chalkley Leeds, the first mayor of Atlantic City, stated that Jeremiah initially acquired land on the island in 1783, but no deeds have as yet proven this assertion, although he was living on the island at that time. It is estimated that he owned most of the land north of Dry Inlet[33] in South Atlantic City (meaning north of Ventnor, Margate, and Longport), other than the 131-acre inlet Chamberlain Tract.[34] The 1830 U.S. Census shows him only as a resident of Egg Harbor Township.[35] Today, he is considered to be the first white settler on what is now Absecon Island and the first person to have built a house in what is now Atlantic City, New Jersey, located on present-day Arctic Avenue between Missouri Avenue and Arkansas Avenue. Leeds later built a larger house at today's Baltic Avenue and Massachusetts Avenue.

In addition to raising livestock, Jeremiah cleared a section of high land on Absecon Beach (the dunes were as high as 50' in those days) and started farming corn, rye, and other produce, which he sold to passing ships.[36] The Leeds family also operated a guest house on the island for select guests desiring to hunt waterfowl.[37] After struggling with lip cancer for 40 years,[38] Jeremiah died on October 10, 1838, at the 251-acre Leeds Plantation in present-day Leeds Point and was interred in the Steelman family burial ground at Northfield.[39] His remains and headstone underwent exhumation in the 1950s and were then moved to Oxford Circle in Northfield to make room for a housing development.

He died intestate (without a will) and the Orphans' Court dispersed his 1058-1/3 acres to his family.[40] The number of acres that each child inherited is listed in the genealogy at the conclusion of this article.[41] The children later sold the inherited 40-cents-per-acre land in 1853–1854 for $5 to $17 per acre when Atlantic City began to expand. Jeremiah's widow Millicent, "Aunt Millie," later turned the Massachusetts Avenue home into a small inn.[42] It was the only licensed tavern on the island and its guests included oystermen, beach goers, and waterfowl hunters.[43]

Family History

Jeremiah Leeds came from a middle-class family of coopers (barrel makers) who emigrated from England directly to New Jersey before late 1676.[44] Thomas Leeds, his great-great grandfather, left Stansted, Mount Fichet, Essex, England, and, after a possible stop in Long Island, took up residence at Little Silver Point in Shrewsbury, Monmouth County. He left England to avoid the religious persecution directed at the Quakers. His three sons probably followed soon after him, possibly in 1678. The *Beach Haven Times* reports an interesting piece of information, but gives no source for the account:

> Thomas had been thrown into prison because of his political opposition to Charles I. When Charles died, Thomas was released from the Tower of London a freeman, but when Charles II took the throne, he decided that England was not a safe place for the Leeds family and so Thomas made his way to America, leaving Daniel to settle the family's affairs.[45]

Professor Brian Regal, a Leeds family scholar at Kean University, has completed recent research that verifies this account.[46] Thomas signed the "Concessions & Agreements" and obtained 240 acres in Shrewsbury in March 1677, meaning that he was in Shrewsbury, New Jersey, by that date. In the account in the British official death records, his wife, Mary Cartwright (listed as wife of Thomas), died July 4, 1677, of smallpox at her sibling John's home on Westbury Street in Stansted, England. The record says she was buried at Chequer Alley, London, England; the smallpox was possibly the reason she did not emigrate with Thomas. There is another family account, although without any proof, that says Thomas' wife emigrated with him and died in Shrewsbury on the same date in 1677, but there is no wife's name associated with this account and no proof of this burial in the Shrewsbury Friends' records. The wife's Stansted, England, death seems more probable.

Regardless, Thomas and Mary had four children while in England: an unnamed child who was born and died in 1648; and three sons: Daniel (1651–1720), William (1653–1753), and Thomas II (1654–?). Some say there may have been a daughter born to this family named Mary Leeds (1665–1727), but it is more likely that this woman was a cousin. The New Jersey will of Mary Leeds states that she died in Burlington in 1727

Grave of Jeremiah Leeds, Oxford Circle Burial Ground, Northfield, Atlantic County, New Jersey. *Photograph courtesy of South Jersey Culture & History Center.*

in a financially comfortable state and was probably the daughter of Thomas' son William.[47]

Thomas married Margaret Collier on August 6, 1678, in Burlington and resided at Shrewsbury until his death on November 23, 1687. His will mentions only his sons, Daniel and William; therefore, it suggests that Thomas II predeceased his father.[48]

As stated earlier, the Thomas Leeds family came to America as barrel-makers (coopers) with enough money in hand to buy property for both the father and two of the sons, plus enough to acquire extra land quickly. In his son Daniel's famous almanac, begun in 1687, there is both a family crest in the masthead as well as a mention that the family was related to a "gentleman" or nobleman from Leeds in Kent (Kent, Essex and London are adjacent counties).

The Philadelphia Quaker hierarchy was highly critical of Daniel for his theology, and his son Titan was likewise criticized by fierce almanac competitor Ben Franklin. It would seem that their detractors would have quickly and gleefully exposed as spurious the claim to a somewhat prestigious English family history and family crest if not true, especially in the case of the Quaker establishment, who had easy access to the English peerage records. According to Professor Regal of Kean University, we should, therefore, assume this claim to peerage and the family crest to be valid.

Thomas' sons, Daniel and William, came to Burlington in 1678. The story that they came on the SHIELD or the KENT cannot be verified. These two ships represent the first two vessels to arrive in West New Jersey from England carrying settlers after Fenwick's arrival in Salem in 1675. Most likely, they came to Shrewsbury first and then Daniel moved to Burlington, rendering the SHIELD story as a probable later family fiction. William owned land in both Shrewsbury and Leeds Point, living in both places at various times. Daniel married Ann Stacey of Trenton on February 21, 1681, and she died in childbirth the same year on December 3, 1681. Daniel then married Dorothy Young of Burlington on March 9, 1683, and they had a "curiously premature" son, Japheth (sometimes spelled Japhet). They went on to have eight other children, all of which experienced the normal nine month gestation period.[49]

Son Japheth was born October 24, 1683, in the family home in present-day Jacksonville, Springfield Township, Burlington County. The house stood on 1,000 acres a half-mile from the current village, on the north side of the turnpike going toward Burlington. Father Daniel was the Surveyor General of West Jersey, a member of the Assembly in 1692,[50] a member of the Governor's Council, a Judge, and a shrewd businessman. He began publishing his almanac in 1687 and continued through 1716. Copies of his almanacs, tracts and *Temple of Wisdom* may be found on microfiche at the Princeton University Library.[51] The Library Company of Philadelphia and the Historical Society of Pennsylvania contain some original publications as well as the microform set that Princeton holds.

Daniel's son Japheth married Deborah Smith in 1703 and moved to a 1,000-acre tract in Leeds Point in eastern Gloucester County. He and Deborah had thirteen children, the third of which was John (1708–1785). Deborah's parentage is uncertain, but perhaps the best guess at her father's identity is Robert Smith of Newark, Essex County. It is this Japheth and Deborah who reputedly parented the Jersey Devil, a story, according to Professor Regal in his forthcoming book, competitor Ben Franklin fabricated in an attempt to diminish Daniel's son Titan's successful almanac business. Japheth remained a devout Quaker, with Quaker meetings held at his home, while his father Daniel reverted to Anglicanism. Japheth died December 15, 1748, and listed each of his children in his will.[52]

Japheth's son John married Rebecca Cordery in 1737 and had four children. After Rebecca's death, John married Sarah Mathis about 1751 and had four more children. He resided the rest of his life in Leeds Point, where he was a farmer producing castor oil, salt hay, corn and rye. John died September 16, 1785,[53] and his New Jersey will lists his son Jeremiah, the subject of this essay.

FAMILY OF JEREMIAH LEEDS

The following is a list of Jeremiah's children and their children, provided for those who wish to join the New Jersey Sons of the American Revolution (SAR), Sons of the Revolution (SR), and Daughters of the Revolution (DAR) by using 1st Lieutenant Leeds as their patriot ancestor. Jeremiah's service can be proven via the Stryker text, as well as Jeremiah's federal Revolutionary War pension application. Since Jeremiah left no written will, direct familial relationship to him must be proven via other documents. Known documents connecting the generations in this writing will be noted below. As an aside, the author acquired a copy of the Atlantic County Orphans' Court 1838 distribution decree to further link Jeremiah with his children and determine which child received the various tracts of land. This Orphans' Court decree, found at the New Jersey Archives, proves the relationship between Jeremiah and all his surviving children.[54] The Leeds children 1853–1854 deeds of sale for the land are also available through the Atlantic County Clerk's Office. For SAR, SR, and DAR applicants, the challenge, albeit an easy one, will be to document the relationship between Jeremiah's children and their progeny. Once one accomplishes that task, the rest of the family can be proven via the federal decennial census information available on Ancestry.com.

On Thursday, March 4, 1954, Atlantic City unveiled a monument at Park Place and the Boardwalk honoring Jeremiah Leeds as Absecon Island's first permanent settler.[55] Another park at Rhode Island and Pacific Avenues in Atlantic City also carries the Leeds name.[56]

∽

Jeremiah Leeds m. Judith Steelman, December 8, 1776
(New Jersey Marriages & Jeremiah Leeds Bible)
- James Leeds (February 26, 1778–1798). Died young with no issue.
- Ruhanna Steelman Leeds (January 21, 1779–August 30, 1862) m. Joseph Conover February 20, 1801. Inherited 50 1/2 acres on Absecon Beach and 185 acres on the mainland.
- Rachel Leeds (October 4, 1782–April 22, 1845) m. Jesse Steelman, m. Mark Read. Inherited 34 acres on Absecon Beach and 66 acres on the mainland.
- Adah Leeds (April 25, 1788–October 25, 1792). Died young with no issue.
- Sarah Leeds (March 26, 1790–October 18, 1792). Died young with no issue.
- Andrew Leeds (April 30 1792–September 5, 1865) m. Armenia Lake (1797–1853) June 1, 1817 (New Jersey Marriages/Gloucester City Marriages)—sonship proven by deed (in DocStar at ACHS); m. Ellen DeKurts-Bennett in 1852. Inherited 347 acres on Absecon Beach.
  - James L. Leeds (Aug 6, 1818–January 10, 1893) m. Abbigail S. Webb (1827–1907) September 4, 1847 (Indenture in DocStar at ACHS).
    - Armenia Lake Leeds (August 15, 1848–?) m. Capt. Israel Nichols July 10, 1875.
    - Sylvester Webb Leeds (December 5, 1849–?) m. Ella Lee June 8, 1879.
    - Lydia Corson Leeds (March 14, 1851–?) m. Elmer P. Reeves December 22, 1869—this is the line from which the article's author was later born.
    - Mary Elizabeth Leeds (April 1853–?) m. Thomas Oakley October 2, 1876.
    - Benjamin Franklin Leeds (April 1, 1855–?) m. Rejoice Treen March 29, 1878.
    - Sarah Abigail Leeds (April 20, 1857–?) never married.
    - Ellen Joanna Leeds (January 31, 1859–?) m. John Baker July 1, 1878.
    - Hannah Rachel Leeds (?–?) m. Edward Shoultes September 5, 1888.
    - Augusta Eveline Leeds (November 15, 1862–?) m. Charles Hommer September 4, 1888.
    - Somers Edwin Leeds (July 15, 1864–?) m. Aura Garwood December 22, 1886.
- John B. Leeds (1819–1867) m. Hannah Webb January 14, 1867.
- Steelman Leeds (1821–1896) (1850 census) m. Rachel Miller October 31, 1854—sonship by NJ will.
- Abigail Leeds (1831–1859) m. John Gill Avery about 1857—daughtership by 1850 census.

Jeremiah Leeds m. Millicent Steelman Ingersoll
- Judith Leeds (1819–1869) m. Richard Hackett January 16, 1840. Inherited 234 acres on Absecon Beach.
  - Matilda Hackett (June 27, 1842–?).
  - Joseph Hackett (December 7, 1848–August 4, 1888) m. Tamar Oakley.
  - Josephine Hackett (January 13, 1850–?) m. Samuel Reeve.
- Aaron Leeds (1820–1820). Died young with no issue.
- Chalkey Steelman Leeds (October 3, 1825–September 10, 1908) m. Margaret Holland Gaskill April 1, 1847; m. Rose Young. He was the first mayor of Atlantic City. Inherited 217 acres on Absecon Beach.
  - Amanda Elizabeth Leeds (December 14, 1847–?) m. George C. Bryant January 26, 1870; m. Thomas J. Horner November 12, 1882.
  - Maria Leeds (August 23, 1849–?) m. Lewis Evans October 1, 1868.
  - Millicent Leeds (March 8, 1852–September 7, 1873) m. William C. Heath.
  - Jeremiah Leeds (July 26, 1854–?) m. Annie Cramer February 11, 1881.
  - Mary Rebecca Leeds (October 29, 1856–?) m. Charles Dougherty November 30, 1881.
  - Charles Gaskill Leeds (September 19, 1857–?).
  - Isaac Steelman Leeds (November 11, 1862–?) m. Mary Parker.
  - Laura Leeds (October 27, 1865–?) m. Fred Hogan December 31, 1890.
  - Nettie Leeds (August 19, 1876–February 22, 1878) probably by wife Rose Young.
- Robert Barclay Leeds (May 2, 1828–March

16, 1905) m. Caroline English April 29, 1852. Inherited 176 acres on Absecon Beach.
- Lurilda Leeds (June 15, 1854–?) m. Oliver T. Nice February 28, 1878.
- Honora Leeds (August 1, 1856–October 25, 1857).
- Neida Leeds (June 5, 1858–?) m. Albert B. Richards.
- Harry Bellerjeau Leeds (August 9, 1860–?) m. Harriet Somers Scull November 24, 1895.
- Albert English Leeds (May 8, 1862–July 25, 1863).
- Alberta Leeds (January 1, 1864–?) m. Fred P. Currie.
- Horace Leeds (November 1, 1865–?).
- Maynard Leeds (questionable).

Bibliography

Note: The author acknowledges that there are family stories that have existed for generations, but that lack confirming documentary evidence. It is the author's decision to include these stories for the purpose of memorializing them, hoping that documentation will be found some day. These family stories have been noted as such in the text or footnotes.

Atlantic County Historical Society (ACHS) Yearbook. Somers Point, NJ: ACHS, 1948 ff. Volume 2, no. 1 (1952) contains a transcription of Jeremiah's federal Revolutionary War pension application, providing his recollections about when and where he served. This has been supplemented by 29 others from Atlantic County residents that this author has collected.

English, A. L. *History of Atlantic City, New Jersey.* Philadelphia: Dickson & Gilling Publishers, 1884.

Hall, John F. *The Daily Union History of Atlantic City and County, New Jersey.* Atlantic City, NJ: The Daily Union Printing Co., 1900. Some of Hall's stories are not verifiable.

Heston, Alfred M. *Absegami: Annals of Eyren Haven and Atlantic City, 1609–1904.* Two volumes. Camden: Sinnickson Chew & Sons Company, 1904.

Hewlett, Joseph M. Jr. *The Leeds Family of South Jersey.* Privately printed, 1972.

Various editors. *Documents Relating to the Colonial History of the State of New Jersey, Calendar of New Jersey Wills.* 1670–1817, various volumes, various publishers.

Stewart, Frank H. *Notes on Old Gloucester County, New Jersey.* Volumes I-IV, various publishers, various dates.

Stryker, William S. *Official Register of the Officers and Men of New Jersey in the Revolutionary War.* Trenton: Wm. T. Nicholson & Co Publishers, 1872. This has been supplemented by copies of the surviving two 3rd Battalion payrolls, one from 1775–1776 and the other from the end of the War in 1783.

Turp, Ralph K. *West Jersey: Under Four Flags.* Philadelphia: Dorrance & Company, 1975, pp. 39, 69–70, 101–114.

About the Author

Rev. Norman Reeves Goos (normangoos@comcast.net) is a member and Past-President (2013–2015) of the New Jersey Society, Sons of the American Revolution, as well as President (2009–present) of the Col. Richard Somers SAR Chapter; SAR Compatriot #169855. Norman is also a member of The New Jersey Sons of the Revolution (2014–#41604) and the Librarian and a Trustee of the Atlantic County Historical Society; he was also recently appointed by the County Freeholders as the Local Historian for Atlantic County. Norm is an ordained minister and retired Senior Pastor in the Wesleyan Church. He is the retired President of The Kairos Institute in Trinidad and Tobago, as well as Professor Emeritus of Ancient Greek in the Graduate School of that institution. Norm is married to Marilyn, a retired middle-school math and science teacher; they have two sons, six grandchildren and a growing quiver of great-grandchildren.

Endnotes

1 *Atlantic County Historical Society (ACHS) Yearbook* 2, no. 1 (October 1952): 205–06.
2 William S. Stryker, *Official Register of the Officers and Men of New Jersey in the Revolutionary War* (Trenton, NJ: Wm. T. Nicholson & Co Publishers, 1872), 438.
3 Franklin Kemp article, undated clipping, *Atlantic City Press*, July 14, 1963, p. 6 in Vertical File in Atlantic City General #1 folder, Atlantic County Historical Society.
4 William A. Nelson and A. Van Doren Honeyman, *Documents Relating to the Colonial History of the State of New Jersey, First Series, Volume XXIX, Tenth Volume of Extracts from American Newspapers Relating to New Jersey, 1773–1774*

(Paterson, NJ: The Call Printing and Publishing Co., 1917), 549.
5. Joseph M. Hewlett Jr., *The Leeds Family of South Jersey* (Privately printed, 1972), 54; reporting unverifiable family tradition.
6. John F. Hall, *The Daily Union History of Atlantic City and County, New Jersey* (Atlantic City, NJ: The Daily Union Printing Co., 1900), 412.
7. Great Egg Harbor Monthly Meeting Minutes, 1726–1843, Haverford College, Quaker Collection, 291. Both the February and late May proceedings occurred at the Cape May Meetinghouse but the May 6 disowning took place at the Egg Harbor Meetinghouse.
8. Ibid., 295.
9. Ibid., 298.
10. United States, Revolutionary War Pension and Bounty Land Warrant Applications, 1800–1900. File S 5686, Jeremiah Leeds, 12–13. Database and image files, http://www/Fold3.com.
11. Alfred M. Heston, *Absegami: Annals of Eyren Haven and Atlantic City, 1609–1904* (Camden, NJ: Sinnickson Chew & Sons, 1904), 138.
12. Pension Application, 13–14.
13. Ibid., 14.
14. Ibid., 14.
15. Ibid., 14–15.
16. Ibid., 15.
17. Ibid.
18. Ibid., 16–18.
19. Barry-Hayes Papers, Independence Seaport Museum, J. Welles Henderson Archives and Library; Series 52, b. 13, f. 3. (Digitized by the Falvey Memorial Library, Villanova University, http://digital.library.villanova.edu/Item/vudl:262289.
20. Frank H. Stewart, *Notes on Old Gloucester County, New Jersey*, vol. 3 ([Woodbury, NJ]: Frank H. Stewart, 1935), 27.
21. Stewart, *Notes on Old Gloucester County*, 63–64.
22. Hall, *The Daily Union History of Atlantic City*, 412.
23. Will Graves, "Pension Acts. An Overview of Revolutionary War Pension and Bounty Land Legislation and the Southern Campaigns Pension Transcription Project," http://revwarapps.org/revwar-pension-acts.htm.
24. Pension Application, multiple pages, but p. 48 summarizes the issues surrounding the application.
25. Ibid., 3.
26. Ibid., 5–10.
27. *ACHS Yearbook* 2, no. 1 (October 1952): 79.
28. Today, Leeds Point is situated in Atlantic County, New Jersey; the county was officially created from the eastern portion of Gloucester County in 1837.
29. Hall, *The Daily Union History of Atlantic City*, 411; reporting unverifiable family tradition.
30. ACHS Bible Records, vol. 9, 53.
31. He is listed in Galloway in 1781 and 1782. He is listed in Egg Harbor Township in 1778, 1780, 1781, 1782, 1784, 1785, 1786, 1787, 1789, 1791, 1793, 1794, and 1802. Based on the listing method, it is impossible to tell if there were multiple properties involved. It is also impossible to determine the location of these properties from the extant tax records.
32. *Beach Haven Times* (Beach Haven, NJ), November 15, 1978.
33. Dry Inlet was in the vicinity of present-day Jackson Avenue. *ACHS* 17, no. 2 (December 2013): 15.
34. ACHS, deed books.
35. The US Censuses for 1790–1820 for NJ have not survived. The 1830 US Census shows Jeremiah in Egg Harbor Township, but with no subdivision listed. No family member names and other info were listed until the 1850 US Census.
36. *Atlantic City Press*, March 26, 1961.
37. *Atlantic City Daily Union*, June 15, 1904, 3.
38. Hall, *The Daily Union History of Atlantic City*, 412; reporting unverifiable family tradition.
39. *ACHS Yearbook*, 2, no. 1 (October 1952): 203–06.
40. A. L. English, *History of Atlantic City, New Jersey* (Philadelphia: Dickson & Gilling Publishers, 1884), 25–28, 33–34, 38. The Orphans' Court Records are found in the New Jersey Archives in Trenton at the following location: 1837–1860 Atlantic County Surrogate, Orphan Court Minutes, and Vol. A, pp. 32, 35, 38, 39, 45 and 47, Microfilm 2–3.
41. *ACHS Yearbook* 2, no. 1 (October 1952): 205–06.
42. Photo of Millicent Leeds from Lantern Slide #2 in ACHS collection.
43. Heston, *Absegami*, 116.
44. Much of the information in this section comes from a recently published study by Professor Brian Regal of Kean University in New Jersey. Professor Regal is a specialist in researching old myths, in this case the myth of the Leeds of the Jersey Devil. The author of this essay has a copy of chapter 2 of this manuscript which is heavily footnoted. Dr. Regal presented his finding about the Leeds family and the source of the famous myth at a monthly dinner meeting of the Col. Richard Somers Chapter of the Sons of the American Revolution on June 12, 2014. A video of this presentation is available at the following web address: http://www.colrichardsomers.com/Pages/JDD.aspx. See Brian Regal and Frank J. Esposito, *The Secret History of the Jersey Devil: How Quakers, Hucksters, and Benjamin Franklin Created a Monster* (Johns Hopkins University Press, 2018).
45. *Beach Haven Times* (Beach Haven, NJ) November, 15, 1978, 6.
46. Professor Regal's footnote, in a study of Leeds underway, is as follows: "Essex County [UK] Records Office. Calendar of Essex Assize file [ASS 35/113/3] Assizes held at Chelmsford, July 15, 1672, ref. code T/A 418/175/25. The present author is not at liberty to reprint any portion of Dr. Regal's text but he did arrange for the copy of the manuscript of chapter 2 to be read in his presence at the Atlantic County Historical Society.
47. William Nelson, *Documents Relating to the Colonial History of the State of New Jersey, Volume XXXIII, Calendar of New Jersey Wills, Vol. I, 1670–1730* (Paterson, NJ: The Press Printing and Publishing Co., 1901), 289.
48. Ibid.

49 The author's usually repressed sense of humor snuck out here!
50 Heston, *Absegami*, 122.
51 The microfiche at Princeton University Library also contain all of the pamphlets from both sides of the vitriolic pamphlet war between Daniel Leeds and the Philadelphia Quaker hierarchy.
52 A. Van Doren Honeyman, editor, *Documents Relating to the Colonial History of the State of New Jersey, Volume XXX, Calendar of New Jersey Wills, Administration, etc., Vol. II, 1730–1750* (Somerville, NJ: The Unionist-Gazette Association, 1918), 295.
53 *ACHS Yearbook* 1, no. 4 (October 1951): 161.
54 ACHS Archives, *ACHS Yearbook* 2, no. 1 (October 1952): 205–06.
55 *Atlantic City Press*, March 5, 1954.
56 *Atlantic City Press* article, undated clipping, *ACHS Yearbook* 2, no. 1 (October 1952): 198; Heston, *Absegami*, 119.

The Hanging of Joshua Huddy

(1735–1782)

Three notices pertaining to the capture and hanging of Joshua Huddy—a Salem-born commander of New Jersey Patriot militia.

The Pennsylvania Evening Post (Philadelphia), March 29, 1782, describes an attack on a Toms River blockhouse that guarded a Patriot salt works. Approximately 100 Loyalists besieged Captain Joshua Huddy and 25 comrades, who defended their small fort until they had expended all ammunition. Upon their surrender, the Patriots witnessed the Loyalists torch all but two houses in Toms River (out of about a dozen structures).

Huddy was briefly interned on a British prison ship until a band of Associated Loyalists removed him and took him to the south coast of Sandy Hook. There, on the beach, Huddy dictated his will on an upturned barrel and was then hanged.

The Providence Gazette, May 4, 1782, describes the Patriot reaction to Huddy's death. Refugees had executed Huddy in retaliation for the death of Philip White, a Loyalist who had recently died in Patriot custody. Using strident language, this notice calls for continuation of the cycle of violence that swirled between Patriot and Loyalist citizens as the war wound down and as relations among former combatants needed to be reestablished.

The Connecticut Currant, May 7, 1782, makes clear the deep discontent Loyalists felt at their treatment by Patriots during this final phase of the war. This particular group of Loyalists, at least, vowed to meet the insults of the triumphant Americans with violence.

Calls to avenge Huddy's death by Patriots forced George Washington and the nascent American government into a diplomatic crisis—the Asgill Affair. When the British refused to surrender the officer responsible for Huddy's execution (in a British court-martial, the officer was found not guilty), Washington reluctantly agreed to execute a British prisoner of equal rank to Huddy, seeking to avoid escalating retributions. The officer chosen by lot was Charles Asgill. Congress eventually granted Asgill a reprieve and returned him to the British lines.

Thus was life near the conclusion of the War for Independence, which, frankly, might be described as America's first civil war.

"Notice is Hereby Given":
Extracts from Colonial Newspapers

During the War, South Jersey experienced its share of battles, skirmishes, military exchanges and troop movements—more than enough to lend credence to the state's later nickname: New Jersey, the cockpit of the American Revolution. But the impact of wartime struggles stretched well beyond the battlefield into the everyday lives of inhabitants. Families and individuals, whether sympathetic to American independence or loyal to the crown, could face terrifying dilemmas as first one army (or armed band) and then an opposing force swept through one's local area. In an attempt to better appreciate common occurrences and concerns during this period, we have reproduced advertisements, notices, and brief news extracts that relate to South Jersey found in contemporary newspapers. Most present perspectives in support of the American cause, but not all. Some detail dramatic events; others describe the mundane. Several are disturbing. Together, though faintly, they suggest something of the texture of daily life throughout the area.

∞

The Pennsylvania Gazette,
April 19, 1775

THE FAMOUS ENGLISH DRAY HORSE COLOSSUS, WILL cover Mares at the Stable of John Dickinson, in the Town of Salem, West Jersey, at Thirty Shillings Cash the Season, and Forty Shillings Credit, until the First of January next. He is a beautiful dark Bay, well marked, rising 4 Years old, and is allowed to be the largest at that Age of any Horse imported into America; he is an excellent Horse for a Draft, and goes very light, fleet and gay under the Saddle, with great Spirits and Ease to the Rider. As he is likely to be very advantageous in enlarging the Breed of Horses (which are so much under Size) I flatter myself the Public will embrace so favourable an Opportunity for the Welfare and Advantage of their Country. Good Pasturage at 2 s. 6 d. Per Week, and proper Attendance provided by DAVID HENRY.

∞

Dunlap's Pennsylvania Packet,
or the General Advertiser,
April 22, 1776

FOUR DOLLARS REWARD.

RAN AWAY from the subscriber, living in Lower Alloways Creek, Salem County, West New-Jersey, in the night of the 12th instant (April), an Irish servant man named DANIEL M'NITE, about five feet nine inches high; had on and took with him, a new led coloured coat without lining, a brown coattee, an old green and red under jacket, old velvet breeches, blue yarn stockings, and strong shoes; was full faced, with yellow thin hair, and very bald; talks broken, and it is supposed intends to get into the Continental service. Whoever takes up said servant and secures him in any gaol in the province, shall have the above Reward. Or if he should inlist in the service aforesaid, I shall be obliged to any officer that will give notice thereof in the public papers, and I shall be willing to come on reasonable terms for his time.

JOHN SMITH.

∞

"Notice is Hereby Given"

The Constitutional Gazette,
May 11, 1776

Extract from a letter from Cumberland county, West-New Jersey, May 6, 1776.

"This serves to inform you of an alarm we had about eleven o'clock this day, a party of regulars landing on Findle's island, in Bacon's neck, about four miles from Greenwich, supposed to be about 30 in number; shooting down the cattle, taking them on board, &c. whereupon I called the militia together as soon as possible, and upon our appearance, a gun was fired from on board one of the vessels for them to repair on board, which they did with the greatest precipitation. Our men pursued so closely, that we were near taking three of them prisoners, one of them left an excellent musket behind, which we got, with some cartridges. They hollowed to our men to go on board the KING-FISHER, and they would pay for the beef. It is supposed they took off between 20 and 30 cattle, 5 they left dead on the shore and wounded many others; which, with all the others, we drove from the water side. They have taken, this morning, a shallop belonging to Daniel Richards, bound from Philadelphia to Morris's river, but the hands got ashore."

The Pennsylvania Evening Post,
May 30, 1776

SIXTEEN DOLLARS Reward.

RAN AWAY last night, from the subscriber living in Gloucester county, Deptford township, two SERVANTS, both about nineteen years of age, and about five feet eight inches high. One an Irishman named ROBERT M'FARLAND; he had on a felt hat almost new, two brownish jackets, the upper one with small cuffs, new homespun shirt and trousers, and good shoes with copper or brass buckles.

The other a Low Dutchman, named PETER DENNEY, has black curly hair, pitted with the smallpox, and is very surly. He had on an old beaver hat, lightish jacket, two new homespun shirts, a pair of trousers, and good shoes with strings.

Whoever apprehends the said servants, and secures them so that their master gets them again, shall have the above reward, or half for either of them, with reasonable charges if brought home.

JOHN JESUP.

The Pennsylvania Journal,
June 26, 1776

TAKEN UP ADRIFT,

IN LITTLE EGG Harbour Inlett, on the 8th day of May, A LARGE LONG BOAT, Supposed to have broke adrift from some vessel at sea; any person proving his property and paying charges, may have the boat again, by applying to RICHARD or HENRY DAVIS, at Chesnutt Neck, in Galway township, Glocester county, New-Jersey.

Dunlap's Pennsylvania Packet, or, the General Advertiser,
September 18, 1776

THREE POUNDS Reward.

RAN AWAY, on Friday, the 6th inst. (September) from the subscriber, living in Pitts-grove, one mile below the Sweed Meeting house, in Salem county, West Jersey, a Mulatto man, named PETER, about 35 years of age, from 5 feet 6 to 7 inches high, stout and well made, is fond of strong liquor, and when drunk very saucy and talks a great deal of his abilities as a farmer; he formerly lived with David Franks, Esq. of Philadelphia, and was purchased of him about 5 years ago, by his present master. As he was seen going towards Salem it is probable he may make for Penn's Neck. He had on and took with him, a light mixed superfine cloth coat and waistcoat, a red hair plush jacket, a white jacket with a belt before, green calimanco breeches, a holland shirt, 3 stocks, a pair of white plain cotton stockings, a pair of light coloured silk ditto, a pair of tow trowsers, one red spotted and one black silk handkerchief, a pair of pumps, one of which is patched on the side, square silver shoe buckles, and an old hat. Whoever secures the said fellow in any gaol, so that his master may have him again, shall receive the above reward, and reasonable charges if brought home, or to Samuel Purviance and Sons, in Philadelphia.

SAMUEL PURVIANCE.

The Pennsylvania Journal,
June 25, 1777

CAME TO the house of the subscriber, living on the Forks of Little Egg Harbour, on the 20th inst. May, a sorrel MARE, about 13 ½ hands high, white face, four white feet, and some white spots on her belly, and is a natural trotter. Whoever has lost said Mare, by applying to the subscriber, proving their property, and paying charges, may have her again.

RICHARD WESCOTT.

The New Jersey Gazette,
December 24, 1777

December 21st, 1777.
WANTED,

As soon as possible, A YOUNG WOMAN, with a good breast of milk, to take the nursing of a child. Such a person applying to the printer hereof, having a good reputation, will meet with proper encouragement.

The Pennsylvania Evening Post,
February 3, 1778

Philadelphia.

This day a number of deserters came in from the rebel army, amongst whom were no less than twelve serjeants, one corporal, and a private, of the regiment of artillery commanded by col. Proctor.

Yesterday about twenty West Jersey loyalists crossed the Delaware, from this city, in order to assist some of their friends, who had expressed a desire of taking refuge here, to avoid the horrid tyranny and implacable persecution of the rebels. At the mouth of Mantua creek, they fell in with a party of the enemy in ambuscade, whom they soon repulsed, advanced four miles into the country, and took one Wilson prisoner, who was a committee man, and, it is said, very active in distressing the friends of the government. They returned this day with the prisoner, and their friends. The loyalists had one man killed, but what the rebels suffered is not known. Wilson is in confinement.

The Connecticut Gazette;
and The Universal Intelligencer,
April 10, 1778

Trenton, March 25, 1778.

By accounts from Salem County we learn, that a number of British troops, supposed to be between fifteen hundred and two thousand, landed last Tuesday at the Town of Salem; with whom our militia has had some skirmishes, but with no great loss on either side. Orders are issued for a reinforcement of the militia to join Col. Ellis in Gloucester County; and Col. Shreve, with his battalion of continental troops, has crossed the Delaware and is on his march to oppose the enemy.—It is reported that the militia of Cumberland have turned out with the most laudable spirit, and it is expected the British rovers will not be able to leave this State without great loss, unless they decamp with the hurry and confusion which distinguished their last visit—or rather their visitation.

The Connecticut Gazette;
and The Universal Intelligencer,
June 5, 1778

Trenton, May 20, 1778.

Two Deserters from our Row-galley's, who went to the Enemy some Time ago, were lately taken by a scouting Party of our Troops, in Gloucester County, and were brought to this Town on Monday last. One of them is named John Gilfroy, who was tried Yesterday by a Court-Martial, and condemned to be hanged. But his Execution is deferred 'till the Sentence is confirmed by his Excellency the President of the State of Pennsylvania. The other, we hear, is shortly to take his Trial at Lancaster.

The New-Jersey Gazette,
June 19, 1778

To whom it may concern.
State of New-Jersey, to wit.

Notice is hereby given, that a court of admiralty will be held at the house of James Esdall, in Burlington, on Wednesday the 26th day of June next, at the hour of ten in the forenoon of the same day, then and there to try to the truth of the facts alledged in the bill of Hope Willets, commander of the armed boat BLACK JOKE; and Joseph Edwards, commander of the armed boat LUCK AND FORTUNE, who as well, &c. against a certain sloop or vessel called the NANCY, which lately sailed from Maurice River in the said state, laden with lumber and tar, was captured at sea by the FAIR AMERICAN, a British cruiser, commanded by William Nelson; and afterwards re-captured by the said Captains, Willets and Edwards, together with her tackle, apparel, furniture and cargo, and two Negro slaves, named Obadiah Gale, and Edward Carter; to the end and intent that the owner or owners of the said vessel, or any other person or persons interested therein, may appear and shew cause, if any they have, why the said vessel, with her tackle, apparel, furniture, cargo and said Negro slaves, should not be

"Notice is Hereby Given"

condemned to the captors thereof, and a decree thereon pass, pursuant to the prayer of the said bill. By Order of the Judge,
JOSEPH BLOOMFIELD, Reg.

∞

The Pennsylvania Evening Post,
July 4, 1778

TAKEN UP, a NEGRO GIRL, who was following the British army. She says she ran from Thomas Short's, Talbot county, Maryland, and took with her a child about three years old. The owner, proving property, and paying charges, may have her again. Apply to David Richards, four miles from Cooper's ferry, upon the Haddonfield Road, West Jersey.

∞

*The Independent Ledger
& American Advertiser* [Boston],
August 21, 1778

August 12.
We hear that on Thursday sennight the ship LOVE AND UNITY from Bristol, with 80 hogsheads of loaf sugar, several thousand bottles of London porter, a large quantity of Bristol beer ale, beside many other very valuable articles, was designedly run on shore near Tom's River; since which, by the assistance of some of our militia, she has been brought into a safe port, and her cargo properly taken care of.

∞

*The Pennsylvania Packet,
or the General Advertiser*,
September 15, 1778

To THE PUBLIC.
A STAGE WAGGON will set out on Monday morning from Peter Wells's, at the Landing at Big Egg-harbour, and to go to the Forks of Little Egg-harbour, and from thence to Samuel Cooper's Ferry on Tuesday evening; On Thursday morning to set out from Samuel Cooper's Ferry, and to go to the Forks of Little Egg-harbour, and from thence to Peter Wells's at the Landing at Big Egg-harbour on Friday evening.
Those Ladies and Gentlemen who please to favour me with their commands, may depend on their being executed with fidelity and dispatch, by
Their much obliged humble servant,
SAMUEL MARRYOTT.

∞

*The Pennsylvania Packet,
or the General Advertiser*,
September 17, 1778

Salem County, Aug. 27, 1778.
NOTICE IS HEREBY given to all persons within the department of the subscriber, in the state of New-Jersey, that have any demands against him as Pay-master to the Militia, to bring in their accounts properly attested, by the 21st of September, and they shall be paid. As it is absolutely necessary the public accounts should be settled as soon as possible, it is expected none will exceed the time specified.
THOMAS CARPENTER, P.M.

∞

The Pennsylvania Evening Post,
October 12, 1778

Piles Grove, Salem county, West Jersey,
Oct 9, 1778.
TWENTY FIVE POUNDS reward. Stole from the Forks of Little Egg harbour, about two o'clock last Thursday morning, a likely quarter blooded sorrel chestnut HORSE, six years old last spring, fourteen hands and a half high, has a blaze down his face, wind galled in his hind legs, his mane hangs on both sides, some of which is worn off by the collar, just below the withers, and has a switch tail. He is a leader in a team. He trots well, carries his head low, and when rained up, he keeps throwing it up and down. Whoever secures the thief and horse, shall, upon conviction of the thief, have Twenty Pounds reward, and for the horse alone, Five Pounds and reasonable charges.
ANTHONY SHARP.

∞

*The Pennsylvania Packet,
or the General Advertiser*,
November 3, 1778

Philadelphia, October 20, 1778.
TO BE SOLD at Public Vendue, on Friday the 6th day of November, at Col. Westcoat's, at the Forks of Little Egg-Harbour, THIRTEEN sails, twenty six coils of running, rigging, and sundry other articles too tedious to mention, belonging to the brig INDUSTRY. Attendance will be given by LUDWIG KUHN & Co.

*The Pennsylvania Packet,
or the General Advertiser*,
March 13, 1779

TO BE SOLD,

A PLANTATION in Piles-grove, Salem county, about four miles from Alloway's Creek, three from the Glass-house, and four from Woodstown, containing one hundred and seventy acres of land, with a frame house and kitchen adjoining, a large peach and apple orchard, plenty of good water, eight or ten acres of meadow, and about thirty more may be made at a small expence; there are about seventy acres of cleared land, the rest woods and swamp. Also another small tenement with a small peach orchard, &c. in which a family has lived for several years; likewise a good outlet for cattle. For terms apply to Mr. WILLIAM RICHMAN, two miles from the Pine tavern in Pitts-grove, Salem county; Messrs. BONSALL and SHOEMAKER, in Philadelphia; or Mr. SAMUEL SHINN, near the New Mills in Jersey.

N. B. The above place will be sold the fifteenth day of March inst. at public vendue, on the premises, if not sold before at private sale. The purchaser may have twelve months credit for half the purchase money, if required, paying interest on proper security.

The New-Jersey Gazette,
August 25, 1779

Burlington, August 4, 1779.

THE GENERAL PROPRIETORS of West-Jersey having received information, that sundry lands and real estates, which, by the late settlement of the line between New-York and New-Jersey, and found to lye within the division of West-Jersey, but have been located under East-Jersey rights only, are likely to be confiscated, and sold as the estate of sundry refugees who have joined the army of the king of Great Britain. The West-Jersey proprietors therefore, at a meeting holden at Burlington, on the 3d and 4th instant, having taken the same into their serious consideration, and it appearing unto them clearly, that no person whatsoever can have derived any title to lands lying within West-Jersey, under East-Jersey rights, located since the year 1718; and being desiring, as far as in them lies, to prevent any misapprehension impacting the title to the said lands, do hereby give notice, that all the lands lying to the westwards of the true line of division; between East and West-Jersey, that is to say, within the angle formed by the ex parte line run by John Lawrence, and the place where the true line will run from the mouth of Mackhockamuck to the station point at Little Egg harbour, which have been located under East-Jersey rights, and not since covered by West-Jersey rights, are claimed by them, (the western proprietors) and that they will be under the disagreeable necessity of instituting suits at law against all and every person, who now does and hereafter may claim title to, and hold the possession of the said lands, or any part thereof, by virtue of a title derived under East-Jersey. By order of the general proprietors.

DANIEL ELLIS, Register.

*The Pennsylvania Packet,
or the General Advertiser*,
March 9, 1780

Philadelphia, March 7, 1780.

TO BE SOLD at Public Auction, on Saturday the 18th instant, at Twelve o'clock, at the Coffee-house, A VALUABLE PLANTATION situate in Greenwich township, Gloucester county, West New Jersey, containing one hundred and eleven acres of excellent land, on which are a good dwelling-house and a young bearing orchard, about four acres of cleared meadow and a considerable quantity more may be made, about twenty acres of the upland cleared and under good fence, the land well timbered with oak and pine fit for sawing, some cedar swamp, and an excellent stream of water running near the house. This place will probably become very valuable, a Glass-house having been lately erected within a mile of it. It is convenient to several saw and grist-mills, and within about six miles of a good landing on Mantua Creek. The above tract is clear of all incumbrances, and binds on land of John Jessops, Benjamin Lodge and Jacob Parks. The terms will be made known on the day of the sale.

WILLIAM BROWN, Auctioneer.

The Pennsylvania Journal,
July 5, 1780

LOST,

FROM THE SUBSCRIBERS SHALLOP, while in the possession of the Refugees, about two weeks ago, between Egg-Island and the Capes of Delaware.

A Large BOAT, which has been cut down and now has strait gunnels, of a very strong built, the ring and bolt drawn from her bow, the stern sheets and thawts painted with

"Notice is Hereby Given"

Spanish brown, and her bottom paid with tar. Whosoever has found said boat, and delivers her to the subscribers, or to William Peterson, at Morris River, in the State of New-Jersey, shall receive Two Hundred Dollars reward.

M'CULLOCH & PETERSON.

∞

*The Pennsylvania Packet,
or the General Advertiser*,
March 13, 1781

Wood-Cutter wanted,

AT BATSTO FURNACE, in New-Jersey, to whom good Wages will be given; the Wood to be cut is chiefly Pine.

For sale or barter, for flour, midlings, pork, corn or molasses, either at the said Furnace, or at the store of CHARLES PETTIT, on Mr. Allen's Wharf, Cannon shot of all sizes, stoves and other Castings; Rolled and Rod IRON.

N. B. Guns, Howitz, or other particular Casting, may be contracted for by applying as above.

∞

*The Pennsylvania Packet,
or the General Advertiser*,
May 5, 1781

The following is communicated by a correspondent at Greenwich, in New-Jersey, April 29, 1781.

"The infamous Levin Turner, commanding the armed barge TRIMMER, having for several days been skulking about in creeks down the Delaware, and picking up defenceless vessels in the bay, collected several of his prizes together in the mouth of Cohansey, which being discovered by the militia on shore, a small party under the command of major Ewing, on Tuesday the 24th inst. fell down the Cohansey, and discovering by scouts that the barge was absent, in pursuit of another vessel, boarded and brought safe to Greenwich, two shallops, loaded with lumber, the Greenwich packet, and a small schooner with oysters. Another small sloop, said to be from Sinepuxent, laden with oats, &c. lay so far out, that the major did not think it prudent to attempt a re-capture, as his party was so small, but thought best to secure what had so fortunately fallen into his hands; the vessels re-captured were delivered to their respective original owners, who made the militia a handsome gratuity for their spirited behaviour."

∞

The Pennsylvania Gazette,
June 6, 1781

Little-Egg-Harbour, April 28, 1781.

THIS IS TO GIVE Public Notice to all whom it may concern, That the subscriber, who has kept a Public House for some time past at Little-Egg-Harbour, has now declined keeping a House of Entertainment any longer, as many wrong censures and difficulties have occurred therefrom; therefore takes this method to acquaint all travellers with the above resolution, as he means to move back into the country to avoid the ill reproach of people.

DAVID FOLKINBURG.

∞

The Pennsylvania Gazette,
January 23, 1782

WOOD CUTTERS WANTED, At the ATSION IRON WORKS, in the township of Evesham, Burlington county, New Jersey. Apply to LAWRENCE SALTAR, at said Works.

∞

*The Pennsylvania Packet,
or the General Advertiser*,
September 17, 1782

To be SOLD on Fifth day, the 19th instant, at two o'clock in the afternoon, by public vendue, on the premises:

A VALUABLE PLANTATION or Tract of Land, containing one hundred and twenty-seven acres and thirteen perches, situate on Cooper's creek, in the township of Newton, Gloucester county, and state of New-Jersey, between two and three miles distant from Cooper's Ferry, on the road leading to Haddonfield:—about fourteen acres of which is drained meadow, within a good bank; and also fifteen acres more of good inland meadow or cleared swamp; the remainder plough and wood-land. There are on said premises, a good dwelling house with a cellar under it, and a large and convenient kitchen, with a good barn, out-houses, and a stone spring-house; and has a convenient wharf on said creek; also a bearing apple orchard, with a variety of good fruit, and a good assortment of other fruit trees.

At the same time and place will also be Sold, eight or nine acres of cedar swamp, lying on a branch of Egg-Harbour river, called Attco-Attco. Any person inclining to purchase, may view the premises, and know the terms by applying to the subscriber any time before the sale.

JOHN BURROUGH

N. B. There is on said place a large Asparagus Bed.

The Pennsylvania Packet, or the General Advertiser, March 15, 1783

GLOUCESTER, December 5.

We have seen within these few days, a considerable order for goods to supply the American market, from some merchants in France, addressed to a manufacturer in this neighbourhood.

The Vermont Gazette, August 7, 1783

CURIOUS ANECDOTE.

An elderly, honest and very religious man, who now resides in West Jersey, some years ago took a voyage to Nova-Scotia, where he was detained on business for eighteen months. Disliking greatly the climate and the soil, he frequently wondered for what particular use that country was created, as his pious principles led him fully to believe that nothing was created in vain. He thought and reflected, but thought and reflected to no purpose! 'Till time, the great revealer of secrets, has abundantly to his satisfaction, removed every difficulty, by disclosing that Nova Scotia was created, and specially designed by an over-ruling Providence, for the dismal habitation of those pests to society, the tories, refugees and ingrates of America, where, on ground as rocky as their hearts, may they long continue unacquainted with, and for ever secluded from the air peculiarly enjoyed by the sons and daughters of freedom.

The Indian King. In 1750, Philadelphia merchant Matthais Aspden completed the earliest construction phase of what became the Indian King Tavern, an eminently recognizable landmark in Haddonfield, Camden County. The original three-and-one-half-story brick structure featured two rooms on each floor. By 1764, Aspden had enlarged the tavern to 24 rooms with a two-story addition. Thomas Redman acquired the tavern in 1775. In January 1777, Redman, a Quaker, ended up being incarcerated in the Gloucester Gaol due to his pacifistic ways and expressions of contempt for the ongoing warfare then raging in America. Shortly after his release from imprisonment in May, he sold the tavern to Hugh Creighton. From May 7 to June 7, 1777, the very first New Jersey State Legislature held their inaugural session at the Indian King Tavern. Legislative action during this session included a resolution that the word "State" should be substituted for "Colony" in all governmental documents. The lawmakers also accepted the official state seal during these days at the Indian King. From September 6 through the 25th, 1777, the state's Privy Council also met at the tavern and on the 22nd of the same month and year, the Council of Safety convened at the tavern.

In 1903, the State of New Jersey purchased the Indian King Tavern as its very first historic site. Its initial "restoration" removed important details and appendages from the tavern, but the building persists as a perennial favorite spot for visitation among area residents.

South Jersey's Revolutionary Battles, Skirmishes, and Future Research

The table on the following pages provides a chronology of virtually every known military engagement that occurred in South Jersey during the American War for Independence, based on the published work of David C. Munn in his 1976 pamphlet, "Battles and Skirmishes in New Jersey of the American Revolution" (unless otherwise noted). A quick glance at the chronology makes it abundantly clear that South Jersey hosted numerous flashpoints in the fight for independence. The thirteen articles comprising this special edition of *SoJourn* provide only a fragmentary glimpse into the intensity that the American War for Independence brought to South Jersey. Much research remains to be conducted. It is the hope of the editors that this chronology will inspire local historians and authors to select some lesser known topics from this table for future research. The unprecedented availability of primary source documents, via repositories and on the Internet, should undergird research into the engagements listed in the chronology and help investigators unearth new information concerning New Jersey in the American Revolution.

Hancock House in the Hancock's Bridge section of Lower Alloways Creek Township, Salem County, New Jersey. The owners' initials and date of construction are recorded on the gable on the west end: H. W. S. stand for William and Sarah Hancock. William Hancock was Justice of the Peace for Salem County and a member of the Colonial Legislature. Upon his death in 1762, his son William inherited the house; William also succeeded his father into the Legislature and was named Judge of the County Court for Salem.

The house was the scene of the massacre at Hancock's Bridge. In the early morning of March 21, 1778, Major John Graves Simcoe led approximately 300 British soldiers and Queen's Rangers to Hancock House, where colonial militia were billetted. In the assault, eight American's were killed including Judge Hancock.

In 1932, the Hancock House was purchased by a commission and the title passed to the State of New Jersey. Photograph taken in 1941 by George Neuschafer. *Courtesy of the Library of Congress.*

1774	December 22	Greenwich	Greenwich Tea Party.
1775	October 16	Brigantine Beach	English transport ship REBECCA & FRANCIS under Captain George Hastings runs aground at Brigantine Beach. Members of Egg Harbor Guard (3rd Regiment, Gloucester County militia), under Colonel Richard Somers, take crew into custody. First ship destroyed in New Jersey during the war.
1776	April 13	Off Cape May	American brigantine POLLY and British schooner LIVELY have engagement off Cape May.
	May 5	Delaware River	British ships ROEBUCK and LIVERPOOL have engagement with American brigantine LEXINGTON.
	May 6	Bacon's Neck, Delaware River	(B) Cumberland County militia chase foraging party from British ships anchored at mouth of Cohansey Creek. British land party at Tindon's or Findles's Island, between Cohansey and Stow Creeks, known as Bacon's neck. (D) British capture Daniel Richards' shallop bound from Philadelphia to Morris [Maurice] River. All hands escape to shore.
	May 8	Delaware River	British ships cannonade Salem County from Delaware River (Day 1).
	May 9	Delaware River	British ships cannonade Salem County from Delaware River (Day 2).
	June	Egg Harbor	June 10, 1776, privateers CONGRESS and CHANCE reported at Egg Harbor with three captured ships, LADY JULIANNA, JUNO and REYNOLDS. Date of capture not given.
	June 28	Off Cape May	Brigantine LEXINGTON and schooner WASP have engagement off Cape May.
	June 29	Cape May	American brigantine NANCY runs aground at Cape May. Local militia remove powder and arms. Exchange with British kills one American, Richard Wickes—the first casualty on New Jersey soil.
	July 5	Egg Harbor	Privateers CONGRESS and CHANCE take TAMAREA.
	December 11	Burlington	Pennsylvania Navy bombards Burlington after Hessian occupation under Count Carl von Donop.

South Jersey's Revolutionary Battles, Skirmishes, and Future Research

1776	December 22	Petticoat Bridge	Skirmish occurs at the bridge between Slabtown (Jacksonville) and Blackhorse (Columbus).
	December 23	Mount Holly	American Colonel Samuel Griffin attacks the British and Hessian position at Petticoat Bridge. The next day British counterattack, forcing Americans to withdraw. Toward evening, a heated engagement at Iron Works Hill results in several casualties on both sides. Hessians wind up in Mount Holly; Americans retreat to Moorestown.
1777	March 1	Off Absecon Beach	Privateers take brig off Absecon Beach.
	April 26	Egg Harbor	British frigate MERMAID destroys schooner at Egg Harbor between April 21 and 28, 1777.
	June 12	Egg Harbor	British sloop HARLEM and brig STANLEY cut out two American brigs in the harbor.
	July 23	Off Absecon Beach	British frigate and American schooner have engagement four miles off beach.
	October 1	Billingsport	Col. Thomas Stirling (British) lands below fort at Billingsport with 42nd Regiment and part of 71st.
	October 2	Billingsport, Mantua, Mickleton	(B) Americans evacuate Fort Billings. On march to Fort Mifflin, small skirmish occurs. (Mantua) Force under General Silas Newcomb meets force under Colonel Thomas Stirling about 9 a.m. and engage in "pretty brisk fire." (Mickleton) British force under Colonel Stirling attacks General Silas Newcomb's troops.
	October 5	Delaware River	Americans scuttle two ships to close gap in *chevaux-de-frise* British made near Billingsport.
	October 7	Delaware River	Skirmish occurs on Province Island near Fort Mifflin.
	October 8	Delaware River	Naval action takes place at mouth of Schuylkill River.
	October 9	Delaware River	A floating battery between Little Mud Island and Fort Island fires on British.

SoJourn

1777	October 11	Delaware River	Commodore John Hazlewood's galleys from the Pennsylvania Navy cannonade Carpenter's Island. Another attack made the next day.
	October 12	Delaware River	Commodore John Hazlewood's galleys from the Pennsylvania Navy cannonade Carpenter's Island.
	October 21	Cooper's Ferry, Haddonfield	American's at Cooper's Ferry snipe at British troops on way to Red Bank. Local Haddonfield militia harasses troops on way to Red Bank.
	October 22	Fort Mercer	Americans have fourteen killed and 23 wounded, Hessians lose 514, killed or wounded, at the Battle of Red Bank.
	October 23	Red Bank	Battery from Fort Mifflin, Pennsylvania, shell British during Battle of Red Bank
	November 1	Mantua, Egg Harbor	(M) General Charles Cornwallis burns barracks at Mantua Creek while marching from Billingsport to Gloucester. (E) Privateers capture boatload of oysters and take to Egg Harbor.
	November 5	Mantua Creek	Americans shell British ships from battery near mouth of Mantua Creek.
	November 15	Mantua Creek	Second battery near mouth of Mantua Creek opens up on British ships in river.
	November 19	Fort Mercer	General Charles Cornwallis attacks Fort Mercer. Americans evacuate the next day.
	November 20	Mantua Creek, Timber Creek	Skirmish at ford in Mantua Creek five miles above bridge British destroyed. Militia fire at bridge over Timber Creek.
	November 21	Delaware River	British shore batteries fire on American vessels attempting to pass Philadelphia along Jersey shore.
	November 24	Haddonfield	American troops bivouac before the Battle of Gloucester. British foraging party harasses them.
	November 25	Gloucester	Reconnaissance force under marquis de Lafayette and British have brief exchange.

South Jersey's Revolutionary Battles, Skirmishes, and Future Research

1777	November 27	Gloucester	General Charles Cornwallis returns to Philadelphia after clearing east bank of rebels. Takes 800 head of cattle. Local militia harasses and British suffer four losses.
	December 1	Thompson's Point	British kill Francis Clark in skirmish.
	December 10	Long Beach Island	Armed sloop Two FRIENDS beaches on Long Beach Island near Barnegat.
	December 15	Cooper's Ferry	Jersey militia takes twenty British sailors.
	December 31	Delaware River	Americans strip and destroy transport, LORD HOWE. Continental troops at Wilmington blow up brigantine with two field pieces. Three other vessels are driven to Jersey Shore, where inhabitants are "taking proper care of their cargoes."
1778	January 5–6	Delaware River	The "Battle of the Kegs" occurs when mines and kegs released between Bordentown and Burlington explode off Philadelphia.
	February 2	Mantua	West Jersey Loyalists out of Philadelphia raid vicinity of Red Bank.
	February 26	Salem	Continental Captain John Barry, under direction of General Anthony Wayne, destroys large quantity of hay before enemy boats appear to stop him.
	February 28	Haddonfield (near)	Continental General Anthony Wayne's foraging party tangles with British patrol. British Major John Simcoe leads raid in Haddonfield vicinity.
	March	Egg Harbor	Privateer takes Brigantine off Egg Harbor.
	March 2	Cooper's Ferry	General Anthony Wayne and Count Casimir Pulaski skirmish with British Major John Simcoe.
	March 12	Mantua	Gloucester County militia and foraging troops under British Colonel Charles Mawhood skirmish at Mantua Creek.
	March 16	Mantua Creek	British Colonel Charles Mawhood's troops march up Salem Road to Mantua Creek Bridge, the only place they could cross. Meet American Captain Samuel Hugg with artillery and others of the colonial militia.

1778	March 17	Alloway's Bridge, Salem, Salem Creek	(A) British foraging party destroys James Smith's house.
			(S) Militia and British foraging party skirmish outside Salem.
			(SC) Americans fire upon British foraging party at mouth of Creek.
	March 18	Quinton's Bridge	Major John Simcoe's Rangers have battle with Salem and Cumberland county militias.
	March 21	Alloway, Hancock's Bridge	(A) British troops overrun local militia at the farm of William Abbott, near bridge over Alloways Creek, during Major John Simcoe's raid on Hancock's Bridge.
			(H) British Major John Simcoe and Rangers with New Jersey Volunteers murder everyone in Hancock House.
	March 22	Swedesboro	Three militiamen take wagon and three horses, the property of Daniel Cozen, a well-known Tory, in foraging raid.
	March 24	Elsinboro	Militiamen capture a wagon and three horses with baggage and stores, the property to Daniel Cozen, Tory captain.
	March 27	Swedesboro	Sixty Tories and marines under a man named Cox take Lieutenant Bateman Lloyd of the 4th Regiment and two recruits and plunder the house of Captain Robert Brown.
	March 31	Woodbury	Party of Refugees and few marines conduct foraging raid.
	April	Egg Harbor	Brigantine from Ireland bound for New York taken off Egg Harbor and brought into port.
	April 4	Gloucester, Spicer's Ferry Bridge, Swedesboro	(G) Foraging parties have skirmish.
			(SP) American and British foraging parties skirmish at bridge.
			(SW) Refugees and British troops arrive hoping to capture local militia. Finding militia gone, they burn schoolhouse and pillage local homes.
	April 5	Haddonfield	British capture Major William Ellis during skirmish.

South Jersey's Revolutionary Battles, Skirmishes, and Future Research

1778	May 8	Burlington	Burlington suffers another naval bombardment, this time by the British.
	June 2	Egg Harbor	Captain Robert Snell's company of Egg Harbor Guards surprise a party of Tories.
	June 18	Evesham	British kill Captain Jonathan Beesley during "an occasional light skirmish" as armies move through New Jersey.
	June 18	Haddonfield, Gloucester	(H) General William Maxwell's brigade harasses British Evacuating Philadelphia. (G) American light horse attack British during evacuation of Philadelphia near Gloucester Point and take prisoners.
	June 20	Mount Holly	Militia harasses British Army on march from Philadelphia to New York.
	June 23	Crosswicks	British shoot Elias Dayton's horse out from under him in action on Crosswicks Creek, four miles from Trenton.
	July	Egg Harbor	Privateers take British transports off Egg Harbor bound from Philadelphia to New York.
	August 1	Egg Harbor	American privateer seizes schooner JOHN & SALLY off Egg Harbor.
	August 20	Egg Harbor	British TRYON sinks rebel GLORY OF AMERICA off Egg Harbor.
	August 21	Cape May	French fleet drives British cruiser ashore.
	August 24	Egg Harbor	Five privateers attack ship SYBELLA off Egg Harbor but fail to capture her.
	September	Egg Harbor	Privateer takes British brigantine RECOVERY to Egg Harbor.
	September 4	Egg Harbor	Several privateers attack British ship off Egg Harbor.
	September 5	Egg Harbor	Americans capture and destroy British ships.
	September 29	Egg Harbor	Privateer retakes sloop with tobacco and brings her to Egg Harbor.
	October 6	Chestnut Neck	British attack privateers' stronghold to stop the piracy of their supply vessels. British easily rout local militia and capture ten prize vessels harbored there. They dismantle and scuttle all vessels and burn tiny village of Chestnut Neck.

1778	October 15	Egg Harbor	British capture two American privateers off Egg Harbor.
	October 16	Egg Harbor	British capture two American privateers off Egg Harbor.
	October 19	Egg Harbor	British capture American privateer off Egg Harbor.
	December 9	Barnegat Beach	British armed vessel runs aground near Barnegat and local militia captures crew.
1779	January 4	Egg Harbor	American Letter of marque brig SIR WILLIAM ERSKINE takes British sloop FRANKLIN off Egg Harbor.
	February	Long Beach Island	Tory John Bacon attacks guards on ship that had beached.
	February 10	Between Egg Harbor and New York	Schooner HUNTER under Captain Douglass from Egg Harbor and the brigantine BELLONA under Captain Buchanan from New York suffer extensive damage during engagement.
	March	Barnegat	Brigantine DILIGENCE captures American sloop SUCCESS.
	March 22	Barnegat Beach	British Frigate DELAWARE takes scow MOLLY 25 leagues to the north of Cape Charles. Prize crew escapes when MOLLY hits the beach. Hornor says crew taken and cargo brought in.
	March 24	Barnegat Beach	Sloop SUCCESS comes ashore. Had been taken previously by the brigantine DILIGENCE. Monmouth County militia takes cargo, sends crew to Princeton.
	April 26	Red Bank	Two divisions of British troops raid Monmouth County. One strikes Tinton Falls and Red Bank. Second party marches on Shrewsbury and Middletown. British plunder inhabitants and burn several houses and barns.
	April 29	Cape May	Brigantine DELIGHT beaches on Peck's Beach (Cape May County). Militia seize crew and vessel.
	May	Egg Harbor	British privateer GENERAL PATTISON leaves Sandy Hook and meets two rebel ships off Egg Harbor. Drives one ashore; the other escapes.
	May 7	Egg Harbor	DILIGENT takes privateer off Egg Harbor.
	May 21	Egg Harbor	Brigantine of sixteen guns comes ashore near Egg Harbor. People from area board her.

South Jersey's Revolutionary Battles, Skirmishes, and Future Research

1779	June	Egg Harbor	Americans take British TRUE BLUE.
	June 7	Egg Harbor	American brigantine MONMOUTH retakes schooner off Egg Harbor.
	June 23	Cape May	Americans take frigate DELAWARE off Cape May.
	July	Egg Harbor	American brig HOLKER captures the snow FRIENDSHIP and sends her to Egg Harbor.
	July 28	Barnegat	Two continental sloops fail to capture cutter INTREPID off Barnegat.
	August 6	Egg Harbor	Americans capture brigantine and send it to Egg Harbor.
	September 10	Egg Harbor	Several armed boats (Br.) destroyed a number of vessels and other property in Egg Harbor.
	October	Absecon	Refugees skirmish with Egg Harbor Guards (3rd Regiment, Gloucester County militia) at Absecon salt works.
	October 1	Egg Harbor	American ship takes ship with 214 Hessians on board.
	October 13	Egg Harbor	British take schooner HAWK with 70 rebels on board off Egg Harbor.
	November 1	Egg Harbor	Americans take British ship and send it to Egg Harbor.
1780	January	Egg Harbor	Americans drive 40-gun British ship ashore near Egg Harbor.
	March 9	Barnegat Inlet	Whaleboat attacks British privateers off Barnegat Inlet.
	March 18	Egg Harbor	Capt. William Marriner (Am.) of New Brunswick has two engagements off coast and takes prizes to Egg Harbor.
	June 9	Red Bank	Col. Ty[e] (a mulatto slave named Titus) with twenty black and white soldiers capture American Capt. Barnes Smock and Capt. Gilbert Vanmater.
	July	Egg Harbor	Privateer brig HOLKER and British brig have battle off Egg Harbor.
	August	Springfield (Burlington County)	Robbers loot several houses.
	September 7	Egg Harbor	HMS IRIS runs a brig ashore near Egg Harbor.
1781	March 27	Chestnut Neck	Skirmish at Chestnut Neck.*
	April 24	Mouth of Cohansey River	Recovery of several vessels previously captured by Refugee Levin Turner.*
	August 20	Maurice River	Tories attempt to take shallop at mouth of the Maurice, but militia repulses them.

1782	January 3	In Delaware Bay	American whaleboat recaptures the cruiser BETSEY from the British.
	March 24	Toms River	A large irregular force of the Associated Loyalists overwhelm the blockhouse and burn most of the town.
	May 5	Egg Harbor	American privateer takes the British OLD RANGER off Egg Harbor.
	May 18	Egg Harbor	Americans capture British ship off Egg Harbor.
	June 1	Forked River (Barnegat)	Tory raid at Forked River, results in a skirmish.
	October 26	Barnegat Beach	Americans take beached British ship, but are killed the same night in a raid led by the Tory, John Bacon.
	December 15	Egg Harbor	Capt. Nathan Jackson of the GREYHOUND captures schooners DOLPHIN and DIAMOND off Sandy Hook and takes them to Egg Harbor.
	December 27	Cedar Creek Bridge	Loyalists skirmish with New Jersey troops in possibly the last land action of the war. Pvt. William Cooke Jr. dies during skirmish.

* Events not noted in Munn's "Battles and Skirmishes in New Jersey of the American Revolution."

Friends Meeting House, Mount Holly. From the founding of the community in the late seventeenth century until the third quarter of the eighteenth century, Mount Holly's members of the Religious Society of Friends (a.k.a. Quakers) met at a frame meetinghouse located adjacent to Woodlane Road. During the 1770s, the membership thought it prudent to relocate to a new meetinghouse closer to downtown Mount Holly. The brick meeting that is still standing today at the corner of High and Garden streets was completed in 1775. It appears the building survived unscathed during the Battle of Iron Works Hill, but during the British army's overland evacuation from Philadelphia through the Jerseys in June 1778, the meetinghouse served as the commissary from June 20 to the 22nd. Evidence of suspended livestock can still be viewed inside the building.

From October 26 through December 26, 1779, the Mount Holly meetinghouse served as the site of the First sitting or session of the Fourth New Jersey Legislature. Beginning November 8 and running to December 26 of the same year, the Privy Council also met in the Mount Holly Friend's Meeting.

Cedar Bridge Tavern

Estimates for the date of construction for the existing Cedar Bridge tavern have varied widely. A Historic American Buildings Survey, completed in 1938, suggested a temporal range between 1761 and 1799. Wikipedia asserts that the tavern dates from "around 1740 and is believed to be the oldest intact bar in the United States."[1] The National Register of Historic Places, basing its dating on recent re-evaluations, places the date of construction during the first twenty years of the nineteenth century: "at what was then the crossroads of two stage routes connecting Mt. Holly in Burlington County with the southern part of Ocean County."[2] A dendrochronology study undertaken on the south sill, an oak timber, returned a date of 1768, but it appears this piece of wood was possibly reused from an earlier structure.[3] The smaller addition to the tavern dates to circa 1836. The previous tavern on the site—standing perhaps forty yards from the current tavern—is purported to have been the site of one of the last actions, if not the last, of the Revolutionary War.[4]

The skirmish, long attributed to the environs of Cedar Bridge Tavern, certainly occurred in the Little Egg Harbor vicinity.[4] Details of the violent clash illustrate the unsettled nature of South Jersey life more than a year after General Cornwallis's surrender at Yorktown (October 19, 1781). New Jersey militia Captains Richard Shreve, of the Burlington County Light Horse, and Edward Thomas, of the Mansfield militia, received information on December 27, 1782, that "John Bacon, with his banditti of robbers, were in the neighbourhood of Cedar Creek."[5] Bacon was a Loyalist—a so-called refugee—who spent much of the war attacking colonial homesteads and shipping along the Jersey coast. From the perspective of Loyalists, Bacon was a man of action who avenged wrongs perpetrated against his majesty's subjects by the rebels. To Patriots, he was a notorious Pine robber and thug.[6]

Two months earlier, a British cutter sailing from Ostend, Belgium, and bound for St. Thomas, West Indies, was blown off course and ran aground on the Barnegat shoals at the north end of Long Beach Island.[7] Andrew Steelman and the crew of the privateer galley ALLIGATOR from Cape May discovered the abandoned wreck, and commenced, with help of local citizens, to salvage the valuable cargo of Hyson tea. Bacon and nine men, in a small boat called the HERO'S REVENGE, attacked under cover of darkness. In the ensuing fray, Steelman and several of his American crew were killed and others wounded.[8] A Tory newspaper reported that Bacon killed or wounded all but a small number of the American plunderers; that he then sent the wounded for treatment; and that the ALLIGATOR was captured and brought to New York.[9] The perspective of the Continentals was quite different: Bacon and his men attacked furtively in the night, stabbing victims as they slept on the beach; he was chased off by reinforcements; and the ALLIGATOR was not captured. Today, the event is known as the "Massacre on Long Beach."[10] Whether Bacon was a hero or murderer depended upon one's perspective.

When in late December Shreve and Thomas received intelligence that Bacon was again disrupting local shipping, this time in a whaleboat named the BLACK-JOKE, the militia captains collected a party of men and went in pursuit, encountering Bacon and his followers at a place named Cedar Creek Bridge.[11] According to contemporary accounts, the militia attacked Bacon and his men with great ferocity, but the Loyalists met the Patriots with "firmness" for a period of time, "several of them having been guilty of such enormous crimes, as to have no expectation of mercy should they surrender."[12] According to one account, the colonials were pressing the Loyalists to the point of breaking "when the militia were unexpectedly fired on from a party of the inhabitants near that place, who had suddenly come to Bacon's assistance."[13] Cedar Creek Bridge, evidently, was a loyalist haunt. In the ensuing confusion, the wounded Bacon and several confederates escaped. One militiaman was killed, William Cooke Jr., and another, Robert Reckless, mortally wounded. One of the Refugees, Ichabod Johnson, was killed.

In the following weeks the militia pursued Bacon and the Refugees. On the evening of April 3, 1783, militia tracked Bacon to the public house of William Rose, located between West Creek and Tuckerton. He was killed after a brief scuffle and his body taken to Jacobstown, where the Americans prepared to bury him in the middle of a road. Bacon's brother arrived before the grave could be finished and successfully pleaded for the body, which he interred at Arneytown.[14] The Treaty of Paris, which brought the conflict between England and its former colonies to an official end, would not be signed for another five months, on September 3, 1783.

The Ocean County Department of Parks and Recreation is working to implement its historic preservation plan for Cedar Bridge Tavern. The spectacular site should be open to the public by the fall of 2018.

Cedar Bridge Tavern. Photographed January 22, 1938, by Nathaniel R. Ewan. *Courtesy of Library of Congress.*

Cedar Bridge Tavern

Endnotes

1. "Cedar Bridge Tavern," *Wikipedia*, https://en.wikipedia.org/wiki/Cedar_Bridge_Tavern.
2. National Register of Historic Places Registration Form for Cedar Bridge Tavern, 2013, 8–5.
3. Ibid., 8–4.
4. David C. Munn, *Battles and Skirmishes in New Jersey of the American Revolution* (Trenton, NJ: Bureau of Geology and Topography, 1976), 20.
5. *The Independent Chronicle and the Universal Advertiser* (Boston), January 30, 1783, 3.
6. For a sound review of John Bacon's life and wartime activities, see Ben Ruset, "The Refugee John Bacon," *NJPineBarrens*, http://www.njpinebarrens.com/the-refugee-john-bacon/. See also Mark P. Donnelly and Daniel Diehl, "John Bacon," *Pirates of New Jersey: Plunder and High Adventure on the Garden State Coastline* (Stackpole Books, 2010).
7. Harry M. Ward, *Between the Lines: Banditti of the American Revolution* (Westport, CT: Praeger Publishers, 2002), 110.
8. *Thomas's The Massachusetts Spy, Or, Worcester Gazette*, November 21, 1782, 3.
9. Ibid.
10. Ruset, "The Refugee John Bacon."
11. *The Pennsylvania Packet or the General Advertiser* (Philadelphia), January 16, 1783, 3; *The Independent Chronicle and the Universal Advertiser* (Boston), January 30, 1783, 3.
12. *The Independent Chronicle and the Universal Advertiser* (Boston), January 30, 1783, 3.
13. Ibid.
14. Henry Charlton Beck, *More Forgotten Towns of Southern New Jersey* (Rutgers, NJ: Rutgers University Press, 1963), 260, as found in Ruset, "The Refugee John Bacon."

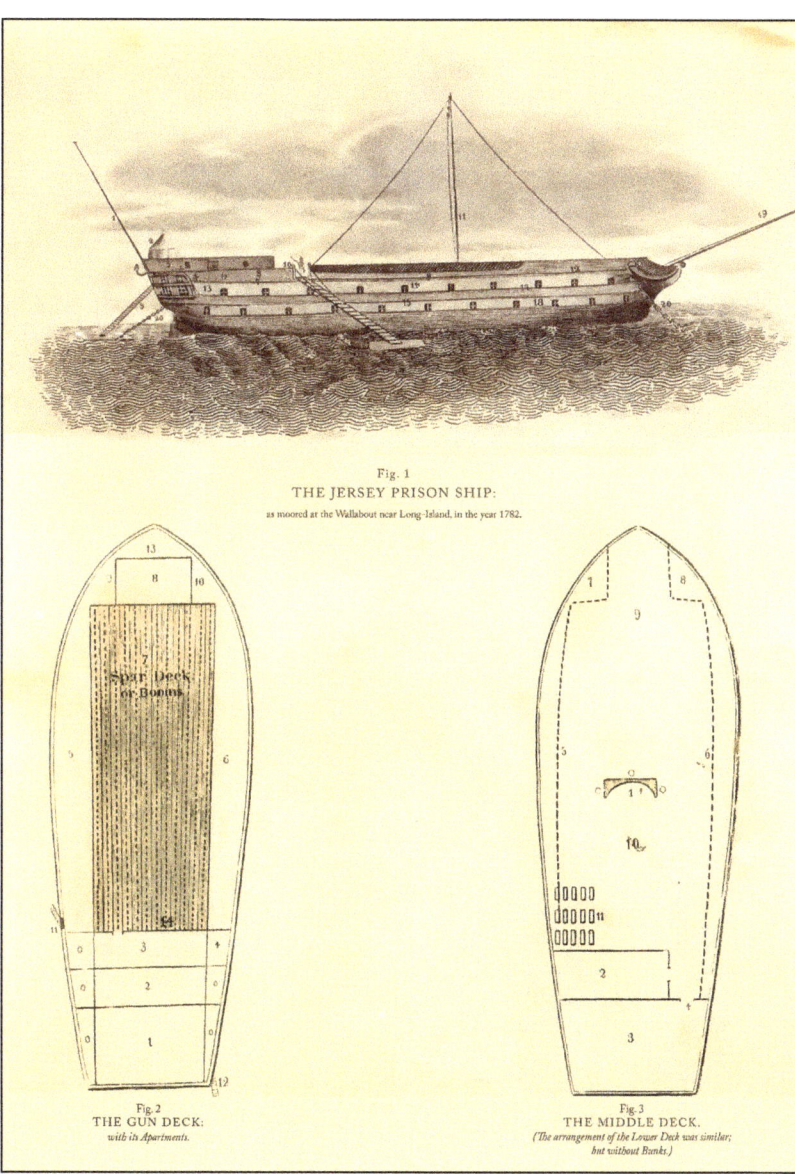

Fig. 1
THE JERSEY PRISON SHIP:
as moored at the Wallabout near Long-Island, in the year 1782.

Fig. 2
THE GUN DECK:
with its Apartments.

Fig. 3
THE MIDDLE DECK.
(The arrangement of the Lower Deck was similar, but without Bunks.)

The Old Jersey. During May 1782, Thomas Dring sailed from Providence, Rhode Island, as master's mate on board the privateer THE CHANCE, commanded by Captain Daniel Aborn, mounted with twelve six pound cannon and a complement of about 65 men. On its maiden voyage it was captured by the British ship of war BELISARIUS, commanded by Captain Graves, with 26 guns.

Dring was interned on the notorious prison ship THE JERSEY, in Wallabout Bay off New York City. His memoir of captivity opens: "Among the varied events of the war of the American Revolution, there are few circumstances which have left a deeper impression on the public mind, than those connected with the cruel and vindictive treatment which was experienced by those of our unfortunate countrymen whom the fortune of war had placed on board the Prison-Ships of the enemy."

Dring's recollections paint a sobering view of conditions aboard British prison ships, where the quantity of food was insufficient, its quality poor, punishment was often arbitrary and cruel, and death through sickness, a daily event.

The work concludes: "At the expiration of the war, in 1783, the prisoners remaining on board, were liberated; and the hulk being considered unfit for further use, was abandoned where she lay. The dread of contagion prevented everyone from venturing on board, and even from approaching her polluted frame. But the ministers of destruction were at work. Her planks were soon filled with worms, who, as if sent to remove this disgrace to the name of common humanity, ceased not from their labour until they had penetrated through her decayed bottom . . . and she sunk. With her, went down the names of many thousands of our countrymen, with which her inner planks and sheathing were literally covered: for but few of the inmates had ever neglected to add their own names to the almost innumerable catalogue. . . ."

Illustration from Albert G. Greene, *Recollections of the Jersey-Prison Ship; Taken and Prepared for Publication, from the Original Manuscript by Thomas Dring of Providence, R. I.* (Providence: H. H. Brown, 1829).

The Whitall House. The expansive plateau that rises above the Delaware River at National Park once hosted the 400-acre plantation of James and Ann Cooper Whitall, who acquired the land in 1748, although James's ancestors had owned land there since 1704. The Whitalls both held memberships in the Religious Society of Friends (the Quakers) and lived their lives as pacifists. The plantation featured expansive orchards, a lumberyard, a shad fishery at the base of the escarpment on the sloping beach, livestock and grazing pastures, and a ferry. The couple brought nine children into the world: six boys and three girls.

In April 1777, John Bull, Colonel Commandant and Superintendent of fortification construction, began building a fortification at Red Bank. Unlike Billingsport, where the Congress purchased 100 acres of land for a fortification there, the government merely usurped the land from James Whitall without any remuneration. It is doubtful that the Whitalls would have sold land for constructing a fortification, given their pacifist ways, so Bull and his laborers just took it. The resultant fort would have required 1000 men or more to defend, so General Washington dispatched Captain Thomas Antoine, the Chevalier de Mauduit Du Plessis, to reduce the fortification down to make it defendable by 400 soldiers. Colonel Nathaniel Greene and two regiments of Rhode Island continental soldiers arrived at the fort in early October. After October 12, Greene and his men commandeered fifteen tons of hay, 60 bushels of wheat, 1000 cedar boards, 8550 rails, 2048 stakes, and 50 white oak posts from James Whitall. The soldiers also tore down a barn and a hayhouse in addition to damaging other outbuildings on the Whitall plantation. The men cut down Whitall's paled gardens and took the produce to the fort and cut down his apple orchard, comprising 300 grafted trees. In 1779, Whitall applied for damages to the state legislature in the amount of £5,760 1/-, but never received any remuneration for his loss. Following the disastrous Hessian attack, James and Ann Whitall allowed their home to be used as a makeshift hospital.

The federal government finally purchased 100 acres of the former Whitall plantation in May 1872, seeking to mine the sand and gravel there for use at the new League Island Navy Yard in Philadelphia. In 1903, the federal government had finished with the land and decided to sell it. Gloucester County purchased it, including the Whitall House, and opened the property as a county park. Today, the Whitall House is an integral part of recounting the story of Fort Mercer and the Battle of Red Bank.

The Atlantic County Veterans Museum:
A Treasure Trove of War History

Jackson Glassey

Beside the eastern corner of Stephen Lake in the lush, pastoral, unassuming surroundings of Estell Manor, New Jersey, is a hidden gem of historical preservation. Have you been to Gettysburg? Richmond's Civil War Museum? New Orleans' WWII Museum? Philadelphia's Museum of the American Revolution? Ready for something more obscure? The Atlantic County Veterans Museum should absolutely be your next stop.

Situated about two-hundred yards northwest of Estell Manor Park's Atlantic County Veterans Cemetery, off of Route 50, the Veterans Museum is a substantial showcasing of South Jersey-centric war history, spanning the spectrum of significance from undeniably important artifacts to more curious ephemera: A cannonball from the Battle of Gettysburg and sand from the beaches of Iwo Jima to Vietnam War first aid kits and Cold War "Drop and Cover" instructional diagrams. It covers every major American conflict from the Revolutionary War to the War on Terror.

The first thing a visitor will notice about the Atlantic County Veterans Museum is that it does not look like a typical museum. While many military museums are constructed for the sole purpose of showcasing war artifacts, the Veterans Museum resides in a building that is itself fascinating. It is the historic Daniel Estell House, once home to Rebecca Estell Bourgeois Winston—the first mayor of Estell Manor and the first female mayor in New Jersey. Originally constructed in 1832 by Daniel Estell, Winston's grandfather, and eventually purchased over a century and a half later in 1993 by Atlantic County for purposes of preservation, this sizeable house has not only gone through several remodeling phases, but also many incarnations of use. According to Nick Leonetti, the former Assistant Administrator of the establishment, it was, at one point, even a home for wayward boys. "We've had families come by who lived in the house," says Leonetti. "As a county-owned property, the decision was made to utilize it in a way to help people appreciate the history of the

The front face of the historic Daniel Estell House, as seen from streetview.

building." Kimberly Brown, the Atlantic County Administrator of Cultural and Heritage Affairs, adds, "It's a place where veterans can come and remember, and have their stories told. The Veterans Cemetery office is actually in this building as well."

A portion of the museum's stained glass sunroom.

The Museum's featured periods are well-organized on two floors. The ground floor covers everything from the American Revolution to the Korean War, while the upstairs floor covers the Vietnam War and on. In particular, the first floor's exhibits wrap around the base of the building like a horseshoe: across the hall near the information desk is the Revolutionary War, and from there the sections loop across the sides of the mansion in chronological order. Also attached to the ground floor is a sunroom that showcases a series of gorgeously radiant stained-glass mosaics depicting images, logos, and scenes from each war, courtesy of the Absecon VFW. Adjacent to the central corridor of the first floor is the "Women's Wall," where one could spend an entire visit perusing artifacts specific to the spellbinding efforts of women in war.

The second-floor displays, detailing more contemporary conflicts, have been designed with great care. Where the first-floor Revolutionary War section features excellent replicas of Patriot uniforms and a life-size Colonial Army tent, the Iraq War section features a framed propaganda poster of Saddam Hussein recovered by Christopher Roeder, a Milmay (Buena Vista Township) resident, while on tour in Iraq.

Quite possibly the most impressive feature of the Museum is its showcasing of the roles of local figures in the United States military since the nation's founding. The organization faithfully compiles stories of Atlantic County veterans such as Alex Forshaw, a member of the 78th Infantry Division of the First World War who hailed from Linwood; Frederick "Fritz" Boling, an Egg Harbor City native who served as a translator during the same war; George A. Carney of Pleasantville, who served in the US Army's 1st Cavalry Division during the Vietnam War; Max Slusher of Somers Point, who served at the al-Asad Airbase in Iraq . . . and many others.

Portraits and memorabilia along the "Women's Wall."

Though it exists to highlight veterans from Southern New Jersey, make no mistake—if you visit the Atlantic County Veterans Museum as an outsider, you will leave with a widened understanding of war on a local level. Leonetti states that the Museum has seen visitors from Colorado, Florida and California. "Scholars have scouted us out," he says.

The Atlantic County Veterans Museum

The World War I bunker exhibit, a popular attraction for visitors that features an authentic Vickers machine gun.

The Atlantic County Veterans Museum is open Thursday, Friday, and Saturday from 10 a.m. to 4 p.m. It is located at 189 Route 50 in Estell Manor. For larger group tours, please call in advance during museum hours (609-909-7305). If you are interested in submitting a donation or want any further details regarding the Atlantic County Veterans Museum, contact Kimberly Brown at "kbrown@aclsys.org.

Longform photographs of World War I companies.

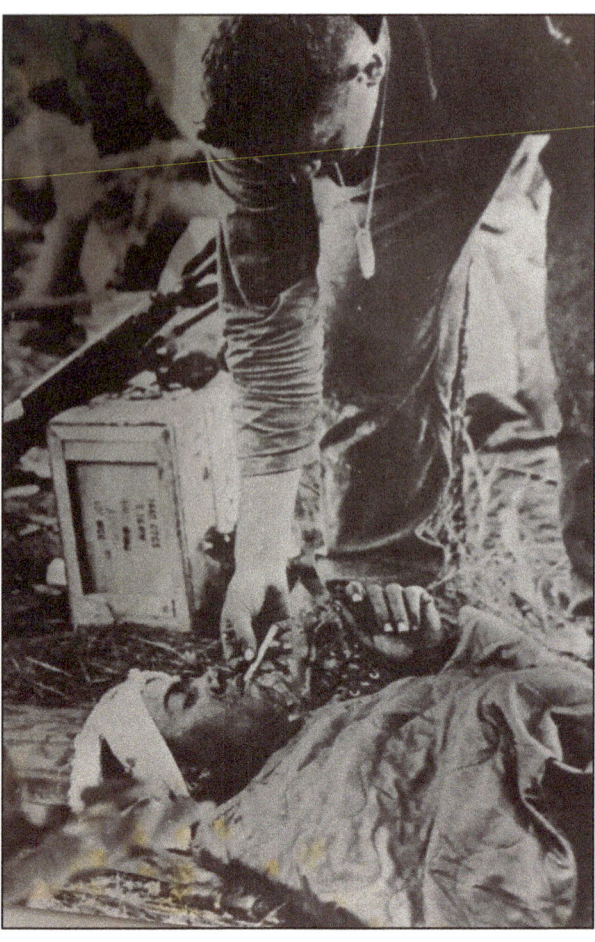
A wounded Vietnam War soldier.

Life-sized replica of a Patriot uniform.

Sections of the Vietnam War exhibit.

The Atlantic County Veterans Museum

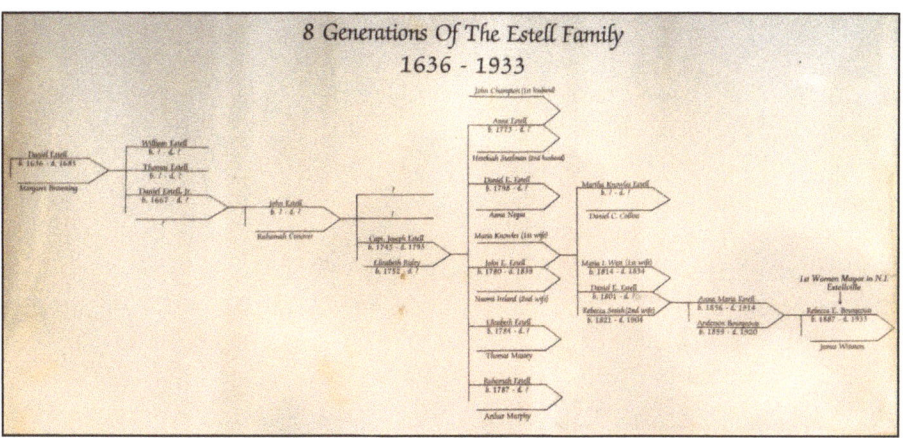

Left: Recovered artifacts from World War II Axis powers.

Above: A generational breakdown of the Estell Family from 1636 to 1933, framed in the Veterans Museum research office.

Below: The beginning of the Revolutionary War exhibit.

> Jackson Glassey is a Literature major at Stockton University. He has served as a managing editor for *Stockpot*, the University's long-standing literary magazine. In fall 2018, he will be co-president of the Stockton Literature Club.

Call for Articles

The South Jersey Culture & History Center at Stockton University publishes twice yearly issues of *SoJourn*. We actively seek community members, avocational historians, and scholars to contribute essays on topics related to South Jersey. Illustrations to accompany these articles will be a plus. Articles should be written for laypersons who are interested and curious about South Jersey topics, but do not necessarily have expertise in the areas covered. Potential authors should check SJCHC's website for a link to a simplified style sheet guide for article preparation—www.stockton.edu/sjchc/—or just follow the style in this issue. Journal editors will be happy to guide any would-be authors. In certain instances, Stockton editing interns may be assigned to help research topics and/or assist authors with writing.

Sample topics might include:

Biographical sketches of important but forgotten local people; the development or succession of a community's roads, bridges or buildings; local transportation (focused by mode, area or era) and what changes it wrought in the served communities; history of community businesses and industries (wineries, garment factories, agriculture, boat building, clamming, etc.); old school houses, old hotels, or meeting halls; narrative descriptions of local geographical features; essays concerned with folklore, music, arts; and reviews of new local interest publications. Photo essays and old photograph and postcard reproductions are welcome with applicable captions. In short, if a South Jersey topic interests you, it will likely interest *SoJourn*'s readers.

Parameters for submissions:

- Submissions must pertain to topics bounded within the eight southernmost counties of New Jersey (Burlington & Ocean Counties and south)
- Manuscripts should be approximately 3,000–4,000 words long (5 to 7 pages of single-spaced text and 9 to 12 pages including images)
- Manuscripts should conform to the *SoJourn* style sheet, available here: https://blogs.stockton.edu/sjchc/sojourn-style-sheet/
- Manuscripts, if at all possible, should be submitted in digital format (Word- or pdf-formatted documents preferred)
- Images should be submitted as high-resolution tiff- or jpeg-formatted files (editors can assist with digital conversion of photos if necessary). 300 dpi resolution, or higher, preferred
- Complete and appropriate citations printed as endnotes should be employed (see style sheet). If using Word, please use its endnote function
- Original submissions only. Copyright licenses for all images must be obtained by the author or should be copyright-free figures and/or figures in the public domain
- If essays are accepted, authors should submit a short 50 to 100 word autobiographical statement
- Articles need to be more than just a chronology of the given topic. The author should be able to properly contextualize the subject by answering such questions as: a) why is this important?; b) what is the impact on the local or regional history? and c) how does it compare to similar events/personages/changes/processes in other localities?

Call for submissions:

Submissions for winter issues are due before September 1; for summer issues, January 15.

Send inquiries or submissions to Thomas.Kinsella@stockton.edu or Paul.Schopp@stockton.edu.

Errata

SoJourn, 2.2, Winter 2017/18
Page 23, paragraph 8 reads:
   Deptford, one of the original townships in Gloucester County, dating to 1695, was on the outskirts of Woodbury. On the morning of January 9, in that year, a local farmer looked up. . . .
Please replace the text above with the following corrected text:
   Deptford, one of the original townships in Gloucester County, dating to 1695, was on the outskirts of Woodbury. On the morning of January 9, 1793, a local farmer looked up. . . .

Page 34, paragraph 2 reads:
   Two other Pine Barrens orchids found a home in the garden, Grass-pink (*Calopogon tuberosus*) and the White Fringed Orchid (*Platanthera blephariglottis*). These three graced the landscape from May into July. Although different species, each was covered with red hairs, tipped with a sticky dew-like droplet to catch and, then, digest small insects.
Please replace the text above with the following corrected text:
   Two other Pine Barrens orchids found a home in the garden, Grass-pink (*Calopogon tuberosus*) and the White Fringed Orchid (*Platanthera blephariglottis*). These three graced the landscape from May into July, sharing their sphagnum-covered niche with three species of sundew. Each of the carnivorous plants was covered with red hairs, tipped with a sticky dew-like droplet to catch and, then, digest small insects.

www.ingramcontent.com/pod-product-compliance
Lightning Source LLC
Chambersburg PA
CBHW060930170426
43193CB00026B/2994